THE VERILOG® HARDWARE DESCRIPTION LANGUAGE

FOURTH EDITION

THE VERILOG® HARDWARE DESCRIPTION LANGUAGE

FOURTH EDITION

by

Donald E. Thomas
Carnegie Mellon University

and

Philip R. Moorby
Synapix, Inc.

KLUWER ACADEMIC PUBLISHERS
Boston / Dordrecht / London

Distributors for North, Central and South America:
Kluwer Academic Publishers
101 Philip Drive
Assinippi Park
Norwell, Massachusetts 02061 USA
Telephone (781) 871-6600
Fax (781) 871-6528
E-Mail <kluwer@wkap.com>

Distributors for all other countries:
Kluwer Academic Publishers Group
Distribution Centre
Post Office Box 322
3300 AH Dordrecht, THE NETHERLANDS
Telephone 31 78 6392 392
Fax 31 78 6546 474
E-Mail <orderdept@wkap.nl>

Electronic Services <http://www.wkap.nl>

 Library of Congress Cataloging-in-Publication Data
Thomas, D.E. (Donald E.,), 1951-
        The Verilog hardware description language / by Donald E. Thomas
    and Philip R. Moorby. -- 4th ed.
            p.   cm.
    Includes index.
    ISBN 0-7923-8166-1
    1. Verilog (Computer hardware description language)   I. Moorby,
Philip R., 1953-   . II.Title
TK7885.7.T48   1998
621.39'2--dc21   98-17941
                                                CIP

(Reference) Reprinted from IEEE Std 1364-1995 IEEE Standard Verilog Hardware Description Language Reference Manual (LRM), Copyright © 1995 by the Institute of Electrical and Electronics Engineers, Inc. The IEEE disclaims any responsibility or liability resulting from placement and use in this publication. Information is reprinted with the permission of the IEEE.

Printed on acid-free paper.
Printed in the United States of America

To Sandie,
and John and Holland,
and Jill.

Preface

The Verilog language is a hardware description language that provides a means of specifying a digital system at a wide range of levels of abstraction. The language supports the early conceptual stages of design with its behavioral level of abstraction, and the later implementation stages with its structural level of abstraction. The language includes hierarchical constructs, allowing the designer to control a description's complexity.

Verilog was originally designed in the winter of 1983/84 as a proprietary verification/simulation product. Later, several other proprietary analysis tools were developed around the language, including a fault simulator and a timing analyzer. More recently, Verilog has also provided the input specification for logic and behavioral synthesis tools. The Verilog language has been instrumental in providing consistency across these tools. Now, the language has been standardized as IEEE standard #1364-1995 and is openly available for any tool to read and write. This book presents the language, providing material for the beginning student and advanced user of the language.

It is sometimes difficult to separate the language from the simulator tool because the dynamic aspects of the language are defined by the way the simulator works. Further, it is difficult to separate it from a synthesis tool because the semantics of the language become limited by what a synthesis tool allows in its input specification and produces as an implementation. Where possible, we have stayed away from simulator- and synthesis-specific details and concentrated on design specification. But, we have included enough information to be able to write working executable models.

The book takes a tutorial approach to presenting the language. Indeed, we start with a tutorial introduction that presents, via examples, the major features of the language and the prevalent styles of describing systems. We then continue with a more complete discussion of the language constructs. Numerous examples are provided to allow the reader to learn (and re-learn!) easily by example. Finally, in the appendix we provide a formal description of the language. Overall, our approach is to provide a means of learning by observing the examples and doing the exercises.

We have provided a set of exercises to stimulate thought while reading the book. It is strongly recommended that you try the exercises as early as possible with the aid of a Verilog simulator. Or, if you have your own designs, try them out too. The examples shown in the book are available in electronic form on the enclosed CD. Alternately, refer to http://www.ece.cmu.edu/~thomas. Also included on the CD is a simulator and a logic synthesis tool. The simulator is limited in the size of description it will handle and the synthesis tool provides a time-limited demonstration of synthesis.

The majority of the book assumes a knowledge of introductory logic design and software programming. As such, the book is of use to practicing integrated circuit design engineers, and undergraduate and graduate electrical or computer engineering students. However, the tutorial introduction is organized in a manner appropriate for use with a course in introductory logic design. It presents structural combinational circuits first, moves to more complex synthesizable combinational and sequential circuits, and ends with cycle-accurate specification of a system. A separate appendix, keyed into the sections of the tutorial introduction, provides solved exercises that discuss common errors as well as exercises for the tutorial section. The book has also been used for courses in upper level logic and integrated circuit design, computer architecture, and computer-aided design (CAD). It provides complete coverage of the language for design courses, and how a simulator works for CAD courses.

The book is organized into ten chapters and seven appendices. We start with the tutorial introduction to the language in chapter 1. Chapters 2 and 3 present the language's behavioral modeling constructs, while chapter 4 presents logic level modeling. Chapter 5 covers advanced topics in timing and event driven simulation. Use of the language for synthesis is presented in chapters 6 and 7. Chapters 8 and 9 then present the more advanced topics of user-defined primitives, and switch level modeling. Chapter 10 suggests two major Verilog projects for use in a university course. One appendix provides tutorial discussion for beginning students. The others are reserved for the dryer topics typically found in a language manual; read those at your own risk.

Have fun designing great systems...

always,

Donald E. Thomas

Philip R. Moorby

Acknowledgments

The authors would like to acknowledge Open Verilog International (http://www.ovi.org), whose role it is to maintain and promote the Verilog standard, and the many CAD tool developers and system designers who have contributed to the continuing development of the Verilog language. In particular, the authors would like to thank Leigh Brady for her help in reviewing earlier manuscripts, and Elliot Mednick for originally organizing the information on the CD that comes with the book.

The authors would also like to thank JoAnn Paul for her help and suggestions on the introduction and the CD, John Langworthy for helping us focus the tutorial material in appendix A toward students in a sophomore course, Tom Martin for his help in developing the exercises in chapter 10, and H. Fatih Ugurdag for providing us with Example 7.4. We also acknowledge many practicing engineers, faculty and students who have used the book and provided feedback to us on it. Finally, we wish to thank Margaret Hanley for the cover and page format designs.

The Institute of Electrical and Electronics Engineers maintains the Verilog Hardware Description Language standard (IEEE #1364-1995). We wish to acknowledge their permission for including the formal syntax specification in appendix G. Complete copies of the standard may be obtained through http://standards.ieee.org.

THE VERILOG® HARDWARE DESCRIPTION LANGUAGE

FOURTH EDITION

1 Verilog —
A Tutorial Introduction

Digital systems are highly complex. At their most detailed level, they may consist of millions of elements, as would be the case if we viewed a system as a collection of logic gates or pass transistors. From a more abstract viewpoint, these elements may be grouped into a handful of functional components such as cache memories, floating point units, signal processors, or real-time controllers. Hardware description languages have evolved to aid in the design of systems with this large number of elements and wide range of electronic and logical abstractions.

The creative process of digital system design begins with a conceptual idea of a logical system to be built, a set of constraints that the final implementation must meet, and a set of primitive components from which to build the system. Design is an iterative process of either manually proposing or automatically synthesizing alternative solutions and then testing them with respect to the given constraints. The design is typically divided into many smaller subparts (following the well-known divide-and-conquer engineering approach) and each subpart is further divided, until the whole design is specified in terms of known primitive components.

The Verilog language provides the digital system designer with a means of describing a digital system at a wide range of levels of abstraction, and, at the same time, provides access to computer-aided design tools to aid in the design process at these levels. The language supports the early conceptual stages of design with its behavioral constructs, and the later implementation stages with its structural constructs. During the design process, behavioral and structural constructs may be mixed as the logical structure of portions of the design are designed. The description may be simulated to determine correctness, and some synthesis tools exist for automatic design. Indeed, the Verilog language provides the designer entry into the world of large, complex digital systems design. This first chapter provides a brief tour of the basic features of the Verilog language.

1.1 **Getting Started**

The Verilog language describes a digital system as a set of *modules*. Each of these modules has an interface to other modules as well as a description of its contents. A module represents a logical unit that can be described either by specifying its internal logical structure — for instance describing the actual logic gates it is comprised of, or by describing its behavior in a program-like manner — in this case focusing on what the module does rather than on its logical implementation. These modules are then interconnected with nets, allowing them to communicate.

1.1.1 **A Structural Description**

We start with a basic logic circuit from introductory logic design courses: part of a binary to seven segment display driver, shown in Example 1.1. A display driver takes a

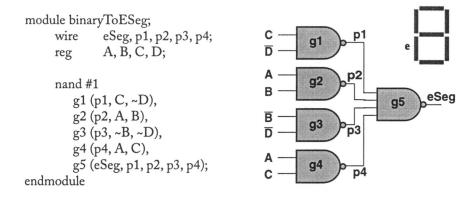

```
module binaryToESeg;
      wire    eSeg, p1, p2, p3, p4;
      reg     A, B, C, D;

      nand #1
          g1 (p1, C, ~D),
          g2 (p2, A, B),
          g3 (p3, ~B, ~D),
          g4 (p4, A, C),
          g5 (eSeg, p1, p2, p3, p4);
endmodule
```

Example 1.1 A Binary To Seven Segment Display Driver (E Segment Only)

four-bit binary input and drives the seven segments needed to display the digits zero through nine and the hexadecimal digits A through F. Only the logic to drive segment E of a display is shown in the example.

A Verilog description of this circuit is also shown in Example 1.1. The description shows the basic *definition* of a module — in this case, of a module named **binaryToE-Seg**. Each module definition includes the keyword *module* followed by the module name and is terminated by the *endmodule* statement. The second line of this definition specifies the names of *wires* used to transmit logic values among the submodules of this module. The third line declares the names of storage elements that will hold values. These *registers* are an abstraction of a flip flop circuit element.

The fifth line, and its continuation onto lines 6 through 10, *instantiates* five NAND gates, each having a delay of one time unit. NAND gates are one of the predefined logic gate types in the language — the others, including AND, OR, and XOR, are detailed later. This statement specifies that five gates, called g1 through g5, exist in the circuit. The "#1" indicates that they each have a delay of one time unit. Finally, the labels in the parentheses indicate the wires and registers to which the gates are connected. The first label in the parentheses is the gate's output and the others are inputs. The NOT operator ("~") is used to specify that the complement of a value is connected to the input. The wire, register, and instance names are included in the schematic drawing to further clarify the correspondence between the logic diagram and its equivalent Verilog description.

Although this example is simple, it illustrates several important points about the Verilog language. The first is the notion of module *definition* versus module *instantiation*. Using the module statement, as shown in the above example, we define a module once specifying all of its inner detail. This module may then be used (instantiated) in the design many times. Each of these instantiations are called instances of the module, and can be separately named and connected differently. Primitive gates, like the NAND, are predefined logic primitives provided by the language. They are presented in more detail in Chapter 4.

The gates are connected by *nets*. Nets are one of the two fundamental data types of the language (registers are the other), and are used to model an electrical connection between structural entities such as gates. A *wire* is one type of net; others include wired-AND, wired-OR, and trireg connections. The different net types are described in more detail in Chapters 4 and 9.

We have also seen how several gates are built into larger modules in a *hierarchical* manner. In this example, NAND gates were used to build the **binaryToESeg** module. This **binaryToESeg** module, if it had input/output ports, could then be used as a piece of a larger module by instantiating it into another module, and so on. The use of hierarchical descriptions allows us to control the complexity of a design by breaking the design into smaller and more meaningful chunks (i.e. submodules). When instantiating the submodules, all we need know about them is their interface; their potentially complex implementation details are described elsewhere and thus do not clutter the current module's description.

As a final comment, we should point out that the designation of **A, B, C,** and **D** as registers might seem anomalous. One would think that these would be inputs to module **binaryToESeg**, and that the value eSeg would be an output. Eventually they

will be changed to inputs and outputs. But for now, we will keep the register definitions as they will aid in simulation in the next section.

References: gate primitives 4.2.1; net specification 4.2.3

1.1.2 **Simulating the binaryToESeg Driver**

Example 1.2 shows a more complete module definition for **binaryToESeg** called
binaryToESegSim. The example includes statements that will provide stimulus to the
NAND gate instances, and statements that will monitor the changes in their outputs.
Although all possible input combinations are not provided, the ones shown will illustrate how to provide input stimuli.

```
module binaryToESegSim;
      wire    eSeg, p1, p2, p3, p4;
      reg     A, B, C, D;

      nand #1
          g1 (p1, C, ~D),
          g2 (p2, A, B),
          g3 (p3, ~B, ~D),
          g4 (p4, A, C),
          g5 (eSeg, p1, p2, p3, p4);

      initial          // two slashes introduce a single line comment
          begin
              $monitor ($time,,,
                  "A = %b B = %b C = %b D = %b, eSeg = %b",
                  A, B, C, D, eSeg);
              //waveform for simulating the binaryToESeg driver
              #10 A = 0; B = 0; C = 0; D = 0;
              #10 D = 1;
              #10 C = 1; D = 0;
              #10 $finish;
          end
endmodule
```

Example 1.2 binaryToESeg Driver To Be Simulated

A simulator for a digital system is a program that executes the statements in
Example 1.2's *initial* statement (and as we will see later, the *always* statement), and
propagates changed values from the outputs of gates and registers to other gate and
module inputs. A simulator is further characterized by its ability to keep track of *time*,
causing the changed values to appear at some specified time in the future rather than

immediately. These future changes are typically stored in a time-ordered event list. When the simulator has no further statement execution or value propagation to perform at the current time, it finds the next time-ordered event from the event list, updates time to that of the event, and executes the event. This event may or may not generate events at future times. This simulation loop continues until there are no more events to be simulated or the user halts the simulation by some other means.

Example 1.2 differs from Example 1.1 with the inclusion of the initial statement to drive the simulation. The simulator begins the simulation by starting the execution of the initial statement. The keywords begin and end bracket the individual statements that are part of the initial statement. The results of the simulation of this example are shown in Figure 1.1.

```
 0  A = x B = x C = x D = x, eSeg = x
10  A = 0 B = 0 C = 0 D = 0, eSeg = x
12  A = 0 B = 0 C = 0 D = 0, eSeg = 1
20  A = 0 B = 0 C = 0 D = 1, eSeg = 1
22  A = 0 B = 0 C = 0 D = 1, eSeg = 0
30  A = 0 B = 0 C = 1 D = 0, eSeg = 0
32  A = 0 B = 0 C = 1 D = 0, eSeg = 1
```

Figure 1.1 Results of Simulating Example 1.2

The first statement in the initial is a simulation command to monitor (and print) a set of values when any one of the values changes. In this case, the time is printed ($time requests that the current time be printed) and then the quoted string is printed with the values of A, B, C, and D substituted for the %b (for binary) printing control in the string. Between $time and the quoted string are several extra commas. One is needed to separate $time and the quoted string; the extras each introduce an extra space. When issued, the monitor command prints the current values in the design, and will automatically print later when at least one of the values changes. (However, it will not print when only $time changes.) As shown in Figure 1.1, they initially print as x, meaning unknown. The first value on the line is the time.

The initial statement continues by scheduling four events to occur in the future. The statement:

    #10 A = 0; B = 0; C = 0; D = 0;

specifies that registers A, B, C, and D will each be loaded with zero 10 time units from the current time. The way to think about the execution of this line is that the simulator suspends the execution of this initial statement for 10 time units. The simulator sees no other action at the current (zero) time and goes to the next event in the time-ordered event list, which happens to reactivate the initial statement. At that time, time 10, the initial statement is reactivated from where it suspended and the next statement is executed. Indeed, it continues executing on the next line where the simulator sees the next #10. At this point the initial statement is suspended, waiting for ten more time units.

But at the current time (time 10), the changed values (for **A, B, C,** and **D**) are propagated. By propagation, we mean that every primitive gate that is connected to any of these is notified of the change. These gates may then schedule their outputs to change in the future. Because the gates in this example are defined to have a time delay of 1, their output changes will be propagated one time unit into the future (at time 11). Thus, the simulator schedules these values to appear one time unit into the future.

As mentioned above, the initial statement continued executing until it found the delay on the next line which specifies that in 10 <u>more</u> time units (i.e., at time 20), **D** will be loaded with a one. The initial block is suspended and scheduled to wake up at time 20. The simulator looks for the next event in time, and it sees that four NAND gates (**g1** through **g4**) are scheduled to change their output values at time 11 and propagate them to the final NAND gate, g5.

Interestingly, gates **g1** through **g4** should update their outputs at the same time. Indeed, they will all happen at the same "simulated time", in this case time 11. However, the simulator can only update them one at a time. All we know about the order of updates is that it will be arbitrary — we cannot assume that one will happen before the other.

The result of propagating these four new values on wires **p1, p2, p3,** and **p4,** is that gate **g5** will be scheduled to change its output value at time 12. Since there are no further events during the current time (11), the next event is taken from the event list at the next time, which is 12. The change to **eSeg** at time 12 will not cause any other gates to be evaluated because it is not connected to any other gates.

The simulation continues until the initial statement executes the finish command. Specifically, at time 20, **D** is set to 1. This will cause a change to **eSeg** two time units later. Then at time 30, **D** is set to 0, **C** is set to 1, and **eSeg** changes its output two time units later. At time 40, the $finish command stops the simulation program.

The simulator output in Figure 1.1 illustrates three of the four values that a bit may have in the simulator: 1 (TRUE), 0 (FALSE), and x (unknown). The fourth value, z, is used to model the high impedance outputs of tristate gates. Note that at the start of a simulation, all values of nets and registers are **x**.

We now can see why **A, B, C,** and **D** were defined as registers for the examples of this section. As the only "external" inputs to the NAND gates, we needed a means of setting and holding their value during the simulation. Since wires do not hold values

— they merely transmit values from outputs to inputs — the register mechanism was used to hold the input values.

It is useful to note that we have seen the use of the two main data types in the language: nets and registers. Primitive gates are used to drive values onto nets; initial statements (and, as we'll later see, always statements) are used to make assignments to the registers.

As a final comment on the simulation of this example, we should note that simulation times have been described in terms of "time units". A Verilog description is written with time delays specified as we have shown above. The *timescale* compiler directive is then used to attach units and a precision (for rounding) to these numbers. The examples in the book will not specify the actual time units.

References: logic values 4.2.2; timescale compiler directive 4.7.3

Tutorial: See the Tutorial Problems in Appendix A.1.

1.1.3 Creating Ports For the Module

Our previous **binaryToESeg** example had neither inputs nor outputs — a rather limiting situation that does not help in developing a module hierarchy. This example extends our notion of defining modules to include ones that have ports.

```
module binaryToESeg (eSeg, A, B, C, D);
    output  eSeg;
    input   A, B, C, D;

    nand #1
        g1 (p1, C, ~D),
        g2 (p2, A, B),
        g3 (p3, ~B, ~D),
        g4 (p4, A, C),
        g5 (eSeg, p1, p2, p3, p4);
endmodule
```

Example 1.3 Adding Ports to a Module

The first line is the opening module definition statement where the module *ports* are shown in parentheses. Within the module, these ports must be declared to be *inputs*, *outputs*, or bidirectional *inouts*. Note that output(s) need not be first, as is the case with the primitive NAND gates. On the second line, this example declares **eSeg** to be an output port. On the third line, four input ports named A, B, C, and D are declared. In contrast to Example 1.2, A, B, C, and D are now wires that connect the input ports to the gates. The **binarytoESeg** module might be drawn in a logic diagram as shown on the right of the example. Note that the port names are shown on the inside of the module in the logic diagram. The port names are only known inside the module.

This module may now be instantiated into other modules. The port list in the module definition establishes a contract between the internal workings of the module and the external uses of it. That is, there is one output and four inputs to connect to. No other connections within the module (say, wire **p1**) can be connected outside of this module. Indeed, the internal structure of the module is not known from the outside — it could be implemented with NOR gates. Thus, once defined, the module is a blackbox that we can instantiate and connect into the design many times. But since we don't have to be bothered with the internal details of the module each time it is instantiated, we can control the descriptive complexity of the design.

One final note on Example 1.3. We no longer declare that **eSeg**, **p1**, **p2**, **p3**, **p4** are wires. (Previously in Example 1.2, we *optionally* chose to declare them as wires.) Since gates only drive nets, these names, by default, are implicitly declared to be wires.

1.1.4 **Creating a Testbench For a Module**

Normally in this book, we will show individual modules that illustrate specific features of the language. This works well given the space we have to present the material. However, when writing Verilog descriptions, it is often appropriate to organize your description using the *testbench* approach. The idea is based on a vague analogy to an engineer's workbench where you have the system being designed wired to a test generator that is going to provide inputs at controlled intervals and monitor outputs. In Verilog, a module is defined and, possibly, given the name testBench. Within this module are two other modules, one representing the system being designed, and the other representing the test generator and monitor. These are shown in Figure 1.2.

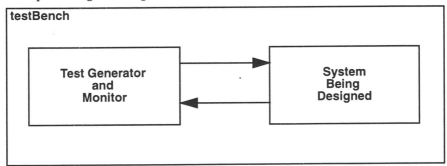

Figure 1.2 General View of a Testbench Module

This is a clean way to separate the design's description and the means of testing it. The system being designed, shown on the right, can be simulated and monitored through its ports, and later the design may be synthesized using other CAD tools. The point is that the descriptions being simulated and synthesized are the same. Further, all testing activity is encapsulated in the module on the left. If you include behavior to test a design within the design's module, then when you synthesize, you may need to remove this behavior — an error prone process. The **binaryToESegSim** module of Example 1.2 showed a module where the design's description (the NAND gate instantiations) and the test behavior (the initial statement) were combined. Example 1.4 shows this description rewritten using the testbench approach.

Module **testBench** instantiates two modules: the design module **binaryToESeg** and the test module **test_bToESeg**. When modules are instantiated, as shown on lines four and five, they are given names. The fourth line states that a module of type **binaryToESeg** is instantiated in this module and given the name d. The fifth line instantiates the **test_bToESeg** module with name t. Now it is clear what the functionality of the system is (it's a binary to seven segment decoder) and what its ports are. Further, it is clear how the system is going to be tested (it's all in the test module). The testbench approach separates this information, clarifying the description, and making it easier to follow on to other design tools such as logic synthesis. The connection of these two modules is illustrated in Figure 1.3.

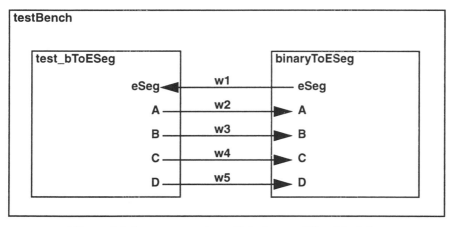

Figure 1.3 Interconnection of Design and Test Modules

Wires need to be declared when connecting modules together. Here, wires **w1** through **w5**, declared on line two of the example, specify the interconnection. We can see that register A in module **test_bToESeg** is connected to an output of the module. In module **testBench**, this port is connected to wire **w2**, which is also connected to port A on module **binaryToESeg**. Inside module **binaryToESeg**, that port is connected to gates **g2** and **g4**. Thus register A drives the inputs of **g2** and **g4**. Simulating module **testBench** will produce the same results as simulating module **binaryToESegSim** in Example 1.2.

```
module testBench;
    wire    w1, w2, w3, w4, w5;

    binaryToESeg    d  (w1, w2, w3, w4, w5);
    test_bToESeg    t  (w1, w2, w3, w4, w5);
endmodule

module binaryToESeg (eSeg, A, B, C, D);
    input   A, B, C, D;
    output  eSeg;

    nand #1
        g1 (p1, C, ~D),
        g2 (p2, A, B),
        g3 (p3, ~B, ~D),
        g4 (p4, A, C),
        g5 (eSeg, p1, p2, p3, p4);
endmodule

module test_bToESeg (eSeg, A, B, C, D);
    input   eSeg;
    output  A, B, C, D;
    reg     A, B, C, D;

    initial         // two slashes introduce a single line comment
        begin
            $monitor ($time,,
                "A = %b B = %b C = %b D = %b, eSeg = %b",
                A, B, C, D, eSeg);
            //waveform for simulating the nand flip flop
            #10 A = 0; B = 0; C = 0; D = 0;
            #10 D = 1;
            #10 C = 1; D = 0;
            #10 $finish;
        end
endmodule
```

Example 1.4 Using the Testbench Approach to Description

Within module **test_bToESeg** we have declared A, B, C, and D to be registers. This is necessary because they are being assigned to in the initial block. Assignments in initial and always blocks must be to registers.

You might think that register A in module **test_bToESeg** and input net A in module **binaryToESeg** are the same because they are named the same. However, in Verilog, each module has its own name space; each A in this example is known only within the module in which it is declared. Thus the two A's are names of distinct entities. In this example though, wire **w2** connects them making them electrically the same.

References: synthesis 6. namespaces 2.6

Tutorial: See the Tutorial Problems in Appendix A.2.

1.2 **Behavioral Modeling of Combinational Circuits**

Our view so far of the Verilog language has mainly highlighted its capabilities of describing structure — module definitions, module instances, and their interconnections. We have only had a very cursory view of the language's capability for describing a module's function behaviorally.

A *behavioral* model of a module is an abstraction of how the module works. The outputs of the module are described in relation to its inputs, but no effort is made to describe how the module is implemented in terms of structural logic gates.

Behavioral models are useful early in the design process. At that point, a designer is more concerned with simulating the system's intended behavior to understand its gross performance characteristics with little regard to its final implementation. Later, structural models with accurate detail of the final implementation are substituted and resimulated to demonstrate functional and timing correctness. In terms of the design process, the key point is that it is often useful to describe and simulate a module using a behavioral description before deciding on the module's actual structural implementation. In this way, the designer can focus on developing the right design (i.e. one that works correctly with the rest of a system and has the intended behavior) before continuing. This behavioral model can then be the starting point for synthesizing several alternate structural implementations of the behavior.

Behavioral models are described in a manner similar to a programming language. As we will see, there are many levels of abstraction at which we may model the behavior of a system. For large systems, we may describe the algorithm that is to be implemented. Indeed, the algorithm may be an almost direct translation from a programming language such as C. At a lower level of abstraction, we may describe the register-transfer level behavior of a circuit, specifying the clock edges and preconditions for each of the system's register transfers. At a still lower level, we may describe the behavior of a logic gate or flip flop. In each case, we use the behavioral modeling constructs of the Verilog language to specify the function of a module without directly specifying its implementation.

1.2.1 Procedural Models

Example 1.5 introduces the behavioral approach to modeling combinational logic. The functionality of the module is described in terms of procedural statements rather than with gate instantiations. The *always* statement, introduced here, is the basis for modeling behavior. The always statement, essentially a "while (TRUE)" statement, includes one or more *procedural* statements that are repeatedly executed. These procedural statements execute much like you would expect a software program to execute: changing register values using the "=" assignment, and executing loops and conditional expressions. Note that within the always statement, all assignments using "=" are made to entities declared as registers. This was also true of the initial statements seen earlier.

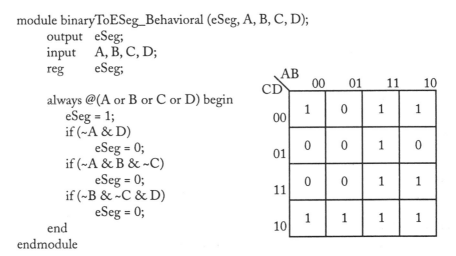

```
module binaryToESeg_Behavioral (eSeg, A, B, C, D);
    output  eSeg;
    input   A, B, C, D;
    reg     eSeg;

    always @(A or B or C or D) begin
        eSeg = 1;
        if (~A & D)
            eSeg = 0;
        if (~A & B & ~C)
            eSeg = 0;
        if (~B & ~C & D)
            eSeg = 0;
    end
endmodule
```

Example 1.5 A Behavioral Model of binaryToESeg

The example shows a behavioral model of our binary to seven segment display driver. The port declarations are the same as before. We have also declared one register, eSeg. This is the register we will make assignments to within the always statement, and it will also be the output of the purely combinational circuit. This always statement starts off with an event control "@" statement. The statement:

@(A or B or C or D) begin … end

states that the simulator should suspend execution of this always block until a change occurs on one of the named entities. Thus, the value of each of A, B, C, and D is sampled. When a change occurs on any one (or more) of these, then execution will continue with the next statement — in this case what is contained in the begin ... end block.

When a change occurs and execution continues, the assignment and if statements shown execute much like you would expect in a programming language. In this case, the statements describe how the output (eSeg) is to be calculated from the inputs. Comparing the statements to the Karnaugh map, one can see that the output is set to one and then, if one of the zeros of the function is on the input, set back to zero. When the begin ... end block finishes, the always block restarts again, waiting for a change on A, B, C, or D. At this point, the simulator will propagate the final value of eSeg to other parts of the design connected to it.

There are two features of the example to note. First, it describes the same functional behavior as the previous example, but there is no mention of the actual gate level implementation; the model is behavioral.

Secondly, the fact that eSeg is declared as a register might make you think that it is not a combinational circuit. But, consider the action of this module when only looking at its ports from the outside. You will quickly conclude that if there is any change on any of the inputs, the output will be re-evaluated based only on the module inputs and driven on the output. This is a fundamental characteristic of a combinational circuit. From the outside of the module, it's clear that this has the behavior of a combinational circuit.

References: always 2.1, if 2.2

1.2.2 **Rules for Synthesizing Combinational Circuits**

Synthesis tools read a behavioral description of a circuit and automatically design a gate level structural version of the circuit. Thus, given Example 1.5 as an input specification, a synthesis tool might produce the design specified in Example 1.3; other implementations are possible too.

Not just any sequence of behavioral statements is appropriate for synthesis of combinational circuits. To use synthesis tools, you need to be very careful with how the description is written. The rules for synthesizing combinational circuits are briefly summarized here but they are covered in far more detail in Chapter 6. To be sure that your synthesized circuit will be combinational:

- Check that all inputs to your combinational function are listed in the control event's sensitivity list (the "or"-separated list of names). That way, if one of them changes, the output is re-evaluated.

The need for this requirement stems from the definition of a purely combinational circuit. The output of a combinational circuit is a function of the current inputs; if one changes, the output should be re-evaluated.

- Check that there is no way to execute the begin...end loop without assigning a value to the combinational output (eSeg in this example). That is, the output must be assigned a value at least once in every execution of the begin...end loop. In Example 1.5, line 7 (eSeg = 1;) assigns a value to eSeg and satisfies this requirement.

  To understand the need for this requirement, consider the situation where you execute the begin...end loop and don't assign to the output. In this case, the circuit needs to remember the previous value. Thus, the output is a function of the current inputs *and* the previous output. This is a fundamental characteristic of a sequential circuit. A synthesized version of such a circuit will have latches to implement the sequential nature of the description. That's not cool, given that we're trying to design a combinational circuit.

Following these two rules will help you in writing behavioral descriptions of combinational circuits that can be used equivalently for either simulation or synthesis.

References: synthesis 6

Tutorial: See the Tutorial Problems in Appendix A.3.

1.3 **Behavioral Modeling of Clocked Sequential Circuits**

Behavioral models also can be used to describe finite state machines. Figure 1.4 shows the state transition diagram for a machine with three states, one input, and one output. The states are encoded by two flip flops named Q1 and Q0. The reset state is encoded with both flip flops being zero. Also shown in the figure is an implementation of the machine using D flip flops and gates.

The traditional diagram of a finite state machine is shown in Figure 1.4. The diagram shows the state registers at the bottom. Their output is the current state of the machine. Their input is the next state of the machine which the registers will load after the clock edge. The next state is a combinational function of the current state and the inputs. The outputs are a combinational function of the current state and (in some systems) the inputs. This traditional structuring appears in the Verilog description. The next state and output combinational functions will be described behaviorally in a single always block following the rules of the previous section. The state registers will be described in a separate always block following a different set of rules.

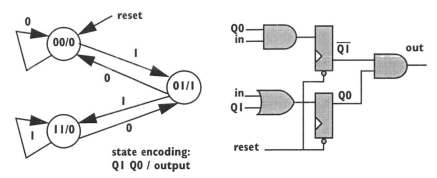

Figure 1.4 State Transition Diagram

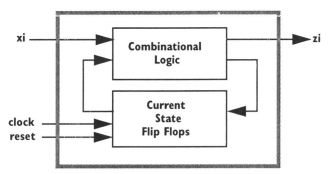

Figure 1.5 Standard Model of a Finite State Machine

1.3.1 Modeling Finite State Machines

A behavioral description of the machine in Figure 1.4 is shown in Example 1.6. We have named the output **out**, the input **in**, and have also provided ports for **clock** and **reset**. The current state of the machine has been named **currentState**. The definition

reg   [1:0]   currentState, nextState;

indicates that **currentState** and **nextState** are two-bit *vectors*. The square brackets ("[ ]") construct declares the range of bit numbers that each register has, the first number being the most-significant bit and the second being the least-significant bit. **out** is also declared to be a register. It and **nextState** are assigned to in the combinational always block that implements the next state and output functions. We have introduced the term *vector* in describing the registers **nextState** and **currentState** in this example. Registers, such as **out**, and nets which are single-bit are said to be *scalar*.

```
module fsm (out, in, clock, reset);
     output          out;
     input           in, clock, reset;
     reg             out;
     reg     [1:0]   currentState, nextState;

     always @(in or currentState) begin  // the combinational portion
         out = ~currentState[1] & currentState[0];
         nextState = 0;
         if (currentState == 0)
              if (in) nextState = 1;
         if (currentState == 1)
              if (in) nextState = 3;
         if (currentState == 3) begin
              if (in) nextState = 3;
              else nextState = 1;
         end
     end

     always @(posedge clock or negedge reset) begin  // the sequential portion
         if (~reset)
              currentState <= 0;
         else
              currentState <= nextState;
     end
endmodule
```

Example 1.6 A Synthesizable Finite State Machine

The first always block describes the combinational behavior of the output and next state logic. The sensitivity list indicates that when a change occurs to **in** or **current-State**, then the begin...end statement is executed. The statements in the begin ... end specify the new values of the combinational outputs **nextState** and **out**. **out** is specified as

out = ~currentState[1] & currentState[0];

indicating that the complement ("~") of bit 1 of **currentState** is AND-ed with bit 0 of **currentState**. The construct "currentState[1]" is called a *bit-select* of a vector — only a single bit from the entire vector is used in the operation. **nextState** is calculated in the following if statements. Consider the third one.

```
        if (currentState == 3) begin
            if (in) nextState = 3;
            else nextState = 1;
        end
```

This states that if **currentState** is equal to 3 (i.e., 11 in two-bit binary, which corresponds to the bottom-left state in the state transition diagram of Figure 1.4), then the new value of **nextState** depends on the value of **in**. If **in** is TRUE, **nextState** is 3 (i.e., 11 in two-bit binary). Otherwise **nextState** is 01 in two-bit binary. The rest of the always statement specifies how **nextState** is calculated when in other states.

The first always block specifies a combinational circuit and it is useful to recheck the combinational rules presented in section 1.2.2. First, the only inputs to this combinational function are **in** and **currentState**. This can be checked by looking at the right-hand sides of the assignment statements and the conditional expressions in the always block. No other named entities appear so these must be the inputs. To be combinational, the or-separated event list must include **in** and **currentState**. It does. Secondly, the combinational outputs **out** and **nextState** must be declared as registers and assigned to in any execution of the always block. They are assigned to in the first two statements of the always block, whether they are overwritten later or not.

The second always block specifies the sequential portion of the finite state machine. We have seen the procedural assignment "=" as it has been used in initial and always statements. This always block introduces the *non-blocking* assignment "<=" — an assignment that might best be described as a concurrent assignment — used in initial and always statements with edge specifications (i.e., posedge or negedge). For now, just think of "=" and "<=" as being the same; later we'll explain the difference.

The sensitivity list in the always block waits for one of two events to occur: either a positive edge on **clock** or a negative edge on **reset**. Think of a positive edge on a signal to be when it changes from a 0 to a 1, and a negative edge to be when a signal changes from a 1 to a 0. When one or both of these occur, the begin...end block is executed. Assume that a negative edge on **reset** occurs. As the begin...end block begins executing, **reset** will be zero and thus **currentState** will be set to zero. As long as **reset** remains zero, even a positive edge on **clock** will only result in **currentState** being set to zero. This is the action of an asynchronous reset signal that overrides the clock on a flip flop.

Now consider the situation where **reset** is one and there is a positive edge on **clock**; the begin...end loop is executed but this time the else clause is taken. The assignment

```
    currentState <= nextState;
```

loads **currentState** with the **nextState**. These statements model the positive edge-triggered behavior of a two-bit register made up of D-type flip flops.

Now we can understand how the whole finite state machine model works. Assume that we are in state 0 (**currentState** is 0), **reset** is 1 (not asserted), **clock** is 0, and **in** is 1. Given these values, then the two combinational outputs are: **out** is 0, and **nextState** is 1. When the positive edge of the **clock** occurs, the second always block will execute and assign the value of **nextState** to **currentState** and then wait again for the next positive edge of **clock** or negative edge of **reset**. Since **currentState** just changed to 1, the first alway block will execute and calculate a new value for **out** and **nextState**. **out** will become 1, and **nextState** will become 3 if **in** remains 1. If **in** becomes 0, the first always block will execute again, recalculating **out** and **nextState** independent of the clock edge; **nextState** will become 0, and **out** will become 0.

References:@ 3.2; if 2.2; bit-select E.1, 2.2;

1.3.2 **Rules for Synthesizing Sequential Systems**

In addition to the rules listed in Section 1.2.2 for combinational circuits, there are rules for sequential systems. The sequential portion of Example 1.6 is the second always block. The rules are:

- The sensitivity list of the always block includes only the edges for the clock, reset and preset conditions.

  These are the only inputs that can cause a state change. For instance, if we are describing a D flip flop, a change on D will not change the flip flop state. So the D input is not included in the sensitivity list.

- Inside the always block, the reset and preset conditions are specified first. If a negative edge on reset was specified, then the if statement should be "if (~reset) …". If a positive edge on reset was being waited for, the if statement should be "if (reset)…".

- A condition on the clock is not specified within the begin…end block. The assignment in the last else is assumed by the synthesis tool to be the next state.

- Any register assigned to in the sequential always block will be implemented using flip flops in the resulting synthesized circuit. Thus you cannot describe purely combinational logic in the same always block where you describe sequential logic. You can write a combinational expression, but the result of that expression will be evaluated at a clock edge and loaded into a register. Look ahead to Example 1.7 for an example of this.

- Non-blocking assignments ("<=") are the assignment operator of choice when specifying the edge-sensitive behavior of a circuit. The "<=" states that all the transfers in the whole system that are specified to occur on the edge in the sensitivity list should occur concurrently. Although descriptions using the regular "=" will synthesize properly, they may not simulate properly. Since both simulation and synthesis are generally of importance, use "<=".

Although these rules may seem to be rather "picky" they are necessary for synthesis tools to infer that a flip flop is needed in the synthesized circuit, and then to infer how it should be connected.

Finally, a note about the **fsm** module. The first is that the use of the names clock and reset have no special meaning for a synthesis tool. We used these names here in the example for clarity; they could be named anything in the model. By using the form of specification shown in Example 1.6, a synthesis tool can infer the need for a flip flop, and what should be connected to its D, clock, and reset inputs.

1.3.3 **Non-Blocking Assignment ("<=")**

The non-blocking assignment is used to synchronize assignment statements so that they all appear to happen at once — concurrently. The non-blocking assignment is used with an edge as illustrated in module **fsm**. When the specified edge occurs, then the new values are loaded concurrently in all assignments that were waiting for the signal's edge. In contrast to the regular assignment ("="), the right-hand sides of <u>all</u> assignments waiting for the signal's edge are evaluated first, and then the left-hand sides are assigned (updated). Think of this as all of these assignments happening concurrently — at the same time — independent of any blocking assignments anywhere in the description. Indeed, when all of the flip flops in a large digital system are clocked from the same clock edge, this is what happens. The non-blocking assignment models this behavior.

Consider an alternate version of the **fsm** module of Example 1.6, shown here in Example 1.7. This time the Verilog is written almost directly from the logic diagram in Figure 1.4. We have modeled the current state flip flops as separately named registers, **cS0** and **cS1**, and we have included the next state equations in the second, sequential always block. Modules **fsm** and **fsmNB** should synthesize to the same hardware.

Consider how the second always block works. The block waits for either a positive edge on **clock** or a negative edge on **reset**. If the negative edge on reset occurs, then both cS0 and cS1 are set to 0. If the positive edge of **clock** occurs, the right-hand sides of the two "<=" assignments are evaluated. Then all of the assignments are made to the registers on the left-hand side. Thus "Q0 & in" (the AND of Q0 and in) and "Q1 | in" (the OR of Q1 and in) are both evaluated, and then the results are assigned to cS1 and cS0 respectively.

When looking at the description, you should think of the two statements

```
cS1 <= in & cS0;
cS0 <= in | cS1;
```

as occurring at the same time (i.e., concurrently). Think of the right-hand sides as the inputs to two flip flops, and that the change in cS1 and cS0 occur when the clock edge occurs. Realize that they occur concurrently. The cS1 on the left-hand side of the first line is not the value cS1 used on the right-hand side of the second line. cS0 and cS1 on the right-hand sides are the values <u>before</u> the clock edge. cS0 and cS1 on the left-hand sides are the values <u>after</u> the clock edge. These statements could have been written in either order with the same resulting values for cS0 and cS1 after the clock edge.

```
module fsmNB (out, in, clock, reset);
    output        out;
    input         in, clock, reset;
    reg           out, cS1, cS0;

    always @(cS1 or cS0)    // the combinational portion
        out = ~cS1 & cS0;

    always @(posedge clock or negedge reset) begin  // the sequential portion
        if (~reset) begin
            cS1 <= 0;
            cS0 <= 0;
        end
        else begin
            cS1 <= in & cS0;
            cS0 <= in | cS1;
        end
    end
endmodule
```

Example 1.7 Illustrating the Non-Blocking Assignment

This example illustrates the functionality being specified with the non-blocking assignment. Across a whole design there may be many always statements in many different modules waiting on the same edge of the same signal. The powerful feature of the non-blocking assignment is that all of these right-hand side expressions will be evaluated before any of the left-hand side registers are updated. Thus, you don't need to worry about which value of cS1 is being used to calculate cS0. With the "<=" you know it is the value before the clock edge.

Tutorial: See the Tutorial Problems in Appendix A.4.

1.4 **Module Hierarchy**

Let's begin building a larger example that includes more and varied components. Figure 1.6 illustrates pictorially what our design looks like. In this section we will

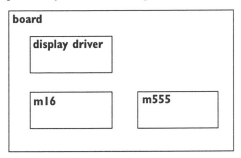

Figure 1.6 The Counter Example

detail each of the modules and their interconnection. The example consists of a board module which contains a **clock** module (**m555**), a four-bit counter (**m16**), and our **binaryToESeg** display driver from section 1.2.

1.4.1 **The Counter**

We look first at the counter module definition shown in Example 1.8. Our counter has two ports: a clock to increment the counter, and the 4-bit counter value **ctr**. The example declares that the internal register **ctr** and its output port are 4-bit *vector*s. The counter is modeled behaviorally using an always block. The module waits for a positive edge on **clock**. When that occurs, **ctr** is incremented and the module waits for the next positive edge on **clock**. Since the generation of the new counter value occurs on an edge of a signal, the non-blocking assignment operator ("<=") is used.

```
module m16 (ctr, clock);
      output   [3:0]   ctr;
      reg      [3:0]   ctr;
      input            clock;

      always @(posedge clock)
          ctr <= ctr + 1;
endmodule
```

Example 1.8 A 4-Bit Counter

1.4.2 **A Clock for the System**

Our counter needs a clock to drive it. Example 1.9 defines an abstraction of a "555" timer chip called **m555** and shows the waveform generated from simulating the description.

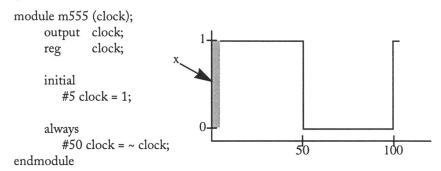

```
module m555 (clock);
    output   clock;
    reg      clock;

    initial
        #5 clock = 1;

    always
        #50 clock = ~ clock;
endmodule
```

Example 1.9 A Clock For the Counter

The **m555** module has an internal register (**clock**) which is also the output of the module. At the start of a simulation, the output has the value x as illustrated by the gray area in the example's timing diagram. The **clock** is initialized to be one after 5 time units have passed. The **m555** is further modeled behaviorally with an always statement which states that after 50 time units **clock** will be loaded with its complement. Since an always statement is essentially a "while (TRUE)" loop, after the first 50 time units have passed, the always statement will be scheduled to execute and change its value in another 50 time units; i.e., this time at time 100. Because **clock** will change value every 50 time units, we have created a clock with a period of 100 time units.

We may want to specify the clock period with real time units. The timescale compiler directive is used to specify the time units of any delay operator (#), and the precision to which time calculations will be rounded. If the compiler directive

`timescale 1ns / 100ps

was placed before a module definition, then all delay operators in that module and any module that followed it would be in units of nanoseconds and any time calculations would be internally rounded to the nearest one hundred picoseconds.

References: timescale 4.7.3

1.4.3 **Tying the Whole Circuit Together**

We have now defined the basic modules to be used in our system. What remains is the tying of these together to complete the design shown in Figure 1.6. Example 1.10 ties together the module definitions in Examples 1.3, 1.8, and 1.9 by defining another module (called **board**) that instantiates and interconnects these modules. This is shown graphically in Figure 1.7.

```
module board;
        wire      [3:0]   count;
        wire              clock, eSeg;

        m16               counter    (count, clock);
        m555              clockGen   (clock);
        binaryToESeg  disp          (eSeg, count[3], count[2], count[1], count[0]);

        initial
            $monitor ($time,,,"count=%d, eSeg=%d", count, eSeg);
endmodule
```

Example 1.10 The Top-Level Module of the Counter

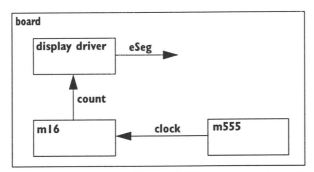

Figure 1.7 The Counter Example With Connections Shown

Most of the statements in the **board** module definition have previously been described, however there are a few details to point out. The module declaration of the counter shows two ports, **ctr** and **clock**.

module m16 (ctr, clock);

ctr is a 4-bit output and **clock** is a 1-bit input. The counter output in Example 1.10 is connected to the **binaryToESeg** module. However, this module is defined to have five 1-bit ports.

module binaryToESeg (eSeg, A, B, C, D);

In the **board** module, we define a 4-bit wire **count** that connects to **m16**. When we connect it to **binaryToESeg** we need to connect each bit (A through D) individually. This we do with a *bit-select* of the count wire, specifying the appropriate bit for each connection. A bit-select allows us to specify a single bit in a register or wire that has been declared to be a vector. Thus, the connection in to **binaryToESeg** in module **board** becomes

binaryToESeg   disp   (eSeg, count[3], count[2], count[1], count[0]);

This connects **count[3]** to A, **count[2]** to B, **count[1]** to C, and **count[0]** to D.

Alternately, as shown in Example 1.11, we could have declared four scalar wires and then *concatenated* them together when connecting to the **m16** module. Here we define scalar wires **w3, w2, w1, w0** and we connect them to ports A, B, C, and D of **binaryToESeg**. However, module **m16** expects a 4-bit vector to connect to its **ctr** port. The concatenation operator "{..., ...}" allows us to combine several wires together to form a multibit wire. Here w3, w2, w1, and w0 are grouped (concatenated) together and treated as one 4-bit entity when connecting to **m16**.

```
module boardWithConcatenation;
    wire            clock, eSeg, w3, w2, w1, w0;

    m16             counter    ({w3, w2, w1, w0}, clock);
    m555            clockGen   (clock);
    binaryToESeg    disp       (eSeg, w3, w2, w1, w0);

    initial
        $monitor ($time,,,"count=%d, eSeg=%d", {w3, w2, w1, w0}, eSeg);
endmodule
```

Example 1.11 An Alternate Top-Level Module

If the module definitions in Examples 1.3, 1.8, 1.9, and 1.10 are compiled together, they form a complete description that can be simulated. Interestingly though, nothing will happen! Since **ctr** is not initialized, it is unknown (**x**). When it is incremented at the positive edge of **clock**, the result of adding one to an unknown is still unknown. To make this simulation model work, **ctr** needs to be initialized. Inserting the statement

initial ctr = 1;

in module **m16** will solve the problem. The simulation trace from simulating these combined examples (with **ctr** initialized) for 802 time units is shown in Figure 1.8.

Initially, all values in the system at time 0 are unknown. Then all of the initial and always blocks are enabled to run; they begin running in an arbitrary order. The initial statements in **m555** begin by delaying for #5 and #50 respectively. The always in **m16** begins by waiting for a positive edge on the **clock**. The gate primitives in **binaryToE-Seg** wait for a change on their inputs. The initial statements in **board** and **m16** can also run. We can see that the one in **m16** runs first, setting **ctr** to 1. Then the initial in **board** runs, executing the $monitor statement and printing the first line in the figure. (If the $monitor had executed before the initialization of **ctr**, **count** would have printed as x.)

Given that **ctr** (**count**) is set to 1 at time 0, two time units later **eSeg** changes its value to 0 (**eSeg** is off when the **ctr** 1 is being displayed). At time 5, **clock** changes from x to 1. In Verilog, this is interpreted as a positive edge, which changes **ctr** (**count**) to 2. Two time units later, at time 7, **eSeg** changes to 1 because the **eSeg** is on when displaying the **ctr** 2. At time 50, **clock** changes to 0. However, this is not shown in our simulation because we were not monitoring the change in the **clock**. At time 100, **clock** changes to 1, creating a positive edge on **clock** and incrementing **ctr** (**count**). **ctr** changes to 3 and **eSeg** changes appropriately two time units later. The simulation continues as shown.

```
  0 count= 1, eSeg=x
  2 count= 1, eSeg=0
  5 count= 2, eSeg=0
  7 count= 2, eSeg=1
100 count= 3, eSeg=1
102 count= 3, eSeg=0
200 count= 4, eSeg=0
300 count= 5, eSeg=0
400 count= 6, eSeg=0
402 count= 6, eSeg=1
500 count= 7, eSeg=1
502 count= 7, eSeg=0
600 count= 8, eSeg=0
602 count= 8, eSeg=1
700 count= 9, eSeg=1
702 count= 9, eSeg=0
800 count=10, eSeg=0
802 count=10, eSeg=1
```

Figure 1.8 Simulation Trace of Examples 1.3, 1.8, 1.9, and 1.10

It is interesting to note that the initial statement is necessary for simulating Example 1.8. However it is not necessary to synthesize it. In fact, logic synthesis ignores the initial block.

References: module instantiation 4.2.4; net declaration 4.2.3; always 2.1; $display F.1

1.4.4 **Tying Behavioral and Structural Models Together**

In several examples, we connected together modules that were defined differently. Some of them were defined structurally using only gate level primitives. And some were defined behaviorally, using always blocks. This is a powerful aspect of the language because it allows us to model parts of a system at a detailed level (i.e., the structural models) and other parts at a less detailed level (the behavioral models). At the start of a design project, most of the system will be at the behavioral level. Then parts will be detailed into structural models. The final simulation could then be with all modules defined at the gate level for accurate timing and functional simulation. Thus the language aids in the complete design process, allowing a design to evolve from behavioral through to structural in evolutionary steps.

Example 1.10 and its submodules partially illustrate how behavioral and structural elements connect together. In this example, the structural **binaryToESeg** module in Example 1.3 is connected together with the behavioral **m16** module from Example 1.8. The register **ctr** in **m16** is declared to be an output. Any changes to **ctr** are propagated through the module ports and eventually to gate inputs. Thus we see that registers specified in behavioral models can drive the inputs of gate primitives. This need not be done in separate modules.

Indeed we could combine the functionality of these two modules as shown in Example 1.12. Here within one module we have both structural and behavioral components. Anytime **ctr** is updated, the gates **g1** through **g4** will re-evaluate their output because their inputs are connected to **ctr**. Thus, the "output" of an always block — the values in the registers assigned to by the always block — can be used as inputs to gate level primitives.

In like manner, the outputs of gate level primitives can be used as "inputs" to always blocks as illustrated in Example 1.13. Here we alter the original structural **binarytoESeg** module to produce **mixedUpESegDriver**. The change is that the final NAND gate that NAND-ed together the outputs of the other NAND gates has been described behaviorally using an always block. This always block waits for any change on **p1**, **p2**, **p3**, or **p4**. When a change occurs, the behavioral statement calculates their NAND storing it in register **eSeg**. This value is the combinational output of the module. Thus the outputs of gate primitives can drive the inputs — values on the right-hand side of behavioral expressions — of behavioral blocks.

```
module counterToESeg (eSeg, clock);
    output          eSeg;
    reg      [3:0]  ctr;
    input           clock;

    initial
        ctr = 0;

    always @(posedge clock)
        ctr <= ctr + 1;

    nand #1
        g1 (p1, ctr[1], ~ctr[0]),
        g2 (p2, ctr[3], ctr[2]),
        g3 (p3, ~ctr[2], ~ctr[0]),
        g4 (p4, ctr[3], ctr[1]),
        g5 (eSeg, p1, p2, p3, p4);
endmodule
```

Example 1.12 Behavior Driving Structure

```
module mixedUpESegDriver (eSeg, A, B, C, D);
    output          eSeg;
    reg             eSeg;
    input           A, B, C, D;

    nand #1
        g1 (p1, C, D),
        g2 (p2, A, ~B),
        g3 (p3, ~B, ~D),
        g4 (p4, A, C);

    always @(p1 or p2 or p3 or p4)
        eSeg = ~(p1 & p2 & p3 & p4);
endmodule
```

Example 1.13 Structure Driving Behavior

These examples serve to illustrate the two main data types in the language, registers and nets, and how they work together. Gate primitives drive their outputs onto nets (in our examples, wires). Gate inputs can either be other nets, or registers. Behavioral models, i.e., always blocks, change register values as a result of their execution. Their inputs can either be other registers, or nets driven by gate primitives.

References: procedural assignment 2.1; continuous assignment 4.4; timing models 5.1

Tutorial: See the Tutorial Problems in Appendix A.5.

1.5 **Finite State Machine and Datapath**

We've used the language to specify combinational logic and finite state machines. Now we'll move up to specifying register transfer level systems. We'll use a method of specification known as finite state machine and datapath, or FSM-D. Our system will be made up of two parts: a datapath that can do computations and store results in registers, and a finite state machine that will control the datapath.

1.5.1 **A Simple Computation**

We begin with a simple computation and show how to specify the logic hardware using Verilog. The computation is shown below in a C-like syntax:

```
...
for (x = 0, i = 0; i <= 10; i = i + 1)
        x = x + y;
if (x < 0)
        y = 0;
else   x = 0;
...
```

The computation starts off by clearing x and i to 0. Then, while i is less than or equal to 10, x is assigned the sum of x and y, and i is incremented. When the loop is exited, if x is less than zero, y is assigned the value 0. Otherwise, x is assigned the value 0. This example will illustrate building larger systems.

We'll assume that these are to be 8-bit computations and thus all registers in the system will be 8-bit.

1.5.2 **A Datapath For Our System**

There are many ways to implement this computation in hardware and we will focus on only one of them. A datapath for this system must have registers for x, i, and y. It needs to be able to increment i, add x and y, and clear i, x, and y. It also needs to be able to compare i with 10 and x with 0. Figure 1.9 illustrates a datapath that could execute these register transfers.

The name in each box in the figure suggests its functionality. Names with overbars are control signals that are asserted low. Looking at the block labeled **register i**, we see

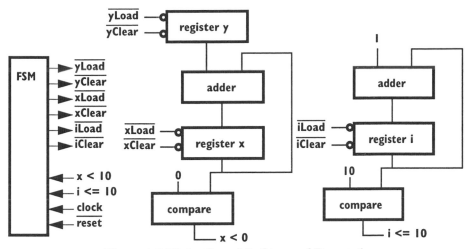

Figure 1.9 Finite State Machine and Datapath

that its output (coming from the bottom) is connected back to the input of an adder whose other input is connected to 1. The output of that adder (coming from the bottom) is connected to the input of **register i.** Given that the register stores a value and the adder is a combinational circuit, the input to **register i** will always be one greater than the current value of **register i.** The register also has two control inputs: **iLoad** and **iClear.** When one of these inputs is asserted, the specified function will occur at the next clock edge. If we assert **iLoad,** then after the next clock edge **register i** will load and store its input, incrementing **i.** Alternately, **iClear** will load a zero into **register i.** The compare modules are also combinational and produce the Boolean result indicated.

The register transfers shown in our computation are x = 0, i = 0, y = 0, i = i + 1, and x = x + y. From the above description of how the datapath works, we can see that all of the register transfers in our computation can be executed on this datapath. Further, all of the conditional values needed for branching in the FSM are generated in the datapath.

The FSM shown on the left sequences through a series of states to cause the computation to occur. The FSM's outputs are **yLoad, yClear, xLoad, xClear, iLoad,** and **iClear.** Its inputs are x<0 and i<=10. A master **clock** drives the state registers in the FSM as well as the datapath registers. A **reset** signal is also connected.

1.5.3 **Details of the Functional Datapath Modules**

The datapath is made up of three basic modules: registers, adders, and comparators. The register module definition is shown in Example 1.14. Looking first at the always block, we see that it is very similar to those we've seen in sequential circuit descriptions so far. The register is positive edge triggered but does not have an asynchronous reset. To go along with the register modules defined for our datapath, it has two control points: clear and load. These control points, when asserted, will cause the register to perform the requisite function. If input **clear** is asserted, it will load 0 at the **clock** edge. If **load** is asserted, it will load input **in** into register **out** at the **clock** edge. If both are asserted, then the register will perform the clear function.

```
module register (out, in, clear, load, clock);
    parameter            Width = 8;
    output  [Width-1:0]  out;
    reg     [Width-1:0]  out;
    input   [Width-1:0]  in;
    input                clear, load, clock;

    always @(posedge clock)
        if (~clear)
            out <= 0;
        else if (~load)
            out <= in;
endmodule
```

Example 1.14 Register Module

This example introduces a new statement, the parameter statement. The parameter defines a name to have a value; in this case **Width** has the value 8. This name is known within the module and can be used in any of the statements. Here we see it being used to define the default value for the left-most bit number in the vector definitions of the output and register **out** and the input **in**. Given that **Width** is defined to be 8, the left-most bit is numbered 7 (i.e., 8-1) and **out** and **in** both have a bitwidth of eight (i.e., bits 7 through 0). What is interesting about a parameter is that the default value can be overridden at instantiation time. That is, this module definition can be used to instantiate registers of different bitwidth. We will see how shortly.

The adder module is shown in Example 1.15. It is parameterized to have a default bitwidth of eight. But, it also makes use of a new behavioral construct: the continuous *assign* statement. The assign statement allows us to describe a combinational logic function without regard to its actual structural implementation — that is, there are no instantiated gates with wires and port connections. In a simulation of the circuit, the result of the logical expression on the right-hand side of the equal sign is evaluated anytime one of its values changes and the result drives the output **sum**. Another way of thinking of the continuous assign statement is that it allows you to write a Boolean expression, but using the larger behavioral operator set of Verilog. The assign statement in this example shows a means of generating our "adder" function. The output sum is assigned the arithmetic sum of inputs **a** and **b** using the "+" operator. The assign statement is discussed further in Chapter 4.

```
module adder (sum, a, b);
    parameter   Width = 8;
    input    [Width-1:0]  a, b;
    output  [Width-1:0]  sum;

    assign sum = a + b;
endmodule
```

Example 1.15 The Adder Module

The **compareLT** and **compareLEQ** modules are shown in Example 1.16, again using the continuous assign statement. In the **compareLT** module, **a** is compared to **b**. If **a** is less than **b**, then **out** is set to TRUE. Otherwise it is set to FALSE. The compareLEQ module for comparing **i** with 10 in our computation is similar to this module except with the "<=" operator instead of the "<" operator. The width of these modules are also parameterized. Don't be confused by the second assign statement, namely:

```
assign out = a <= b;
```

This does not assign **b** to **a** with a non-blocking assignment, and then assign **a** to **out** with a blocking assignment. Only one assignment is allowed in a statement. Thus by their position in the statement, we know that the first is an assignment and the second is a less than or equal comparison.

```
module compareLT (out, a, b);    // compares a < b
    parameter   Width = 8;
    input        [Width-1:0]  a, b;
    output                    out;

    assign out = a < b;
endmodule

module compareLEQ (out, a, b); // compares a <= b
    parameter   Width = 8;
    input        [Width-1:0]  a, b;
    output                    out;

    assign out = a <= b;
endmodule
```

Example 1.16 The CompareLT and CompareLEQ Modules

The **adder, compareLEQ,** and **compareLT** modules could have written using the combinational version of the always block discussed earlier in section 1.2. As used in these examples, the two forms are equivalent. Typically, the continuous assign approach is used when a combinational function can be described in a simple statement. More complex combinational functions, including ones with don't care specifications, are typically easier to describe with a combinational always statement.

References: continuous assign 4.4

1.5:4 **Wiring the Datapath Together**

Now we build a module to instantiate all of the necessary FSM and datapath modules and wire them together. This module, shown in Example 1.17, begins by declaring the 8-bit wires needed to connect the datapath modules together, followed by the 1-bit wires to connect the control lines to the FSM. Following the wire definitions, the module instantiations specify the interconnection shown in Figure 1.9.

```
module sillyComputation (yIn, y, x, ck, reset);
    parameter    Width = 8;
    input                    ck, reset;
    input    [Width-1:0]  yIn;
    output   [Width-1:0]  y, x;
    wire     [Width-1:0]  i, addiOut, addxOut;
    wire                    yLoad, yClear, xLoad, xClear, iLoad, iClear;

    register    #(Width)    I    (i, addiOut, iClear, iLoad, ck),
                            Y    (y, yIn, yClear, yLoad, ck),
                            X    (x, addxOut, xClear, xLoad, ck);

    adder       #(Width)    addI (addiOut, 1, i),
                            addX (addxOut, y, x);

    compareLT   #(Width)         cmpX (xLT0, x, 0);
    compareLEQ  #(Width)         cmpI (iLEQ10, i, 10);

    fsm            ctl
    (xLT0, iLEQ10, yLoad, yClear, xLoad, xClear, iLoad, iClear, ck, reset);
endmodule
```

Example 1.17 Combining the FSM and Datapath

Note that this module also defines a **Width** parameter, uses it in the wire definitions, and also in the module instantiations. Consider the module instantiation for the register I from Example 1.17.

register   #(Width)   I   (i, addiOut, iClear, iLoad, ck),

What is new here is the second item on the line, "#(Width)". This value is substituted in the module instantiation for its parameter. Thus, by changing the parameter **Width** in module **sillyComputation** to, say 23, then all of the module instantiations for the datapath would be 23 bits wide. Parameterizing modules allows us to reuse a generic module definition in more places, making a description easier to write. If #(Width) had not been specified in the module instantiation statement, then the default value of 8, specified in module **register**, would be used.

1.5.5 **Specifying the FSM**

Now that the datapath has been specified, a finite state machine is needed to evoke the register transfers in the order and under the conditions specified by the original computation. We first present a state transition diagram for this system and then describe the Verilog **fsm** module to implement it.

The state transition diagram is shown in Figure 1.10 along with the specification for the computation. The states marked "..." represent the computation before and after the portion of interest to us. Each state "bubble" indicates the FSM outputs that are to be asserted during that state; all others will be unasserted. The arrows indicate the next state; a conditional expression beside an arrow indicates the condition in which that state transition is taken. The diagram is shown as a Moore machine, where the outputs are a function only of the current state. Finally, the states are labeled **A** through **F** for discussion purposes.

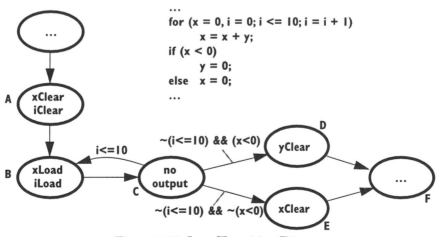

Figure 1.10 State Transition Diagram

Following through the computation and the state transition diagram, we see that the first action is to clear both the **x** and **i** registers in state A. This means that while the machine is in state A, xClear and iClear are asserted (low). Note though that the registers i and x will not become zero until after the positive clock edge and we're in state B. State B then asserts the load signals for x and i. The datapath in Figure 1.9 shows us what values are actually being loaded: x + y and i + 1 respectively. Thus, state B executes both the loop body and the loop update. From state B the system goes to state C where there is no FSM output asserted. However, from state C there are three possible next states depending on whether we are staying in the loop (going to state B), exiting the loop and going to the then part of the conditional (state D), or exiting the loop and going to the else part of the conditional (state E). The next state after D or E is state F, the rest of the computation.

It is useful to understand why state C is needed in this implementation of the system. After all, couldn't the conditional transitions from state C have come from state B where x and i are loaded? The answer is no. The timing diagram in Figure 1.11 illustrates the transitions between states A, B, and C. During the time when the system is in state B, the asserted outputs of the finite state machine are xLoad and iLoad, meaning that the x and i registers are enabled to load from their inputs. But they will not be loaded until the next clock edge, the same clock edge that will transit the finite state machine into state C. Thus the values of i, on which the end of loop condition is based, and x, on which the if-then-else condition is based, are not available for comparison until the system is in state C. In the timing diagram, we see that since i is less than or equal to 10, the next state after C is B.

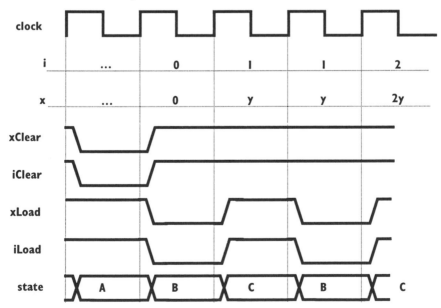

Figure 1.11 Timing Diagram For States A, B, and C.

It is interesting to note that in this implementation of the system, the exit condition of the for loop is not checked before entering the loop. However, given that we just cleared i before entering the loop, it is not necessary to check that is less than or equal to 10. Further, with a different datapath, state C might not be necessary. For instance, the comparisons with i and x could be based on the input value to these registers, thus comparing with the future value. Or the constants with which the comparisons are made could be changed. Of course, these are all at the discretion of the designer.

Now consider the Verilog model of the finite state machine for this system shown in Example 1.18. The machine's inputs are the two conditions, x < 0 and i <= 10. Internal to the **fsm** module, they are called LT and LEQ respectively. Module **fsm** also has a **reset** input and a clock (ck) input. The module outputs are the control points on the registers (yLoad, yClear, xLoad, xClear, iLoad, iClear). Like our previous fsm examples, there are two always blocks, one for the sequential state change and the other to implement the next state and output combinational logic. Registers are declared for all of the combinational outputs.

Our state machine will only implement the states shown in the state transition diagram, even though there would be many more states in the rest of the computation. Thus, the width of the state register (cState) was chosen to be three bits. Further, the reset state is shown to be state 0 although in the full system it would be some other state. A very simple state assignment has been chosen, with state A encoded by 0, B encoded by 1, and so on.

The first always block is very similar to our previous state machine examples. If **reset** is asserted, then the reset state is entered. Otherwise, the combinational value **nState** is loaded into **cState** at the positive **clock** edge.

The second always block implements the next state and output combinational logic. The inputs to this combinational logic are the current state (cState) and **fsm** inputs (LT and LEQ). The body of the always block is organized around the value of cState. A case statement, essentially a multiway branch, is used to specify what is to happen given each possible value of cState. The value of the expression in parentheses, in this case cState, is compared to the values listed on each line. The line with the matching value is executed.

Following through this case statement, the line following the case keyword specifies a numeric value followed by a colon. The number 3'b000 is the Verilog notation for a 3-bit number, specified here in binary as 000. The b indicates binary — other options include h for hexadecimal and d for decimal.

If the current state changes to state A, then the value of **cState** is 0 given our encoding. Thus, when this change occurs, the always block will execute, and the statement on the right side of the 3'b000: will execute. This statement specifies that all of the outputs are unasserted (1) except **iClear** and **xClear**, and the next state is 3'b001 (which is state **B**). If the current state is **B**, then the second case item (3'b001) is executed, asserting **iLoad** and **xLoad**, and unasserting all of the other outputs. The next state from state **B** is **C**, encoded as 3'b010. State **C** shows a more complex next state calculation; the three if statements specify the possible next states from state **C** and the conditions when each would be selected.

The last case item specifies the **default** situation. This is the statement that is executed if none of the other items match the value of **cState**. For simulation purposes, you might want to have a $display statement to print out an error warning that you've reached an illegal state. The $display prints a message on the screen during simulation, acting much like a print statement in a programming language. This one displays the message "Oops, unknown state: %b" with the binary representation of **cState** substituted for %b.

To make this always block a combinational synthesizable function, the default is required. Consider what happens if we didn't have the default statement and the value of **cState** was something other than one of the five values specified. In this situation, the case statement would execute, but none of the specified actions would be executed. And thus, the outputs would not be assigned to. This breaks the combinational synthesis rule that states that every possible path through the always block must assign to every combinational output. Thus, although it is <u>optional</u> to have the default case for debugging a description through simulation, the default is <u>required</u> for this always block to synthesize to a combinational circuit. Of course a default is not required for synthesis if all known value cases have been specified or **cState** was assigned a value before the case statement.

Consider now how the whole FSM-Datapath system works together. Assume that the current state is state **C** and the values of **i** and **x** are 1 and **y** respectively, as shown in the timing diagram of Figure 1.11. Assume further that the clock edge that caused the system to enter state **C** has just happened and **cState** has been loaded with value 3'b010 (the encoding for state **C**). Not only has **cState** changed, but registers **x** and **i** were also loaded as a result of coming from state **B**.

In our description, several always blocks are were waiting for changes to **cState**, **x**, and **i**. These include the **fsm**'s combinational always block, the adders, and the compare modules. Because of the change to **cState**, **x**, and **i**, these always blocks are now enabled to execute. The simulator will execute them, in arbitrary order. Indeed, the simulator may execute some of them several times. (Consider the situation where the **fsm**'s combinational always block executes first. Then after the compare modules execute, it will have to execute again.) Eventually, new values will be generated for the outputs of the comparators. Changes in LT and LEQ in the **fsm** module will cause its combinational always block to execute, generating a value for **nState**. At the next positive clock edge, this value will be loaded into **cState** and another state will be entered.

```verilog
module fsm (LT, LEQ, yLoad, yClear, xLoad, xClear, iLoad, iClear, ck, reset);
input    LT, LEQ, ck, reset;
output   yLoad, yClear, xLoad, xClear, iLoad, iClear;
reg      yLoad, yClear, xLoad, xClear, iLoad, iClear;
reg      [2:0]    cState, nState;

always @(posedge ck or negedge reset)
    if (~reset)
            cState <= 0;
    else    cState <= nState;

always @(cState or LT or LEQ)
    case (cState)
        3'b000 :  begin      // state A
                    yLoad = 1; yClear = 1; xLoad = 1; xClear = 0;
                    iLoad = 1; iClear = 0; nState = 3'b001;
                 end
        3'b001 :  begin      // state B
                    yLoad = 1; yClear = 1; xLoad = 0; xClear = 1;
                    iLoad = 0; iClear = 1; nState = 3'b010;
                 end
        3'b010 :  begin      // state C
                    yLoad = 1; yClear = 1; xLoad = 1; xClear = 1;
                    iLoad = 1; iClear = 1;
                    if (LEQ) nState = 3'b001;
                    if (~LEQ & LT) nState = 3'b011;
                    if (~LEQ & ~LT) nState = 3'b100;
                 end
        3'b011 :  begin      // state D
                    yLoad = 1; yClear = 0; xLoad = 1; xClear = 1;
                    iLoad = 1; iClear = 1; nState = 3'b101;
                 end
        3'b100 :  begin      // state E
                    yLoad = 1; yClear = 1; xLoad = 1; xClear = 0;
                    iLoad = 1; iClear = 1; nState = 3'b101;
                 end
        default : begin // required to satisfy combinational synthesis rules
                    yLoad = 1; yClear = 1; xLoad = 1; xClear = 1;
                    iLoad = 1; iClear = 1; nState = 3'b000;
                    $display ("Oops, unknown state: %b", cState);
                 end
    endcase
endmodule
```

Example 1.18 FSM For the Datapath

References: case 2.4; number representation B.3

Tutorial: See the Tutorial Problems in Appendix A.6.

1.6 Cycle-Accurate Behavioral Descriptions

As we have progressed through this tutorial, the level of abstraction of the Verilog descriptions has increased. We again move up to a higher level: *cycle accurate*, sometimes called *scheduled behavior*. At this level, we describe systems in a clock-cycle-by-clock-cycle fashion, specifying the behavior that is to occur in each state. The term *cycle-accurate* is used because the values in the system are specified to be valid only at the time of the system's state change — at a clock edge. The resulting description can be simulated, or it can be synthesized, using behavioral synthesis tools, producing the FSM-D style of description presented in section 1.5.

1.6.1 Specification Approach

Scheduled behavior is specified using always blocks, and "@(posedge clock);" statements are used to break the specification into clock cycles or states. Example 1.19 illustrates a scheduled behavioral description of the simple calculation from section 1.5. The module has ports for registers x, y, and the **clock**. Register i, a loop counter, is only used inside the module.

Before discussing the cycle accurate nature of the description, let's explain the always block and the new statement used in it: the while statement. The while statement is similar to the while statements used in programming languages. This statement evaluates the while condition ("i <= 10"). If this condition is TRUE the loop is entered and the loop body is executed; in this case we add y to x and increment i. We then continue on to evaluate the while condition and execute the loop body as long as the condition is still TRUE. It the condition is FALSE, the loop body is not executed. Given that, in this example, i will be less than or equal to 10 when the while condition is first evaluated, the loop is entered. (However, if the while condition was false when first evaluated, the loop body is not executed and control passes to the next statement after the while.) Thus, the while statements loop body will only execute when the condition is TRUE.

Using this style of description, an "@(posedge clock);" statement is followed by behavioral statements and then by another "@(posedge clock) statement. We'll call this "@(posedge clock)" the *clock event*. The statements between the two clock events constitute a state. The clock event statements need not appear in pairs; if there is only one clock event statement in a loop body, then the loop executes in one state and the next clock event is, indeed, itself.

```
module simpleTutorial (clock, y, x);
    input            clock;
    output  [7:0]    x, y;
    reg     [7:0]    x, y, i;

    always begin
        @(posedge clock) x <= 0;
        i = 0;
        while (i <= 10) begin
            @(posedge clock);
            x <= x + y;
            i = i + 1;
        end
        @(posedge clock);
        if (x < 0)
                y <= 0;
        else   x <= 0;
    end
endmodule
```

> state A

> state B

> state C

Example 1.19 Description Using Scheduled Behavioral Approach

In example 1.19, consider state C, the last clock event and the statement that follows it as shown in Figure 1.12. The statement that follows the clock event here is an if-else statement. Given that the always continuously loops, the next clock event is the one at the top of the always block, which starts state A. Thus, these statements show the specification of one state. In that state, either y or x is assigned the value 0, depending on whether x is less than 0. On the right of the figure the state corresponding to the description is shown. Mealy notation is used (where outputs are a function of inputs and current state), indicating that if x is less than 0 then we'll follow the top arc to state A and load register y with 0 (using a non-blocking assignment). The bottom arc shows the inverse condition when x is set to zero. In simulation, when the clock event before the if statement is being waited for, we are executing state C.

```
@(posedge clock);
if (x < 0)
        y <= 0;
else   x <= 0;
```

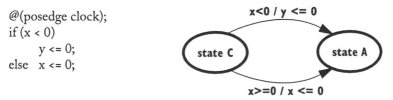

Figure 1.12 State C

The full state transition diagram is shown in Figure 1.13. The state **A** initializes x and i to 0 and enters the loop. The state **B** is the loop body and state **C** is the if-else as described above. The state **B** is of particular interest because it shows two possible next states. The beginning of the state is the clock event statement in the loop body. However, the next clock event statement is either the one found by executing the loop body and staying in the loop (i.e., the same statement), or the one found by executing the loop body and exiting to the one just after the while statement. These account for the two next states possible from state B.

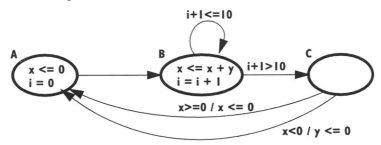

Figure 1.13 State Transition Diagram of Cycle-Accurate Behavior

1.6.2 **A Few Notes**

There are a few interesting notes to be made about this example and the scheduled behavior or cycle-accurate style of description.

This style of description is used at the point in system design when we want to specify the cycle-by-cycle behavior of the system but we are not too concerned with the actual datapath for the design. We have specified the simple calculation and which states the new values will be produced in. But, we haven't specified any datapath for it; that is left for a later stage of the design process.

The use of blocking ("=") and non-blocking ("<=") assignments was mixed in this specification. Non-blocking assignments were used for registers x and y which are used outside of the always block. This effectively synchronizes their loading to the clock edge specified. For registers used only in one always block, such as register i, this is not necessary. Remember that when you assign using non-blocking assignments, the value is not available by the register's name until after the clock edge. i.e, it's not available on the next line of the description! Further, only one unconditional non-blocking assignment can be made to any register in a state. However, you can use blocking assignments to calculate intermediate values and values only used inside the always block. Of course, these are immediately available on the next line of the description. In this example, the i used in comparison at the end of the loop is the i calculated in the loop because we used a blocking assignment.

Finally, the two state transition diagrams for the two implementations of the simple calculation (shown in Figures 1.10 and 1.13) are different. This was intentional, and not a limitation of either style of specification.

References: cycle-accurate 7.2

Tutorial: See the Tutorial Problems in Appendix A.7.

1.7 **Summary of Assignment Statements**

When developing Verilog models of digital systems, an important aspect is capturing how new values (outputs) are generated over time. Indeed, this tutorial has presented four different methods for generating new values: gate primitives, continuous assignment, procedural assignment ("="), and non-blocking assignment ("<="). Within the Verilog language, these four methods fall into two major categories. These categories differ in the way in which outputs are generated over time. Thus we call them timing models. These models are the *gate-level* timing model and the *procedural* timing model.

The gate-level timing model is illustrated by the gate primitive (e.g., Example 1.3) and continuous assignment (e.g., Example 1.15). When writing a simple AND expression, we could write either:

    and   (a, b, c);

or

    assign   a = b & c;

These two statements as shown are equivalent; both perform a bitwise AND of **b** and **c**, and assign the result to **a**. The way to think about these statements is that any time any of the inputs (**b** or **c**) changes, the output **a** is re-evaluated. Further, in both of these statements, **a** is a net.

The procedural timing model uses procedural statements found in initial and always blocks to generate new values. Regular procedural assignment ("=") was illustrated in Example 1.5 and non-blocking procedural assignment ("<=") was illustrated in Example 1.7. The always block:

    always @(posedge clock)
      Q <= D;

has two inputs (**clock** and **D**) and one output **Q**. In contrast to the gate-level timing model, the procedural assignment is not sensitive to all of its inputs; only certain ones at certain times. Here, the always block is only sensitive to positive edge changes on clock. When the positive edge occurs, Q is updated with the value of D. However, if D, another input to the always block changes, Q is not updated. Procedural models are only sensitive to the inputs they are explicitly waiting for. Further, the left-hand sides of all procedural assignments are registers.

The loading of the value into the register or memory is done only when control is transferred to the procedural assignment statement. Control is transferred to a procedural assignment statement in a sequential manner, flowing from one statement to the next. In this way, procedural assignments function similar to a normal software programming language assignment statement. However, the flow of control can be interrupted by an event (@) statement (and as we'll see later, wait and #delay statements), and then is only reactivated when the event occurs.

The procedural assignments "=" and "<=" can be further categorized by when the left-hand side is updated. As discussed in section 1.3.3, the "=" updates its left-hand side immediately so that this new value is available in the next procedural statement. In contrast, "<=" updates its left-hand side only after all of the right-hand sides of "<=" statements waiting on the same edge in the whole design have been calculated. Thus, the new value on the left-hand side is not available in the next procedural statement. This leads to anomalous descriptions such as:

```
@(posedge clock)      // somewhere in an evil always block
m = 3;
n = 75;
n <= m;
r = n;
```

The question is what value is assigned to r? The answer is 75. Even though the third statement changes r to 3, the left-hand side isn't updated immediately. Indeed the always block doesn't stop (i.e., block) to update n; rather it keeps going (thus the name non-blocking), using the value of n from before the clock edge. Eventually, n will be updated with the value of 3, but only after all other right-hand sides of non-blocking assignments have been evaluated. It's better not to write models such as the evil one above; they are hard to read. Further, they are not accepted by synthesis tools, so their use is limited. Use non-blocking assignments when describing concurrent transfers in edge-sensitive systems.

In essence, the two timing models are closely aligned with the two fundamental data types of the language: nets and registers. Continuous assigns and primitive gates may only drive nets, and procedural assignments may only be made to registers (and memories).

References: procedural assignment 2.1; continuous assignment 4.4; timing models 5.1

1.8 **Summary**

This brief tour has illustrated the basic capabilities of the language. Important among these are:

- The ability to partition a design into modules which can then be further divided until the design is specified in terms of basic logic primitives. This hierarchical modularization allows a designer to control the complexity of the design through the well-known divide-and-conquer approach to large engineering design.

- The ability to describe a design either in terms of the abstract behavior of the design or in terms of its actual logical structure. The behavioral description allows for early design activities to concentrate on functionality. When the behavior is agreed upon, then it becomes the specification for designing possibly several alternate structural implementations, possibly through the use of synthesis tools.

- The ability to synchronize concurrent systems. The concurrent parts of a system that share data must synchronize with each other so that the correct information is passed between the current parts. We illustrated how systems can be synchronized to signal edges (e.g. a clock).

This tutorial chapter was meant to give a quick introduction to the language. As such, many details were skimmed over with the goal of giving the reader a feel for the language. The approach was to present and describe examples that illustrate the main features and uses of the language. The goal of the later chapters is to cover the language in more depth, while still presenting the language with an example-oriented approach. Our goal here and in the rest of the book is not to present the Verilog language just as a formal syntax specification. But, realizing that the examples we give cannot illustrate the entire language syntax, we will begin introducing some of the language's formal syntax specification. This specification will probably not be useful for the first-time reader. However, it will be invaluable for the reference reader and description writer. The complete formal syntax specification is in Appendix G.

The rest of the book illustrates in more depth the syntax and semantics of the Verilog language.

1.9 **Exercises**

For more exercises, see Appendix A.

1.1   Rewrite the eSeg module in Example 1.4 with continuous assignment statements.

1.2   Write three different descriptions of a 2-bit full adder including carry-in and carry-out ports. One description should use gate-level models, another should use continuous assignment statements, and the third — combinational always.

1.3   Change the clock generator **m555** in Example 1.9 such that the clock period remains the same but that the low pulse width is 40 and high pulse width is 60.

1.4   Write a two-phase clock generator. Phase two should be offset from phase one by one quarter of a cycle.

1.5   Keeping the same output timing, replace the initial and always statements in the clock generator **m555** in Example 1.9 with gate primitives.

1.6   Write a behavioral description for a serial adder. The module definition is:

```
module serialAdder (clock, a, b, sum, start);
    input    clock, a, b, start;
    output   sum;
    ...
endmodule
```

A. The bits will come in to the module low order first. The carry into the low-order bits is assumed to be zero. The inputs are all valid right before the negative edge of the clock. **a** and **b** are the two bits to add and **sum** is the result. If **start** is 1, then these two bits are the first of the word's bits to add. Just after the negative edge of the clock, **sum** will be updated with its new value based on the values of **a** and **b** (and the carry from the previous bits) just before the clock edge.

B. Create a test module to demonstrate the serial adder's correctness.

1.7   Oops, forgot the declarations! Here's a Verilog module that is complete except for the register, input, and output declarations. What should they be? Assume **a**, **b**, and **c** are 8 bit "things" and the others are single-bit. Note that you may have to add to the input-output list. Do not add any more assignments — only input, output, and register declarations.

```
module sillyMe (a, b, c, q, ... );

// oops, forgot the declarations!

    initial
      q = 1'b0;

    always
      begin
            @ (posedge y)
                #10 a = b + c;
            q = ~q;
      end

    nand    #10      (y, q, r);
endmodule
```

2 | Behavioral Modeling

We now begin a more in-depth discussion of the constructs used to model the behavior of digital systems. These have been split into two groups. The first are statements that are, for the most part, similar to those found in programming languages: if-then-else, loops, etc. In the next chapter we take up the statements that are oriented toward modeling the concurrent nature of digital hardware.

2.1 Process Model

The basic essence of a behavioral model is the *process*. A process can be thought of as an independent thread of control, which may be quite simple, involving only one repeated action, or very complex, resembling a software program. It might be implemented as a sequential state machine, as a microcoded controller, as an asynchronous clearing of a register, or as a combinational circuit. The point is that we conceive the behavior of digital systems as a set of these independent, but communicating, processes. Their actual implementation is left to the context of the description (what level of abstraction we are dealing with) and the time and area constraints of the implementation.

The basic Verilog statement for describing a process is the *always* construct:

always_construct
    ::= **always** statement

The always continuously repeats its statement, never exiting or stopping. A behavioral model may contain one or more always statements. (A module that contains none is purely a specification of hierarchical structure — instantiated submodules and their interconnections.)

The *initial* construct is similar to the always statement except that it is executed only once.

initial_construct
    ::= **initial** statement

The initial provides a means of initiating input waveforms and initializing simulation variables before the actual description begins its simulation. Once the statements in the initial are exhausted it does not repeat; rather it becomes inactive.

There are many types of statements in the language. Some, such as "if", "while", and procedural assignments ("out = ~currentState[1] & currentState[0];"), have already been seen in earlier examples. These and most of the rest of the statement types will be covered in the next two chapters.

When modeling a system using the statements in an always or initial block, we must be cognizant of the execution model of these statements. The statements are executed in the order specified in the description. Assignments made using the *blocking assignment* ("=") take effect immediately and the value written to the left-hand side of the = is available for use in the next statement. When an event statement ("@"), a delay statement ("#"), or, as we'll see later, a wait statement where the expression is FALSE is executed, the execution of the initial or always statement is suspended until (respectively): the event occurs, the number of time units indicated in the delay has passed, or the wait statement expression becomes TRUE. At that time, execution of statements in the initial or always statement continues.

Further, even though the statements in an always or initial block are executed in order, it is possible that statements from other always or initial blocks will be interleaved with the statements of the current process. When an always or initial block is waiting to continue (due to @, #, or wait), other always or initial blocks, gate primitives, and continuous assign statements can execute. Thus, concurrent/overlapping behavior is modeled.

Unlike gate primitives and continuous assign statements, behavioral models do not execute because one of their inputs change. Rather, they only execute when one of the three conditions above is being waited for, and then occurs. Behavioral models follow the *procedural timing model* as discussed in Section 5.1.

At the start of the simulation, all of the initial and always statements are allowed to execute until they are suspended due to an event, delay, or wait. At this point, register values set in an initial or always may activate a gate input, or time may advance to the next event that will probably allow one or more of the suspended processes to become active again. When there are multiple processes that can execute at any particular time, the order in which they begin executing is indeterminate. Care must be taken when writing them to insure that register and wire values are assigned in an appropriate order.

In summary, the initial and always statements are the basic constructs for describing concurrency. When using these statements, we should be thinking conceptually of concurrently active processes that will interact with each other. Although it is possible to mix the description of behavior between the always and initial statement, it is more appropriate to describe the behavior of the hardware in the always, and describe initialization for the simulation in the initial.

References: contrast to continuous assign 4.4; contrast to gate level modeling 4.1; interleaving 5.3; procedural timing model 5.1

2.2 **If-Then-Else**

Conditional statements are used in a sequential behavior description to alter the flow of control. The *if* statement and its variations are common examples of conditional statements. Example 2.1 is a behavioral model of a divide module that shows several new features, including two versions of the if statement, with and without an else clause.

The **divide** module determines the output **quotient** from the two inputs, **dvInput** and **ddInput**, using an iterative subtract and shift algorithm. First, four text macros are defined. The `compiler directive provides a macro capability by defining a name and gives a constant textual value to it. The name may then be used in the description; on compilation, the text value will be substituted. The general form is:

`define A alpha

Then, anytime the description is compiled, alpha will be substituted for all occurrences of " `A ". Note that the left single quote (" ` ") is required at all uses of the macro. Example 2.1 illustrates a means of entering constant numeric data into the description using the more mnemonic macro.

```
`define DvLen 15
`define DdLen 31
`define QLen 15
`define HiDdMin 16

module divide (ddInput, dvInput, quotient, go, done);
     input    [`DdLen:0]   ddInput, dvInput;
     output   [`QLen:0]    quotient;
     input                 go;
     output                done;

     reg      [`DdLen:0]   dividend;
     reg      [`QLen:0]    quotient;
     reg      [`DvLen:0]   divisor;
     reg                   done, negDivisor, negDividend;

     always begin
        done = 0;
        wait (go);
        divisor = dvInput;
        dividend = ddInput;
        quotient = 0;
        if (divisor) begin
             negDivisor = divisor[`DvLen];
             if (negDivisor)      divisor = - divisor;
             negDividend = dividend[`DdLen];
             if (negDividend)   dividend = - dividend;
                repeat (`DvLen + 1)  begin
                    quotient = quotient << 1;
                    dividend = dividend << 1;
                    dividend[`DdLen:`HiDdMin] =
                        dividend[`DdLen:`HiDdMin] - divisor;
                    if (! dividend [`DdLen])   quotient = quotient + 1;
                    else
                        dividend[`DdLen:`HiDdMin] =
                            dividend[`DdLen:`HiDdMin] + divisor;
                end
                if (negDivisor != negDividend)   quotient = - quotient;
        end
        done = 1;
        wait (~go);
     end
endmodule
```

Example 2.1 A Divide Module

The divide starts by zeroing the **done** output and waiting for **go** to be TRUE. These two signals are the handshake signals that allow the **divide** module to communicate and synchronize with other modules. **done** indicates when the divide module has completed a division and stored the result in the **quotient**. Since at the beginning no quotient has been calculated, **done** is set to FALSE (or zero). Then we wait for the **go** input to be one (or TRUE) signifying that the **dvInput** and **ddInput** inputs are valid. When **go** becomes TRUE, **dvInput** and **ddInput** are copied into **divisor** and **dividend** respectively.

The wait statement, waits for an external condition to become TRUE. When it is executed, execution continues if the condition in the parentheses is TRUE. However, if the condition is FALSE, the always block stops executing and waits for the condition to become TRUE. At that point, execution continues with the statement after the wait. The wait statement is discussed further in section 3.3.

The first example of an **if** tests whether the divisor is zero or not with the statement:

```
if (divisor)
    begin
        // ... statements
    end
```

This shows the basic form of the **if** statement. The **if** is followed by a parenthesized expression; a zero expression evaluates to FALSE and any value other than zero evaluates to TRUE. Comparison with an unknown (**x**) or high impedance (**z**) may produce a result that is either unknown or high impedance. Such a result is interpreted as FALSE. In this case, we are testing the **divisor**. If it is not zero, then we follow the normal divide algorithm. The begin-end block following the **if** statement allows all of the encompassed statements to be considered as part of the **then** statement of the **if**.

More formally:

statement
    ::=   conditional _statement
    | ...

conditional_statement
    ::= **if** (expression) statement_or_null [**else** statement_or_null]

Continuing with the divide algorithm, the absolute value of each of the inputs is determined and their original signs are saved. More specifically, the statements

```
          negDivisor = divisor[`DvLen];
          if (negDivisor)
              divisor = - divisor;
```

first assign (procedurally) bit **DvLen** (i.e., bit 15) of the **divisor** to **negDivisor**. If this bit is a one, indicating that the value was negative in the two's complement number representation, then the **then** part will be executed and **divisor** will be negated, making it positive. It should be noted that since there is no begin-end block with this **if**, the **then** statement is the first statement (up to the semicolon) following the **if**.

This statement also illustrates a *bit-select*. A bit-select is used to specify that only one of the bits of a vector are to be used in the operation. A range of bits may also be specified by separating the bit numbers specifying the range with a colon. This is called a *part-select*. More formally, a bit- or part-select occurs either as an expression or as part of an expression as shown below:

```
primary
    ::=  identifier [ expression ]
    |    identifier [ msb _constant_expression : lsb_constant_expression ]
    |    ...
```

In the formal syntax, a primary is one definition of an expression. The first definition of the primary is a bit-select and the second is the part-select. The indices of the bit- and part-select may be positive or negative numbers.

After the initialization to determine the final arithmetic sign, the **repeat** statement executes the statements in the begin-end block 16 times. Each time, the **quotient** and **dividend** are shifted left one position, as described by the << operator, and then the **divisor** is subtracted from the top part of the **dividend**. If the result of this subtract is positive, one is added to the **quotient**. However, if the result is negative (the top most bit is a one), the **else** part of the **if** conditional statement is executed, adding the **divisor** back into the top part of the **dividend**.

Following this more closely, if the sign bit is 1, then the result is negative. This nonzero value would be interpreted as TRUE by the if statement. However, the ! operator complements the result and the **if** expression evaluates to FALSE. Thus, if the **dividend** is negative, the **else** part is executed.

Finally, if the signs of the original operands are different, then the **quotient** is negated. After the **quotient** output is calculated, the **done** bit is set to one signalling another module that the output may be read.

Before continuing on, this example illustrates some other facets of the language that should be discussed.

Vector nets and registers all obey the laws of arithmetic modulo 2^n where n is the number of bits in the vector. In effect, the language treats the numbers as unsigned quantities. If any of these values were printed by a $display or $monitor statement, they would be interpreted and printed as unsigned values. However, that does not stop us from writing descriptions of hardware that use the two's complement number representation — the laws of arithmetic modulo 2^n still hold. Indeed, the unary minus provided in the language performs the correct operation.

The relational operators typically used in conditional expressions are listed in Appendix B. These include > (greater than), >= (greater than or equal), == (equal), and != (not equal). In the case where unknown or high impedance values are present, these comparisons may evaluate to a quantity which contains unknown or high impedance values. Such values are considered to be FALSE by the simulator. However, the case equality operator (===) and inequality operator (!==) can be used to specify that individual unknown or high impedance bits are to take part in the comparison. That is, a 4-valued logic comparison is done where the value of each bit being compared, including the unknowns and high impedances, must be equal. Thus, if the statement

```
if (4'b110z === 4'b110z)
    then_statement;
```

was executed, the **then** part of the **if** would be taken. However, if the statement

```
if (4'b110z == 4'b110z)
    then_statement
```

was executed, the **then** part of the **if** would not be taken.

Conditional expressions may be more complex than the single expression examples given so far. Logical expressions may be connected with the && (AND), || (OR), and ! (NOT) logical operators as shown in the following example:

```
if ((a > b) && ((c >= d) || (e == f)))
    then_statement
```

In this example, the **then** statement will execute only if **a** is greater than **b**, and either (or both) **c** is greater than or equal to **d**, or **e** equals **f**.

References: bit-select, part-select E.1; $display F.1; $monitor F.2; Verilog operators C

2.2.1 **Where Does The ELSE Belong?**

Example 2.1 also shows the use of an else clause with an if statement. The else clause is optional, and if it exists, it is paired with the nearest, unfinished if statement. Formally speaking:

conditional_statement
      ::= **if** (expression) statement_or_null [**else** statement_or_null]
      | ...

In the example we find:

```
if (! dividend [`DdLen])
    quotient = quotient + 1;
else
    dividend[`DdLen:`HiDdMin] =
        dividend[`DdLen:`HiDdMin] + divisor;
```

In this case, if the **dividend** is positive after subtracting the **divisor** from it, then the low order bit of the **quotient** is set to one. Otherwise, we add the **divisor** back into the top part of the **dividend**.

As in most procedural languages, care must be taken in specifying the else clause where multiple if statements are involved. Consider the following situation.

```
if (expressionA)
    if (expressionB)
        a = a + b;
    else
        q = r + s;
```

In this example, we have nested **if** statements and a single **else**. In general, the language attaches the **else** to the nearest **if** statement. In the above situation, if **expressionA** and **expressionB** are both TRUE, then **a** is assigned a new value. If **expressionA** is TRUE and **expressionB** is FALSE, then **q** is assigned a new value. That is, the **else** is paired with the second **if**.

Consider an alternate description giving different results.

```
if (expressionA)
        begin
            if (expressionB)
                a = a + b;
        end
    else
        q = r + s;
```

In this example, the begin-end block in the first **if** statement causes the **else** to be paired with the first **if** rather than the second. When in doubt about where the **else** will be attached, use begin-end pairs to make it clear.

2.2.2 **The Conditional Operator**

The conditional operator (?:) can be used in place of the if statement when one of two values is to be selected for assignment. For instance, the statement determining the final sign of the **quotient** in Example 2.1 could have been written with the same result as

> quotient = (negDivisor != negDividend) ? -quotient: quotient;.

This operator works as follows: first the conditional expression in the parentheses is evaluated. If it is TRUE (or nonzero), then the value of the right-hand side of the statement is found immediately after the question mark. If it is FALSE, the value immediately after the colon is used. The result of this statement is that one of the two values gets assigned to **quotient**. In this case, if it is TRUE that the signs are not equal, then **quotient** is loaded with its negative. Otherwise, **quotient** remains unchanged. As in Example 2.1, we are describing hardware that will use the two's complement number system, and we use the fact that a Verilog's unary minus operation implements a two's complement negate.

The general form of the conditional operator is:

expression
      ::=   expression ? expression : expression
      | ...

If the first **expression** is TRUE, then the value of the operator is the second **expression**. Otherwise the value is the third **expression**. The operator is right-associative.

There is a major distinction between if-then-else and the conditional operator. As an operator, the conditional operator may appear in an expression that is either part of a procedural or continuous assignment statement. The if-then-else construct is a statement that may appear only in the body of an initial or always statement, or in a task or function. Thus whereas if-then-else can only be used in behavioral modeling, the conditional operator can be used both in behavioral and gate level structural modeling.

References: if-then-else 2.2; comparison with multiway branch 2.4

2.3 **Loops**

Iterative sequential behavior is described with looping statements. Four different statements are provided, including the *repeat, for, while,* and *forever* loops.

2.3.1 **Four Basic Loop Statements**

An excerpt from Example 2.1 illustrated in Example 2.2 shows the use of the repeat loop. In this form of loop, only a loop count is given in parentheses after the keyword

```
repeat (`DvLen + 1)
begin
    quotient = quotient << 1;
    dividend = dividend << 1;
    dividend[`DdLen:`HiDdMin] =
        dividend[`DdLen:`HiDdMin] - divisor;
    if (! dividend [`DdLen])
        quotient = quotient + 1;
    else  dividend[`DdLen:`HiDdMin] =
        dividend[`DdLen:`HiDdMin] + divisor;
end
```

Example 2.2 An Excerpt from Example 2.1

repeat. The value of the loop count expression is determined once at the beginning of the execution of the loop. Then the loop is executed the given number of times. The loop count expression is sampled once at the beginning of the loop, and thus it is not possible to exit the loop execution by changing the loop count variable. The *disable* statements described later allow for early loop exits.

The general form of the repeat statement is:

```
statement
    ::=  loop_statement
    |    ...

loop_statement
    ::=  repeat ( expression ) statement
    |    ...
```

The loop in Example 2.2 could have been written as a *for* loop as:

```
for (i = 16; i; i = i - 1)
    begin
        ...//shift and subtract statements
    end
```

In this case, a register must be specified to hold the loop counter. The for loop is very similar in function to for loops in the C programming language. Essentially, this for loop initializes i to 16, and while i is not zero, executes the statements and then decrements i.

The general form of the for loop is

loop_statement
    ::= **for** (reg_assignment; expression; reg_assignment) statement
    | ...

Specifically, the first assignment is executed once at the beginning of the loop. The expression is executed before the body of the loop to determine if we are to stay in the loop. Execution stays in the loop while the expression is TRUE. The second assignment is executed after the body of the loop and before the next check for the end of the loop. The statement is the body of the loop. The difference between the for and repeat loop statements is that repeat is simply a means of specifying a constant number of iterations. The for loop is far more flexible and gives access to the loop update variable for control of the end-of-loop-condition.

As in the C programming language, the above for statement could have been written using a *while* statement as:

```
i = 16;
while (i)
    begin
        ... // shift and subtract statements
        i = i - 1;
    end
```

The general form of the while is

loop_statement
    ::= **while** (expression) statement
    | ...

The expression is evaluated and if it is TRUE, the statement is executed. The while expression is then evaluated again. Thus, we enter and stay in the loop while the expression is TRUE.

The while expression must be updated as part of the loop statement execution, in this case "i = i - 1". The while statement <u>cannot</u> be used to wait for a change in a value generated external to its always statement as illustrated in the following example.

```
module sureDeath (inputA);        //This will not work!!
input    inputA;

    always
        begin
            while (inputA)
                ;        // wait for external variable
            // other statements
        end
endmodule
```

Here, the while statement expression is dependent on the value of **inputA** and the while statement is null. The above while statement appears to have the effect of doing nothing until the value of **inputA** is TRUE, at which time the other statements are executed. However, since we are waiting for an external value to change, the correct statement to use is the *wait*. For further discussion, see section 3.3 on the wait statement.

Finally, the forever loop loops forever. An example of its use is in the abstract description of a microprocessor. Here we see that certain initializations occur only at

```
module microprocessor;

    always
        begin
            powerOnInitializations;
            forever
                begin
                    fetchAndExecuteInstructions;
                end
        end
endmodule
```

Example 2.3 An Abstract Microprocessor

power-on time. After that, we remain in the forever loop fetching and executing instructions. A forever loop may be exited by using a *disable* statement, as will be discussed in the next section. If the forever loop is exited, then the always statement will start the power-on initializations and begin the forever loop again.

The general form of the forever loop is:

```
loop_statement
        ::= forever statement
      |    ...
```

References: disable 2.3, 3.6; wait 3.3; comparison with wait 3.3.2; intra-assignment repeat 3.7

2.3.2 **Exiting Loops on Exceptional Conditions**

Generally, a loop statement is written to execute to a "normal" exit; the loop counter is exhausted or the while expression is no longer TRUE. However, any of the loop statements may be exited through use of the *disable* statement. A disable statement disables, or terminates, any named begin-end block; execution then begins with the statement following the block. Begin-end blocks may be named by placing the name of the block after a colon following the begin keyword. An example of the C programming statements break and continue are illustrated in Example 2.4.

```
begin :break
      for (i = 0; i < n; i = i + 1)
            begin : continue
                  if (a == 0)
                        disable continue;        // proceed with i = i + 1
                  ... // other statements
                  if (a == b)
                        disable break;           // exit for loop
                  ... // other statements
            end
end
```

Example 2.4 Break and Continue Loop Exits

Example 2.4 shows two named blocks, **break** and **continue**. Recall that the continue statement in C skips the rest of the loop body and continues the loop with the loop update, and that the break statement breaks out of the loop entirely, regardless of the loop update and end-of-loop condition. The disable statements in the example perform the analogous actions. Specifically, the **disable continue** statement stops execution of the begin-end block named **continue** and passes control to the update of the for loop. The **disable break** statement stops execution of the block that contains the for loop. Execution then proceeds with the next statement.

The general form of the disable statement is:

```
statement
      ::= disable_statement
      |    ...

disable_statement
      ::= disable task_identifier;
      |    disable block_identifier;
```

References: disable named blocks 3.6; tasks 2.5

2.4 **Multi-way branching**

Multi-way branching allows the specification of one or more actions to be taken based on specified conditions. Verilog provides two statements to specify these branches: *if-else-if,* and *case.*

2.4.1 **If-Else-If**

If-else-if simply uses if-then-else statements to specify multiple actions. It is the most general way to write a multi-way decision in that it allows for a variety of different expressions to be checked in the if conditional expressions. Consider the description of a simple computer shown in Example 2.5. The example is reminiscent of the early Mark-1 computer (a few details have been changed) and is used here for its simplicity. A cycle-accurate style of specification is used, separating the instruction fetch and execution into two separate clock periods.

This example uses the if-else-if statement to specify the instruction decode of the computer. Bits fifteen through thirteen of the instruction register (**ir[15:13]**) are compared with seven of the eight possible combinations of three bits. The one that matches determines which of the instructions is executed.

References: if-then-else 2.2; conditional operator 2.2.2

2.4.2 **Case**

The *case* statement can be used for multi-way branches when each of the if conditionals all match against the same basic expression. In Example 2.6, the Mark-1 description is rewritten using the case statement for instruction decoding.

The case expressions are evaluated linearly in the order given in the description. In this case, bits fifteen through thirteen of the instruction register (the *controlling expression*) are compared with each of the seven *case expressions*. Bit widths must match exactly. The first expression to match the controlling expression causes the statement following the colon to be executed. Then execution continues with the statement after the case. The comparison is done using 4-valued logic; thus a 2-bit case condition can evaluate to sixteen different values.

```
module mark1;
    reg [15:0]  m [0:8191];   // 8192 x 16 bit memory
    reg [12:0]  pc;           // 13 bit program counter
    reg [12:0]  acc;          // 13 bit accumulator
    reg [15:0]  ir;           // 16 bit instruction register
    reg         ck;           // a clock signal

    always
        begin
            @(posedge ck)
                ir = m [pc];              // fetch an instruction
            @(posedge ck)
                if (ir[15:13] == 3'b000)          // begin decoding
                    pc = m [ir [12:0]];           // and executing
                else if (ir[15:13] == 3'b001)
                    pc = pc + m [ir [12:0]];
                else if (ir[15:13] == 3'b010)
                    acc = -m [ir [12:0]];
                else if (ir[15:13] == 3'b011)
                    m [ir [12:0]] = acc;
                else if ((ir[15:13] == 3'b101) || (ir[15:13] == 3'b100))
                    acc = acc - m [ir [12:0]];
                else if (ir[15:13] == 3'b110)
                    if (acc < 0) pc = pc + 1;
                pc = pc + 1;              //increment program counter
        end
endmodule
```

Example 2.5 The Mark-1 Processor With If-Else-If

The general form of the case statement is

statement
        ::= case_statement
        | ...

case_statement
        ::= **case** (expression) case_item { case_item} **endcase**
        | ...

case_item
        ::= expression {, expression } : statement_or_null
        | **default** [:] statement_or_null

```
module mark1Case;
    reg [15:0]    m [0:8191];    // 8192 x 16 bit memory
    reg [12:0]    pc;            // 13 bit program counter
    reg [12:0]    acc;           // 13 bit accumulator
    reg [15:0]    ir;            // 16 bit instruction register
    reg           ck;            // a clock signal

    always
        begin
            @(posedge ck)
                ir = m [pc];
            @(posedge ck)
                case (ir [15:13])
                    3'b000 :    pc = m [ir [12:0]];
                    3'b001 :    pc = pc + m [ir [12:0]];
                    3'b010 :    acc = -m [ir [12:0]];
                    3'b011 :    m [ir [12:0]] = acc;
                    3'b100,
                    3'b101 :    acc = acc - m [ir [12:0]];
                    3'b110 :    if (acc < 0) pc = pc + 1;
                endcase
            pc = pc + 1;
        end
endmodule
```

Example 2.6 The Mark-1 With a Case Statement

A default may be specified using the *default* keyword in place of a case expression. When present, the default statement will be executed if none of the other case expressions match the controlling expression. The default may be listed anywhere in the case statement.

The example also illustrates how a single action may be specified for several of the case expressions. The commas between case expressions specify that if either of the comparisons are TRUE, then the statement is executed. In the Mark-1 example, if the three bits have either of the values 4 or 5, a value is subtracted from the accumulator. The first line of case_item, above, details the syntax.

Finally, note that the controlling expressions and case expressions do not need to be constants.

References: casez, casex 2.4.4; comparison with if-else-if 2.4.3; conditional operator 2.2.2; register specification E.1; memory specification E.2

2.4.3 **Comparison of Case and If-Else-If**

In the Mark-1 examples above, either case or if-else-if could be used. Stylistically, the case is more compact in this example and makes for easier reading. Further, since all of the expressions were compared with one controlling expression, the case is more appropriate. However, there are two major differences between these constructs.

- The conditional expressions in the if-else-if construct are more general. Any set of expressions may be used in the if-else-if whereas with the case statement, the case expressions are all evaluated against a common controlling expression.

- The case expressions may include unknown (x) and high impedance (z) bits. The comparison is done using 4-valued logic and will succeed only when each bit matches exactly with respect to the values 0, 1, x, and z. Thus it is very important to make sure the expression widths match in the case expressions and controlling expression. In contrast, if statement expressions involving unknown or high impedance values may result in an unknown or high impedance value which will be interpreted as FALSE (unless case equality is used).

An example of a case statement with unknown and high impedance values is shown below in a debugging example.

```
reg   ready;                // a one bit register
      // other statements
      case (ready)
          1'bz:    $display ("ready is high impedance");
          1'bx:    $display ("ready is unknown");
          default: $display ("ready is %b", ready);
      endcase
```

In this example, the one bit **ready** is compared with high impedance (z) and unknown (x); the appropriate display message is printed during simulation. If **ready** is neither high impedance or unknown, then its value is displayed.

References: four-level logic 4.2.2; casez, casex 2.4.4; case equality 2.2

2.4.4 **Casez and Casex**

casez and *casex* are two types of case statements that allow don't-care values to be considered in case statements. **casez** allows for z values to be treated as don't-care values, and **casex** allows for both z and x to be treated as don't-care. In addition to specifying bits as either z or x, they may also be specified with a question mark ("?") which also indicates don't-care. The syntax for **casex** and **casez** is the same as with the case statement, except the **casez** or **casex** keyword is substituted for case.

case_statement
       ::= **case** (expression) case_item { case_item} **endcase**
       | **casez** (expression) case_item { case_item} **endcase**
       | **casex** (expression) case_item { case_item } **endcase**

```
module decode;
    reg[7:0]    r;

    always
        begin
            // other statements
            r = 8'bx1x0x1x0;
            casex (r)
                8'b001100xx:  statement1;
                8'b1100xx00:  statement2;
                8'b00xx0011:  statement3;
                8'bxx001100:  statement4;
            endcase
        end
endmodule
```

Example 2.7 An Example of Casex

Consider the **casex** shown in Example 2.7. In this example we have loaded register r with the eight bit value x1x0x1x0, indicating that every other bit is unknown. Since the unknown x is treated as a don't-care, then only statement 2 will be executed. Although statement 4 also matches, it will not be executed because the condition on statement 2 was found first.

        x1x0x1x0   value in register r
        1100xx00   matching case expression

The difference between the two case types is in whether only z is considered as a don't-care (**casez**), or whether z and x are considered don't-cares (**casex**).

References: Verilog operators C; case 2.4.2

2.5 Functions and Tasks

In software programming, functions and procedures are used to break up large programs into more-manageable pieces. In Verilog, modules break a design up into more-manageable parts, however the use of modules implies that there are structural boundaries being described. These boundaries may in fact model the logical structure or the physical packaging boundaries. Verilog provides *functions* and *tasks* as constructs analogous to software functions and procedures that allow for the behavioral description of a module to be broken into more-manageable parts.

As in software programming, functions and tasks are useful for several reasons. They allow often-used behavioral sequences to be written once and called when needed. They also allow for a cleaner writing style; instead of long sequences of behavioral statements, the sequences can be broken into more readable pieces, regardless of whether they are called one or many times. Finally, they allow for data to be hidden from other parts of the design. Indeed, functions and tasks play a key role in making a behavioral description more readable and maintainable.

Consider defining opcode 7 of the Mark-1 description in the previous sections to be a multiply instruction. Early in the behavioral modeling process, we could use the multiply operator as shown in Example 2.8. This is a perfectly reasonable behavioral

```
module mark1Mult;
    reg [15:0]    m [0:8191];    // 8192 x 16 bit memory
    reg [12:0]    pc;            // 13 bit program counter
    reg [12:0]    acc;           // 13 bit accumulator
    reg [15:0]    ir;            // 16 bit instruction register
    reg           ck;            // a clock signal

    always
        begin
            @(posedge ck)
                ir = m [pc];
            @(posedge ck)
                case (ir [15:13])
                    3'b000 :    pc = m [ir [12:0]];
                    3'b001 :    pc = pc + m [ir [12:0]];
                    3'b010 :    acc = -m [ir [12:0]];
                    3'b011 :    m [ir [12:0]] = acc;
                    3'b100,
                    3'b101 :    acc = acc - m [ir [12:0]];
                    3'b110 :    if (acc < 0) pc = pc + 1;
                    3'b111 :    acc = acc * m [ir [12:0]];    //multiply
                endcase
            pc = pc + 1;
        end
endmodule
```

Example 2.8 The Mark-1 With a Multiply Instruction

model for early in the design process in that the functionality is thoroughly described. However, we may want to further detail the multiply algorithm used in the design. Our first approach will be to use functions and tasks to describe the multiply algorithm. Later, we will contrast this approach to that of describing the multiply as a separate, concurrently operating module. Table 2.1 contrasts the differences between tasks and functions.

Table 2.1 Comparison of Tasks and Function

Category	Tasks	Functions
Enabling (calling)	A task call is a separate procedural statement. It cannot be called from a continuous assignment statement.	A function call is an operand in an expression. It is called from within the expression and returns a value used in the expression. Functions may be called from within procedural and continuous assignment statements.
Inputs and outputs	A task can have zero or more arguments of any type.	A function has at least one input. It does not have inouts our outputs.
Timing and event controls (#, @, and wait)	A task can contain timing and event control statements	Functions may not contain these statements
Enabling other tasks and functions	A task may enable other tasks and functions	A function can enable other functions but not other tasks.
Values returned	A task does not return a value to an expression. However, values written by the task into its inout or output ports are copied back at the end of the task execution.	A function returns a single value to the expression that called it. The value to be returned is assigned to the function identifier within the function.

2.5.1 **Tasks**

A Verilog *task* is similar to a software procedure. It is called from a calling statement and after execution, returns to the next statement. It cannot be used in an expression. Parameters may be passed to it and results returned. Local variables may be declared within it and their scope will be the task. Example 2.9 illustrates how module Mark-1 could be rewritten using a task to describe a multiply algorithm.

```
module mark1Task;
    reg [15:0]    m [0:8191];    // 8192 x 16 bit memory
    reg [12:0]    pc;            // 13 bit program counter
    reg [12:0]    acc;           // 13 bit accumulator
    reg           ck;            // a clock signal

    always
        begin: executeInstructions
            reg [15:0]    ir;    // 16 bit instruction register

            @(posedge ck)
                ir = m [pc];
            @(posedge ck)
                case (ir [15:13])
                    // other case expressions as before
                    3'b111 :    multiply (acc, m [ir [12:0]]);
                endcase
            pc = pc + 1;
        end

    task multiply;
    inout    [12:0]  a;
    input    [15:0]  b;

        begin: serialMult
            reg    [5:0]  mcnd, mpy; //multiplicand and multiplier
            reg    [12:0] prod;        //product

            mpy = b[5:0];
            mcnd = a[5:0];
            prod = 0;
            repeat (6)
                begin
                    if (mpy[0])
                        prod = prod + {mcnd, 6'b000000};
                    prod = prod >> 1;
                    mpy = mpy >> 1;
                end
            a = prod;
        end
    endtask
endmodule
```

Example 2.9 A Task Specification

A task is defined within a module using the *task* and *endtask* keywords. This task is named **multiply** and is defined to have one inout (**a**) and one input (**b**). This task is called from within the always statement. The order of task parameters at the calling site must correspond to the order of definitions within the task. When **multiply** is called, **acc** is copied into task variable **a**, the value read from memory is copied into **b**, and the task proceeds. When the task is ready to return, **prod** is loaded into **a**. On return, **a** is then copied back into **acc** and execution continues after the task call site. Although not illustrated here, a task may include timing and event control statements. Twice within Example 2.9 named begin-end blocks are used, illustrating that within these blocks, new register identifiers may be defined. The scope of these names (**ir, mcnd, mpy,** and **prod**) is the named begin-end block. The general form of the task declaration is:

```
task_declaration
    ::=  task task_identifier ;
            {task_item_declaration}
            statement_or_null
            endtask

task_argument_declaration
    ::=  block_item_declaration
    |    output_declaration
    |    inout_declaration

block_item_declaration
    ::=  parameter_declaration
    |    reg_declaration
    |    integer_declaration
    |    real_declaration
    |    time_declaration
    |    realtime_declaration
    |    event_declaration
```

The multiply algorithm uses a shift and add technique. The low-order sixteen bits of the operands are multiplied producing a 32-bit result that is returned. The statement

```
mpy = b[5:0];
```

does a part-select on **b** and loads the low order six bits into **mpy**. Six times, the low-order bit of the multiplier (**mpy**) is checked. If it is one, then the multiplicand (**mcnd**) is concatenated (using the "{ , }" operator) with six bits of zeros on its right and added to the product (**prod**). The product and multiplier are both shifted right one place and the loop continues.

The general forms of a concatenation are shown below:

concatenation
    ::= { expression {, expression} }

multiple_ concatenation
    ::= { expression { expression {, expression } } }

The first form is that shown in the example. The second allows for the concatenation in the inner braces to be repeated **n** times where **n** is given by the first expression.

The input, output, and inout names declared in tasks (and as we will later see, functions) are local variables separate from the variables named at the calling site. Their scope is the task-endtask block. When a task is called, the internal variables declared as inputs or inouts receive copies of the values named at the calling site. The task proceeds executing. When it is done, then all of the variables declared as inouts or outputs are copied back to the variables listed at the call site. When copying values to and from the call site, the variables at the call site are lined up left-to-right with order of the input, output, and inout declarations at the task definition site.

A task may call itself, or be called from tasks that it has called. However, as in a hardware implementation, there is only one set of registers to hold the task variables. Thus, the registers used after the second call to the task are the same physical entities as those in the previous call(s). The simulator maintains the thread of control so that the returns from a task called multiple times are handled correctly. Further, a task may be called from separate processes (i.e., always and initial statements) and the task may even be stopped at an event control when the task is enabled from another process. There is still only one set of variables for the two invocations of the task to use. However, the simulator does keep track of the control tokens so that the appropriate return to the calling process is made when the task exits.

The general form of a task call is:

task_enable
    ::= *task*_identifier [(expression {, expression })] ;

It is useful to comment on the concatenation operation in the example. The "{ , }" characters are used to express concatenation of values. In this example, we concatenate two 6-bit values together to add to the 13-bit **prod**. **mcnd** has 6 binary zeros (expressed here in binary format) concatenated onto its right-hand side. Notice that in this case, an exact bit width must be specified for the constant so that **mcnd** is properly aligned with **prod** for the add.

References: functions 2.5.2; Identifiers B.5, G.10

2.5.2 **Functions**

A Verilog function is similar to a software function. It is called from within an expression and the value it returns will be used in the expression. The function has one output (the function name) and at least one input. Other identifiers may be declared within the function and their scope will be the function. Unlike a task, a function may <u>not</u> include delay(#) or event control (@, wait) statements. Although not illustrated here, a function may be called from within a continuous assignment. Functions may call other functions but not other tasks. During the execution of the function, a value must be assigned to the function name; this is the value returned by the function.

Example 2.10 shows module **mark1Fun** specified with a multiply function. The function is defined within a module using the *function* and *endfunction* keywords. The function declaration includes the function name and bit width. At calling time, the parameters are copied into the function's inputs; as with tasks, the declaration order is strictly adhered to. The function executes, making assignments to the function's name. On return, the final value of the function's name (**multiply**) is passed back to the calling site and copied into register **acc**. Note that named begin-end blocks are used illustrating that new register definitions may be made within them. The general form of a function declaration is:

function_declaration
    ::= **function** [range or type] *function* _identifier ;
           function_item_declaration { function_item_declaration }
           statement
           endfunction

range_or_type
    ::= range | **integer** | **real** | **realtime** I **time**

range
    ::= [*msb*_constant_expression : *lsb* _constant_expression]

function_item_declaration
    ::= block_item_declaration
    I   input_declaration

A function is called from inside a procedural expression or from inside a continuous assignment where the call takes the form:

function_call
    ::= *function* _identifier (expression {, expression})

References: functions in continuous assignment 4.4.1; tasks 2.5.1; Identifier B.5, G.10

```
module mark1Fun;
    reg [15:0]   m [0:8191];    // 8192 x 16 bit memory
    reg [12:0]   pc;            // 13 bit program counter
    reg [12:0]   acc;           // 13 bit accumulator
    reg          ck;            // a clock signal

    always
        begin: executeInstructions
            reg  [15:0]    ir;   // 16 bit instruction register

            @(posedge ck)
                ir = m [pc];
            @(posedge ck)
                case (ir [15:13])
                    //case expressions, as before
                    3'b111:    acc = multiply(acc, m [ir [12:0]]);
                endcase
            pc = pc + 1;
        end

    function [12:0] multiply;
    input    [12:0]  a;
    input    [15:0]  b;

        begin: serialMult
            reg    [5:0]        mcnd, mpy;

            mpy = b[5:0];
            mcnd = a[5:0];
            multiply = 0;
            repeat (6)
                begin
                    if (mpy[0])
                        multiply = multiply + {mcnd, 6'b000000};
                    multiply = multiply >> 1;
                    mpy = mpy >> 1;
                end
        end
    endfunction
endmodule
```

Example 2.10 A Function Specification

2.5.3 **A Structural View**

The task and function examples of the previous sections have illustrated different organizations of a behavioral model. That is, we can choose to model the behavior in different ways with the same result. When we used the * operator, we were probably only interested in simulation of the model. There are many ways to implement a multiply in hardware, but early in the design process we were content to let the simulator substitute its method.

As the design progresses, we want to specify the multiply algorithm that we want our hardware to implement. This we did by using the task and function statements in the above examples. The implication of the description using a task or function is that this divide algorithm will be part of the final data path and state machine synthesized to implement the Mark-1 processor. That is, we enlarged the behavioral description by specifying the details of the multiply algorithm and thus we would expect the final state machine that implements this behavior to have more states. Likewise, the data path may need more components to hold the values and perform the operations.

Another design decision could have been to use a possibly pre-existing multiply module in conjunction with the Mark-1 module. This case, shown in Example 2.11, illustrates the multiply as an instantiated module within the **mark1Mod** module. This description approach would be used if a previously designed multiply module was to be used, or if the designer wanted to force a functional partitioning of the modules within the design. The **multiply** module ports are connected to the **mark1Mod** and the **mark1Mod** module starts the **multiply** module with the **go** line. When done, the **multiply** module signals the Mark-1 with the **done** line which Mark-1 waits for. This structural description leads to a very different design. Now we have two state machines, one for **mark1Mod** and one for multiply. To keep the two modules synchronized, we have defined a handshaking protocol using wait statements and signalling variables **go** and **done**. At this point in the design process it is not possible to point to one of these solutions as being the best. Rather we can only suggest, as we have done above, why one would describe the system solely with behavioral modeling constructs (*, function, task) or suggest structural partitioning of the behavior.

References. Functions in continuous assign 4.4.1

```
module mark1Mod;
    reg [15:0]    m [0:8191];    // 8192 x 16 bit memory
    reg [12:0]    pc;            // 13 bit program counter
    reg [12:0]    acc;           // 13 bit accumulator
    reg [15:0]    ir;            // 16 bit instruction register
    reg           ck;            // a clock signal

    reg     [12:0]  mcnd;
    reg             go;
    wire    [12:0]  prod;
    wire            done;
    multiply        mul (prod, acc, mcnd, go, done);

    always
        begin
            @(posedge ck)
                go = 0;
                ir = m [pc];
            @(posedge ck)
                case (ir [15:13])
                    //other case expressions
                    3'b111:begin
                        wait (~done) mcnd = m [ir [12:0]];
                        go = 1;
                        wait (done);
                        acc = prod;
                    end
                endcase
            pc = pc + 1;
        end
endmodule

module multiply (prod, mpy, mcnd, go, done);
    output  [12:0]  prod;
    input   [12:0]  mpy, mcnd;
    input           go;
    output          done;

    reg     [12:0]  prod;
    reg     [5:0]   myMpy;
    reg             done;
```

```
        always
            begin
                done = 0;
                wait (go);
                myMpy = mpy[5:0];
                prod = 0;
                repeat (6)
                    begin
                        if (myMpy[0])
                            prod = prod + {mcnd, 6'b000000};
                        prod = prod >> 1;
                        myMpy = myMpy >> 1;
                    end
                done = 1;
                wait (~go);
            end
    endmodule
```

Example 2.11 The Multiply as a Separate Module

2.6 **Rules of Scope and Hierarchical Names**

An identifier's *scope* is the range of the Verilog description over which the identifier is known. The rules of scope define this range. Verilog also has a hierarchical naming feature allowing any identifier in the whole design to be accessed from anywhere in the design.

2.6.1 **Rules of Scope**

Module names are known globally across the whole design. Verilog then allows for identifiers to be defined within four entities: modules, tasks, functions, and named blocks. Each of these entities defines the *local scope* of the identifier, the range of the description over which the identifier is known. This local scope encompasses the module-endmodule, task-endtask, function-endfunction, and begin:name-end pairs. Within a local scope, there may only be one identifier with the given name.

Identifiers can be known outside of the local scope. To understand the scope rules we need to distinguish between situations which allow forward referencing and those which do not.

- Forward referenced. Identifiers for modules, tasks, functions, and named begin-end blocks are allowed to be forward referencing and thus may be used before they have been defined. That is, you can instantiate a module, enable a task, enable a function, or disable a named block before either of these entities has been defined.

- Not forward referenced. Forward referencing is not allowed with register and net accesses. That is, before you can use them, they must be defined. Typically, these are defined at the start of the local scope (i.e., module, task, function or named begin-end) in which they are being used. An exception to this is that output nets of gate primitives can be declared implicitly (See section 4.2.3).

For the case of the forward referencing entities (module, task, function, and named begin-end blocks), there is also an *upward scope* defined by the module instantiation hierarchy. From the low end of the hierarchy, forward referenced identifiers in each higher local scope are known within the lowest scope. This path up the module instantiation hierarchy is the *upward scope*.

Consider Example 2.12. The identifiers in the local scope of module **top** are: **top**, **instance1, y, r, w,** and **t.** When module **b** is instantiated within module **top**, procedural statements in **b** can enable tasks and functions defined in the local scope of module **top** and also disable a named block in its local scope. However, task **t** in module **top** has a named block (**c**) within its scope. **c** cannot be disabled from module **b** because **c** is not in **top**'s local scope and thus it is not in **b**'s upward scope (rather, it is down a level from it in task **t**'s local scope). Further, named block **y** in **top**'s local scope can be disabled from module **b** and it can be disabled from within a task or function defined in module **top**, or from within named blocks within the task or function.

Note however, that register **r** and wire **w**, although in the upward scope of module **b**, are not accessible from it; registers and nets are not forward referencing and thus can only be accessed in the local scope. The rule is that forward-referencing identifiers (i.e. module, task, function, and named block identifiers) are resolved after the instantiations are known by looking upward through the module instantiation tree. When the top of the hierarchy is reached (at a module that is not instantiated elsewhere) the search for the identifier is ended. Non-forward referenced registers and nets are resolved immediately in the local scope.

It is important to note that tasks and functions defined in a module can be enabled from within any of the modules instantiated (to any level) in that module. Thus functions and tasks used in many parts of the design should be defined in the top module.

It is also useful to think of the upward identifier tree as arising from two sources: the module hierarchy, and procedural statement hierarchy. The module hierarchy tree was described above. The procedural statement hierarchy arises from nested named blocks within always and initial statements, tasks, and functions. Procedural statement hierarchies are rooted in modules (essentially, they are always and initial state-

```
module top;
     reg      r;          //hierarchical name is top.r
     wire     w;          //hierarchical name is top.w
     b instance1();

     always
        begin: y
              reg      q;    //hierarchical name is top.y.q
        end

     task t;
        begin: c              //hierarchical name is top.t.c
              reg      q;     //hierarchical name is top.t.c.q
              disable y;      //OK
        end
     endtask
endmodule

module b;
     reg      s;          //hierarchical name is top.instance1.s

     always
     begin
        t;                 //OK
        disable y;         //OK
        disable c;         //Nope, c is not known
        disable t.c;       //OK
        s = 1;             //OK
        r = 1;             //Nope, r is not known
        top.r = 1;         //OK
        t.c.q = 1;         //OK
        y.q = 1            //OK, a different q than t.c.q
     end
endmodule
```

Example 2.12 Scope and Hierarchical Names

ments) and are separate from the module hierarchy. When accessing non-forward referencing identifiers (registers and wires), statements at the deepest point of nesting look up the procedural hierarchy for the identifier. When the root of the procedural hierarchy is found, the search is stopped. The reason is that non-forward referencing identifiers only have access to the current local scope and its procedural statement hierarchy for identifier resolution.

Thus, identifiers representing registers and nets are searched up the procedural hierarchy, but not searched across module instantiation boundaries. Identifiers representing tasks, functions, and named blocks are searched up the procedural and module instantiation hierarchy.

2.6.2 **Hierarchical Names**

The previous section discussed the upward scope of identifiers within a description. When possible, these identifiers should be used — they are easier to read and easier to type. On the other hand, hierarchical names can uniquely specify any task, function, named block, register, or wire in the whole description.

Hierarchical names are forward referencing — they are not resolved until all modules are instantiated. Hierarchical names consist of a path name which has identifiers separated by periods ("."). The first identifier is a forward referencing identifier found by searching up the procedural and module hierarchy name tree. From where the first identifier is found, each succeeding identifier specifies the named scope within which to continue searching downward. The last identifier specifies the entity being search for.

Consider Example 2.12. Within module b, register r is not known because register and wire identifiers are not searched for across module instantiations; they are only known in the local scope. However, the hierarchical reference **top.r** in module **b** will access **r** in **top**. Similarly, from module b, t.c.q accesses register q in task t (which, by the way is different than register q in named block y). Further, block c can be disabled from b through the hierarchical name **t.c**. Note that these last two did not start with **top** (although they could have). When searching up the module hierarchy from b, the next scope up includes forward referencing names **top**, **y**, and **t**. Any of these (and actually any forward referencing identifier — modules, tasks, functions, or named blocks) can be used as the root of the hierarchical name. Indeed, when using a hierarchical name to specify a register or wire, the first identifiers in the name must be forward referencing identifiers. The last is the register or wire. When specifying the name, you need not start from the top. **top.t.c.q** and **t.c.q** are, from module **b**'s perspective, the same.

Although we can gain access to any named item in the description with this mechanism, it is more appropriate to stay within the local and upward scope rules which enforce better style, readability, and maintainability. Use hierarchical names sparingly because they violate the stylistic rules of localizing access to elements of the design, rather than allowing any statement in the whole design to access anything.

Yes, anything <u>can</u> access anything else through hierarchical naming. However, it <u>may</u> not be appropriate stylistically. Stick with the rules of local and upward scope as much as possible.

2.7 **Summary**

The behavioral modeling statements that we have covered so far are very similar to those found in software programming languages. Probably the major difference seen so far is that the Verilog language has separate mechanisms for handling the structural hierarchy and behavioral decomposition. Functions and tasks are provided to allow for the behavior of a module to be "software engineered". That is, we can break long and sometimes repetitious descriptions into behavioral subcomponents. Separately, we can use module definitions to describe the structural hierarchy of the design and to separate concurrently operating behaviors into different modules. The examples of Section 2.5 have shown how these two approaches to modeling allow us to represent a design in a wide range of stages of completion. The next chapter continues with the topic of describing concurrent behaviors.

2.8 **Exercises**

2.1   Change the expressions containing the right shift operator in Example 2.9 to use bit and part selects and concatenations only.

2.2   Does replacing the repeat loop in Example 2.2 with the register declaration and **for** loop below achieve the same results?

    reg [3:0]   i;

        for (i = 0; i <= `DvLen; i = i+1)
            begin
                //shift and subtract statements
            end

2.3   Shown below is a case statement with two case items defined. The items call different tasks. If we want to enumerate all of the possible case items, how many would there be in all?
        reg   [3:0] f;
        case (f)
            4'b 0110:   taskR;
            4'b 1010:   taskS;
        endcase

2.4   Write a **for** loop statement which is equivalent to the **casez** statement in the following function without introducing any new variables.

```
function [7:0] getMask;
input [7:0]    halfVal;
    casez (halfVal)
        8'b???????1: getMask = 8'b11111111;
        8'b??????10: getMask = 8'b11111110;
        8'b?????100: getMask = 8'b11111100;
        8'b????1000: getMask = 8'b11111000;
        8'b???10000: getMask = 8'b11110000;
        8'b??100000: getMask = 8'b11100000;
        8'b?1000000: getMask = 8'b11000000;
        8'b10000000: getMask = 8'b10000000;
        8'b00000000: getMask = 8'b11111111;
    endcase
endfunction
```

2.5 Simulate the **multiply** task and show the value of **mpy**, **mcnd**, and **prod** initially, and at the end of each of the 6 iterations of the loop. Add a $display statement to show these values.

2.6 Write the hierarchical name of every task, function, and register in Examples 2.9 and 2.10.

2.7 In Example 2.12, we saw that from module **b**, register **q** in task **t** could be referred to either as **top.t.c.q** or **t.c.q**. Why is there only one way to refer to register **r** from module **b**?

2.8 Look ahead to Example 4.18 on page 147.

A. How would a behavioral statement in module **slave** call task **wiggleBusLines**?

B. If both modules **master** and **slave** needed to call task **wiggleBusLines**, where would be the appropriate place for the task to be defined?

3 Concurrent Processes

Most of the behavioral modeling statements discussed to this point have been demonstrated using single process examples. These statements are part of the body of an always statement and are repetitively executed in sequential order. They may operate on values that are inputs or outputs of the module or on the module's internal registers. In this chapter we present behavioral modeling statements that by their definition interact with activities external to the enclosing always. For instance, the *wait* statement waits for its expression to become TRUE as a result of a value being changed in another process. As in this case and the others to be presented here, the operation of the wait statement is dependent on the actions of concurrent processes in the system.

3.1 Concurrent Processes

We have defined a process to be an abstraction of a controller, a thread of control that evokes the change of values stored in the system's registers. We conceive of a digital system as a set of communicating, concurrent processes or independent control activities that pass information among themselves. What is important is that each of these processes contains state information and that this state is altered as a function of the process' current inputs and present state.

Example 3.1 shows an abstract description of a computer. An implementation of the hardware controller for the process described in the always statement is a sequential state machine with output and next state logic. This state machine would control a data path that includes the registers, arithmetic-logic units, and steering logic such as buses and multiplexors.

```
module computer;
     always
          begin
               powerOnInitializations;
               forever
                    begin
                         fetchAndExecuteInstructions;
                    end
          end
endmodule
```

Example 3.1 An Abstract Computer Description

Consider that this process may interact with another process in the system, possibly an input interface that receives bit-serial information from a modem. The process abstraction is necessary in this case because there are two independent, but communicating, threads of control: the computer, and the input interface. The input interface process watches for new input bits from the modem and signals the computer when a byte of data has been received. The other process, the computer described in Example 3.1, would only interact with the input interface process when a full byte of information has been received.

These two processes could have been described as one, but it would have been quite messy and hard to read. Essentially, each statement of the computer process would have to include a check for new input data from the interface and a description of what to do if it is found. In the worst case, if we have two processes that have n and m states respectively, then the combined process with equivalent functionality would have $n*m$ states — a description of far higher complexity. Indeed, it is necessary to conceive of the separate processes in a system and describe them separately.

When, when several processes exists in a system and information is to be passed among them, we must synchronize the processes to make sure that correct information is being passed. The reason for this is that one process does not know what state another process is in unless there is some explicit signal from that process giving such information. That is, each of the processes is asynchronous with respect to the others. For instance, they may be operating at their own clock rate, or they may be producing data at intervals that are not synchronized with the intervals when another process can consume the data. In such instances, we must synchronize the processes, providing explicit signals between them that indicate something about their internal state and that of the data shared among them.

In hardware, one approach to synchronization is implemented with "data-ready" handshakes — one process will not read the shared data until the other signals with a "data-ready" signal that new data is present. When the other signals that the data has been read, the first unasserts the "data-ready" signal until new information is available. Alternately, a clock signal is used to synchronize multiple processes. Values are guaranteed to be valid and actions are specified to occur on one or both of the clock edges. Synchronizing signals such as handshakes and clocks are necessary when information is to be passed correctly among separate processes.

The statements presented in this chapter pertain to describing behavior that involves the interactions among concurrent processes.

References: always, initial 2.1; procedural timing model 5.1; non-determinism 5.3

3.2 **Events**

Event control statements provide a means of watching for a change in a value. The execution of the process containing the *event control* is suspended until the change occurs. Thus, the value must be changed by a separate process.

It is important to note that the constructs described in this section trigger on a change in a value. That is, they are edge-sensitive. When control passes to one of these statements, the initial value of the input being triggered on is checked. When the value changes later (for instance, when a positive edge on the value has occurred), then the event control statement completes and control continues with the next statement.

This section covers two basic forms of the event control: one that watches for a value change, and another, called the *named event*, that watches for an abstract signal called an event.

3.2.1 **Event Control Statement**

Example 3.2 will be used to motivate the discussion of event control statements. In this example, the statement:

    @(negedge clock) q <= data;

models the negative edge triggering of a D-type flip flop. This procedural *event control* statement watches for the negative transition of **clock** and then assigns the value of **data** to q. The value assigned to **q** is the value of **data** just before the edge of the clock.

```
module dEdgeFF (q, clock, data);
output   q;
reg      q;
input    clock, data;

    always
        @(negedge clock) q <= data;
endmodule
```

Example 3.2 A D-Type Edge-Triggered Flip Flop

In addition to specifying a negative edge to trigger on, we may also specify a positive edge ("posedge") or make no specification at all. Consider:

@ (ricky) lucy = crazy;

Here, **lucy** will be loaded with the value **crazy** if there is any change on **ricky**.

The general form of the event control statement is:

```
event_control
    ::=  @ event_identifier
    |    @ ( event_expression )

event_expression
    ::=  expression
    |    event_identifier
    |    posedge_expression
    |    negedge_expression
    |    event_expression or event_expression
```

The qualifier may be "posedge", "negedge", or it may be left blank. The expression is a gate output, wire, or register whose value is generated as a result of activity in another process. The event control begins watching for the specified change from the time procedural control passes to it. Changes prior to the time when control passed to the event control statement are ignored. After the event occurs, the statement is executed. If, while waiting for the event, a new value for the expression is generated that happens to be the same as the old value, then no event occurs.

At times, the event control expression may take on unknown values. In such cases, a negative edge is defined as a transition from 1 to 0, 1 to x, or x to 0. A positive edge is defined as a transition from 0 to 1, 0 to x, or x to 1.

Any number of events can be expressed in the event control statement such that the occurrence of any one of them will trigger the execution of the statement. A time-out example is shown in Example 3.3.

```
always
    begin
        // start the timer that will produce the timeOut signal;

        @(posedge inputA or posedge timeOut)
            if (timeOut)
                // ... error recovery
            else regA = regB;            // normal operation
        // ... other statements
    end
```

Example 3.3 ORing Two Events in an Event Control Statement

In this example, we are watching for either of two events, a positive edge on **inputA**, or a positive edge on **timeOut**. The two events are separated by the keyword **or**. In this case, we can trigger on the intended event — the change on **inputA**. However, if the **InputA** event does not occur with a reasonable amount of time, the process can extricate itself from the deadlock situation and begin some form of error recovery.

The *or* construct is important in concurrent process applications. If a process needs to wait for <u>any</u> of several events to occur, it does not want to prematurely commit itself to waiting for one specific event before waiting for another. Indeed, since the events may not occur in a given sequential order — the order of arrival may be data dependent — waiting for individual events in a specific sequential order will probably cause the system to *deadlock*. That is, one process will be waiting for an event that will never occur. The or construct allows us to wait for any of several events.

References: level sensitive wait 3.3; compare event and wait 3.3.3; intra-assignment delay 3.7

3.2.2 **Named Events**

The event control statements described above require that a change be specified explicitly. A more abstract version of event control, the *named event*, allows a trigger to be sent to another part of the design. The trigger is not implemented as a register or wire and thus is abstract in nature. Further, even if it crosses module boundaries, it requires no port specification. Other parts of the design may watch for the occurrence of the named event before proceeding.

Example 3.3 shows a Fibonacci number generator example using a named event to communicate between the two modules. The **topFib** module instantiates only two modules (**fnc** and **ng**).

The always statement in module **numberGen** illustrates the triggering of event **ready**:

   #50 -> ready;

The event must have been previously declared as on the fourth line of the module description. The always statement will continuously delay for 50 time units, increment the value **number**, delay for 50 more time units, and then trigger event **ready**.

Module **fibNumCalc** watches for the event on the first line of its always statement:

   @ng.ready
         count = startingValue;

The name "ng.ready" is a *hierarchical name* for event **ready** and will be explained after we dispense with how the named event works. For module **fibNumCalc** to receive the trigger, it must first have started to execute the @event statement, and then the trigger statement in module **numberGen** must be executed. At this time, module **fibNum-Calc** will continue executing with the statement **count= startingValue;**.

Note that the act of triggering an event is, itself, a statement and need not be combined with a delay operator as in the example. The general form for activating the named event is:

statement
       ::=   event_trigger

event_trigger
       ::=   - > *event* _identifier;

This description of the Fibonacci number generator does have a race condition in it if module **fibNumCalc** takes longer than 100 time units to execute the always loop. Module **numberGen** produces a value every 100 time units and sends a trigger. If module **fibNumCalc** did not get around its always loop in less than that time, it would miss **numberGen**'s trigger. The result would be that the Fibonacci number of every other number produced by **numberGen** would be calculated.

Note that there is no register to hold the trigger, nor any wire to transmit it; rather it is a conceptual event which when it occurs in one module, can trigger other modules that were previously stopped at an @event statement. Further, the named event is more abstract than the event control in that no hardware implementation clues are given. By comparison, a posedge event control implies that some form of edge trig-

```
module topFib;
    wire [15:0]   number, numberOut;

    numberGen      ng      (number);
    fibNumCalc     fnc     (number, numberOut);
endmodule

module numberGen (number);
    output   [15:0]  number;
    reg      [15:0]  number;
    event            ready;        //declare the event

    initial
        number = 0;

    always
        begin
            #50 number = number + 1;
            #50 -> ready;        //generate event signal
        end
endmodule

module fibNumCalc (startingValue, fibNum);
    input    [15:0]  startingValue;
    output   [15:0]  fibNum;

    reg      [15:0]  count, fibNum, oldNum, temp;

    always
        begin
            @ng.ready            //wait for event signal
                count = startingValue;
            oldNum = 1;
            for (fibNum = 0; count != 0; count = count - 1)
                begin
                    temp = fibNum;
                    fibNum = fibNum + oldNum;
                    oldNum = temp;
                end
            $display ("%d, fibNum=%d", $time, fibNum);
        end
endmodule
```

Example 3.4 Fibonacci Number Generator Using Named Events

gering logic will be used to detect that such a transition has occurred. The named event is typically used in simulation.

References. Hierarchical names 2.6

3.3 **The Wait Statement**

The wait statement is a concurrent process statement that waits for its conditional expression to become TRUE. Conceptually, execution of the process stops until the expression becomes TRUE. By definition, the conditional expression must include at least one value that is generated by a separate, concurrent process — otherwise, the conditional expression would never change. Because the wait must work with inputs from other processes, it is a primary means of synchronizing two concurrent processes.

The wait statement condition is level-sensitive. That is, it does not wait for a change in a value. Rather it only checks that the value of the conditional is TRUE. If it is, execution continues. If it is FALSE, the process waits.

The wait is often used in handshaking situations where we are synchronizing two processes. Example 3.5 illustrates the situation where a process will only read the **dataIn** input if the **ready** input is TRUE. The wait synchronizes the two processes by insuring that the consumer process does not pass the wait statement and consume the data until the producer process generates **dataIn** and sets the **ready** signal to TRUE. The **ready** signal is a synchronization signal that tells the consumer process that the producer process has passed the state where **dataIn** is generated. In this way, the two processes become synchronized by the **ready** signal.

```
module consumer (dataIn, ready);
    input    [7:0]   dataIn;
    input            ready;
    reg      [7:0]   in;

    always
        begin
            wait (ready)
                    in = dataIn;
            //... consume dataIn
        end
endmodule
```

Example 3.5 The Consumer Module

The general form of the wait statement is

statement
      ::= wait_statement
      | ...

wait_statement
      ::= **wait** (expression) statement_or_null

statement _or_null
      ::= statement
      | ;

The expression is evaluated and if it is TRUE, the process proceeds to execute the statement. If it is FALSE, the process stops until it becomes TRUE. At that time, the process will proceed with the statement. Note that the wait statement does not, itself, have a semicolon at its end; the statement_or_null contains the semicolon. Again, the change in the expression must come about from the actions of another concurrent process.

It is interesting to note that there would be a problem simulating Example 3.5 if there were no other event control or delay operations in the always statement. If this were true, then once the wait condition becomes TRUE, the loop would continue to be executed forever as the wait will never be FALSE. In one sense, this problem comes about because the simulator is simulating concurrent processes in a sequential manner and only switching between simulating the concurrent processes when a wait for a FALSE condition, delay, or event control is encountered. Since none of these are encountered in this loop, a simulation would loop forever in this always statement.

Actually, this is a more general problem in describing concurrent systems. In general, we cannot assume much about the speed of the processes in relation to each other, and thus, we need to introduce more synchronization signals to insure their correct execution. If Example 3.5 had another synchronization point, say a wait (~ready), then the producer and consumer in the example would be more tightly synchronized to each other's operating rate. Further, the simulation would also run correctly! The next section illustrates this with further examples.

References: compare to while 3.3.2

3.3.1 **A Complete Producer-Consumer Handshake**

Example 3.5 could exhibit some synchronization errors. Specifically, the consumer never signals to the producer that the **dataIn** has been consumed. Two possible errors could occur because of this incomplete handshake:

- The producer may operate too fast and change **dataIn** to a new value before the consumer has a chance to read the previous value. Thus the consumer would miss a value.

- The consumer may operate too fast and get around its always statement and see **ready** still TRUE. Thus it would read the same data twice.

We need to synchronize the processes so that regardless of the speed of their implementation they function correctly. One method of synchronizing two processes is with a fully-interlocked handshake as shown in Figure 3.1.

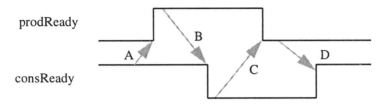

Figure 3.1 A Fully Interlocked Handshake

The handshake illustrated above is described in Example 3.6 and the following paragraphs. The description consists of two always blocks, the first modeling the consumer and the second modeling the producer. At the start of time, both of these blocks can run. Of course one of them will go first, as chosen arbitrarily by the simulator. Initially all registers and wires have unknown value. Thus, when producer reaches "wait (consReady)" or the consumer reaches "wait (prodReady)", that always block will stop and wait because **consReady** and **prodReady** are unknown. If the consumer starts first, it will wait for **prodReady** after setting **consReady** to 1. The producer will then run, setting **prodReady** to 0 and continue through the wait for **consReady**. If the producer starts first, it will set **prodReady** to zero, produce some data, and wait for **consReady**. Then the consumer will execute, setting **consReady** to 1 and wait for **prodReady**. Since **consReady** was just set to 1, the producer will continue again.

Assume we are at the point where the producer has set producer-ready (**prodReady**) to FALSE (or zero) indicating that it is not ready to send any information, and the consumer has set consumer-ready (**consReady**) to TRUE (or one) indicating that it is ready to receive information. When producer has generated a value, and it sees that **consReady** is one (arrow A in Figure 3.1), it loads the value into the output register **dataOut** and sets **prodReady** to one. It then waits for the consumer to receive the value and set **consReady** to zero. The consumer, seeing **prodReady** at level one, makes a copy of the input and sets **consReady** to zero (arrow B in Figure 3.1).

```
module ProducerConsumer;
    reg                consReady, prodReady;
    reg      [7:0]     dataInCopy, dataOut;

    always        // The consumer process
        begin
            consReady = 1;            // indicate consumer ready
            forever
                begin
                    wait (prodReady)
                        dataInCopy = dataOut;
                    consReady = 0;                // indicate value consumed
                    //...munch on data
                    wait (!prodReady)             // complete handshake
                        consReady = 1;
                end
        end

    always        // The producer process
        begin
            prodReady = 0;        // indicate nothing to transfer
            forever
                begin
                    // ...produce data and put into "dataOut"
                    wait (consReady)               // wait for consumer ready
                        dataOut = $random;
                    prodReady = 1;                 //indicate ready to transfer
                    wait (!consReady)              //finish handshake
                        prodReady = 0;
                end
        end
endmodule
```

Example 3.6 The Consumer With Fully Interlocked Handshake

The producer now knows that the consumer has received the data so it sets **pro-dReady** back to zero, signalling the end of its half of the transfer (arrow C in Figure 3.1). The producer proceeds with its business and the consumer consumes the data. Then, seeing that the producer has finished its transfer, the consumer indicates that it is ready for another transfer by setting **consReady** (arrow D in Figure 3.1). The consumer then watches for the next transfer. At this point, the transfer is complete.

Note that we have introduced the **random** system function in the **producer**. This function returns a new random number each time it is called.

This method of transferring data between two concurrent processes will work correctly regardless of the timing delays between the processes and regardless of their relative speeds of execution. That is, because each process waits on each level of the other process' synchronization signal (i.e. the producer waits for both **consReady** and **!consReady**), the processes are guaranteed to remain in lockstep. Thus, the consumer cannot get around its always loop and quickly reread the previously transferred data. Nor, can the producer work so quickly to make the consumer miss some data. Rather, the producer waits for the consumer to indicate that it has received the data. Systems synchronized in this way are called *self-timed* systems because the two interacting processes keep themselves synchronized; no external synchronization signal, such as a clock, is needed.

References: $random F; comparison of event and wait 3.3.3

3.3.2 **Comparison of the Wait and While Statements**

It is incorrect to use the while statement to watch for an externally generated condition. Even though the final implementation of the state machine that waits for the condition generated by another concurrent process may be a "while" (i.e. stay in state Q while ready is FALSE), conceptually we are synchronizing separate processes and we should use the appropriate wait construct.

A further explanation of the differences between the wait and while involves the use of the simulator. Assuming a uniprocessor running a simulator, each always and initial statement is simulated as a separate process, one at a time. Once started, the simulator continues executing a process until either a delay control (#), a wait with a FALSE condition, or an event (@) statement is encountered. In the case of the delay control, event, or a wait with a FALSE condition, the simulator stops executing the process and finds the next item in the time queue to simulate. In the case of the wait with a TRUE expression, simulation continues with the same process. A while statement will never stop the simulator from executing the process.

Therefore, since the while statement shown in Example 3.7 waits for an external variable to change, it will cause the simulator to go into an endless loop. Essentially, the process that controls **inputA** will never get a chance to change it. Further, if the loop were corrected by using a wait statement in place of the while, an infinite loop would still occur. Since the wait is level sensitive, once its condition becomes TRUE, it will continue to execute unless stopped by a wait with a FALSE condition, event control, or delay statement within the loop.

Substituting a wait statement in Example 3.7 would be correct only if the body of the loop contained either a delay, wait (FALSE), or event control. These would all stop simulation of this process and give the process that controls **inputA** a chance to change its value.

```
module endlessLoop (inputA);
    input        inputA;
    reg[15:0]    count;

    always
      begin
            count = 0;
            while (inputA)
                count = count + 1; // wait for inputA to change to FALSE
            $display ("This will never print if inputA is TRUE!");
      end
endmodule
```

Example 3.7 An Endless Loop

References: while 2.3; delay control 2.1; event control 3.2

3.3.3 Comparison of Wait and Event Control Statements

In essence, both the event and wait statements watch for a situation that is generated by an external process. The difference between the two is that the event control statement is edge-triggered whereas the wait is a level-sensitive statement.

Thus the event control is appropriate for describing modules that include edge-triggering logic, such as flip flops. When active, the event statement must see a change occur before its statement is executed. We may write:

@(posedge clock)   statement;

When control passes to this statement, if clock has the value one, the execution will stop until the next transition to one. That is, the event operator does not assume that since clock is one that a positive edge must have occurred. Rather, it must see the positive edge before proceeding.

The wait, being level-sensitive, only waits if its expression is FALSE.

References: while 2.3

3.4 **A Concurrent Process Example**

The Producer-Consumer example presented in section 3.3 illustrated how two processes could communicate and transfer information by waiting for appropriate levels on interprocess handshake lines. In this section, we specify a simple synchronous bus protocol and develop a simulation model for it using the event control (@) constructs. The cycle-accurate style of description will be used.

Figure 3.2 illustrates the synchronous bus protocol to be used in our example. A **clock** signal is transmitted on the bus and is used to synchronize the actions of the bus master and bus slave. A write bus cycle takes one full clock period and a read cycle takes two. The type of bus cycle being performed is indicated by the **rwLine** bus line; a zero indicates a read and a one indicates a write.

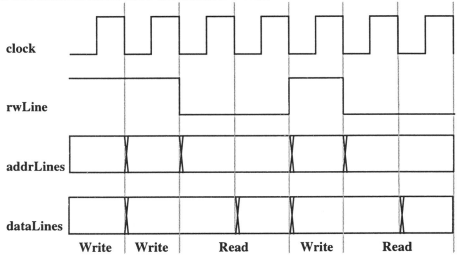

Figure 3.2 A Synchronous Bus Protocol

At the beginning of a write cycle the bus master drives the **rwLine, addrLines,** and **dataLines** lines and waits for the end of the clock cycle. At the end of the clock cycle, the values will have propagated down the bus to the slave. On the negative edge of **clock,** the slave loads the **dataLines** into the memory location specified by the **addrLines** lines.

A read cycle takes two clock periods to complete. During the first, and continuing through the second, the bus master drives the **rwLine** and **addrLines** lines. During the second clock period, the bus slave drives the **data** lines with the value read from memory at address **addrLines**. On the negative edge of second clock cycle, the master loads **dataLines** into an internal register.

The x'ed areas in **addrLines** and **dataLines** show values changing at the clock edge. In our description, they change in zero time; the x's in the figure necessarily take up physical space on the horizontal axis.

Although the bus protocol is simple, it will illustrate the cycle-accurate specification of a clock-synchronous system and bring together a number of modeling constructs illustrated in smaller examples.

Example 3.8 is organized as one module containing four processes described using always and initial statements. Three processes model the clock, the bus master, and the bus slave. The fourth initializes the system and sets up a monitor to display changes in values. The **wiggleBusLines** task is used by the master to encapsulate the actions of the bus protocol, hiding the details from other possible actions of the master. The processes communicate through the global variables **clock**, **rwLine**, **addressLines**, and **dataLines** instead of through nets. (Example 4.18 extends this example to using nets between the master and slave.)

The description begins by defining two constants of the system, **READ** and **WRITE**. These definitions will make the **wiggleBusLines** task call more readable. Within the **sbus** module, a parameter is defined. Parameter **tClock** is one half of the clock period and is set to 20. At this point we can consider this to be default value for the **tClock**. This value will be substituted when the parameter name is used. (Later in Chapter 4, parameters will be discussed more fully and we will see that this generic value can be overridden at instantiation time.) Finally, the registers are defined. Since we are only implementing 32 16-bit words in memory **m**, we have only defined **addressLines** to be 5 bits wide.

When simulation of the two always and two initial statements begins, they will start executing in arbitrary order. The description must be written so that it will work correctly under any starting order.

The first initial statement in the example performs three important functions. First, it loads memory **m** from an external file called "memory.data" using the $readmemh system task. The operation of this task will be described later. Secondly, **clock** is initialized to 0; it is important to initialize values that are used to synchronize processes. Finally, the $monitor statement displays the values **rwLine**, **dataLines**, **addressLines**, and **$time** anytime any of the first three change.

The first always statement in the description simply inverts **clock** every **tClock** time units (which is 20 in this case). It waits for **tClock** time units before executing. Even if this always statement started executing first, it will not access the value of **clock** until it is set to 0 by the initial statement described above. Thus, the time delay

```
`define READ 0
`define WRITE 1

module sbus;
    parameter    tClock =  20;

    reg          clock;
    reg [15:0]   m[0:31]; //32 16-bit words
    reg [15:0]   data;
    // registers names xLine model the bus lines using global registers
    reg          rwLine;   //write = 1, read = 0
    reg [4:0]    addressLines;
    reg [15:0]   dataLines;


    initial
       begin
           $readmemh ("memory.data", m);
           clock = 0;
           $monitor ("rw=%d, data=%d, addr=%d at time %d",
                         rwLine, dataLines, addressLines, $time);
       end

    always
       #tClock clock = !clock;

    initial    // bus master end
       begin
           #1
           wiggleBusLines ( `READ, 2, data);
           wiggleBusLines ( `READ, 3, data);
           data = 5;
           wiggleBusLines ( `WRITE, 2, data);
           data = 7;
           wiggleBusLines ( `WRITE, 3, data);
           wiggleBusLines ( `READ, 2, data);
           wiggleBusLines ( `READ, 3, data);
           $finish;
       end
```

```
            task wiggleBusLines;
                input           readWrite;
                input [5:0]    addr;
                inout [15:0]  data;

                begin
                    rwLine <= readWrite;
                    if (readWrite) begin    // write value
                        addressLines <= addr;
                        dataLines <= data;
                    end
                    else begin                  //read value
                        addressLines <= addr;
                        @ (negedge clock);
                    end
                    @(negedge clock);
                    if (~readWrite)
                        data <= dataLines;    // value returned during read cycle
                end
            endtask

        always    // bus slave end
            begin
                @(negedge clock);
                if (~rwLine) begin    //read
                    dataLines <= m[addressLines];
                    @(negedge clock);
                end
                else    //write
                    m[addressLines] <= dataLines;
            end
    endmodule
```

Example 3.8 Behavioral Description of a Synchronous Bus

orders the start of these two statements and insures that this always statement won't
be complementing an unknown value.

The bus master process calls the **wiggleBusLines** task with three parameters, indicating the type of cycle, the memory address, and the data. The third parameter is
defined in the task to be an inout, and represents the data to be written during a write
bus cycle, or the data read during a read cycle. The task is called six times by the master process, passing different values to it. The first task call will cause **wiggleBusLines**
to read from address 2 and return the read value in **data**. The third call will cause a
write of the value 5 into memory address 2.

The bus master is written assuming that **clock** has just fallen and a new bus cycle is beginning. If the bus cycle is a **WRITE**, the **then** part of the **if** is executed, loading **addressLines** and **dataLines** with the values passed to the task. The task then waits for the next negative edge of the **clock** (i.e. the end of the write cycle) before returning from the task. When that negative edge occurs, we know that the end of the **WRITE** cycle has occurred and, as we will see, the bus slave has loaded the value in **dataLines** into **m** at the address in **addressLines**. The #1 assures that all other always and initial blocks execute first.

Let's trace the action of the slave during the write cycle. The bus slave process begins by waiting for the negative edge of the clock. Remember that these models are written assuming that a negative clock edge has just occurred and that a bus cycles is just beginning. Thus the "@(negedge clock)" statement waits until the end of the cycle just started, at which point it executes its **if** statement. Since we are tracing a write cycle, the **else** part of the **if** is executed and the value in **dataLines** is copied into **m** as addressed by **addressLines**. The slave process then waits for the end of the next clock cycle.

Let's assume that two back-to-back writes are going to be done to memory. It is instructive to examine how the two "@(negedge clock)" statements at end of the write cycle work; the one clock event is near the end of the **wiggleBusLines** task and the other is the clock event at the start of the slave process. Both processes are waiting for this edge to occur. When it does, one or the other will execute first; we do not know which. The value at issue is **dataLines**. If **wiggleBusLines** executes first and starts the second write, it will assign **dataLines** with a new value of **data** in the first **then** part. If the slave starts first, it will write the value of **dataLines** into memory. So, which value of **dataLines** will be written into memory? Given that both transfers are non-blocking, the transfers are synchronized and order independent. Indeed, care must be taken to insure the order independence of data transfers. In cycle-accurate descriptions, non-blocking assignments insure this.

The read cycle requires an extra clock period in the master and slave models. Task **wiggleBusLines** loads **addressLines** with the address to read from and waits for the end of the <u>second</u> clock cycle before continuing. At the end of the second cycle, the value in **dataLines** is loaded into **data** and that value is returned from the task to the bus master.

The bus slave waits for the end of the first clock cycle and then puts the value read from address **addressLines** of **m** into **dataLines**. Thus the value read appears at the beginning of the second clock cycle. The slave then waits for the next negative clock edge event (i.e. the end of the read cycle) before looping around for the next bus cycle.

The results of simulating Example 3.8 are shown in Figure 3.3. The simulation is driven by the bus master process and its calls to the **wiggleBusLines** task. Essentially, the process reads from addresses 2 and 3, writes the values 5 and 7 respectively to them, and then rereads them to see that the values are written correctly. The $finish system task is called to end the simulation.

The printing is controlled by the $monitor statement in the initial statement. Since values only change on the clock edges, each line of the simulation trace shows the values in the system at the end of a clock cycle. The first line shows values in the system when the $monitor first executes. The second line shows the values when the wiggle-BusLines task first executes (it shows the system reading from address 2). **dataLines** has not been written yet and thus it appears as x. The next line represents the values at the ends of the two clock cycles in the read cycle. The value read is 29. (This corresponds to the value that was in the **memory.data** file.) Following through the simulation trace, we can see that the 29 in address 2 is overwritten with the value 5 by the first write operation. Evidence that the value was actually stored in the memory is seen in the second to last read operation where address 2 is reread.

rw=x, data=	x, addr= x at time	0	
rw=0, data=	x, addr= 2 at time	1	> Read
rw=0, data=	29, addr= 2 at time	40	
rw=0, data=	29, addr= 3 at time	80	> Read
rw=0, data=	28, addr= 3 at time	120	
rw=1, data=	5, addr= 2 at time	160	— Write
rw=1, data=	7, addr= 3 at time	200	— Write
rw=0, data=	7, addr= 2 at time	240	> Read
rw=0, data=	5, addr= 2 at time	280	
rw=0, data=	5, addr= 3 at time	320	> Read
rw=0, data=	7, addr= 3 at time	360	

Figure 3.3 Simulation Trace For Behavioral Model of Synchronous Bus

There are several features of the description that should be emphasized:

- The bus master and slave processes are synchronized to the clock signal. At the end of the clock period when the negative edge occurs, these processes execute. It is important to note that none of these processes immediately changes any of the registers used to pass information between the processes (i.e. **rwLine, addrLines, dataLines**). If one of the processes had changed any of these registers, the result of the simulation would have relied on the order in which the simulator executed these events — not good. Non-blocking assignments insure correct operation.

- The memory array **m** is initialized from an external text file using the $readmemh system task. This technique is quite useful for loading machine instructions into a simulation model of a processor, initializing data in a memory as shown here, and loading test vectors that will be applied to other parts of the system. In this case, the $readmemh task reads whitespace-separated hexadecimal numbers from the **memory.data** file and loads them consecutively into memory locations starting at address 0. See Appendix F.8 for more details and options.

- Note that **READ** and **WRITE** were defined to be constants but **tClock** was defined to be a parameter. Parameters provide a means of specifying a default constant to use for a module. However, when the module is instantiated, the values of the parameters may be overridden. Section 4.5 discusses parameters in more detail.

- In one statement we use the operator "!" to specify the complement of **clock**, and in another statement we use the operator "~" to specify the complement of **rwLine**. In this context, either is correct because the values being complemented are one-bit. The "~" specifies a bitwise complement of its operand (i.e. ~4'b0101 is 4'b1010). The "!" specifies the complement of the operand's value. Assume the operand is multibit. Then if the value is 0 (FALSE), the "!" complement is TRUE. If the multibit operand is nonzero (TRUE), the "!" complement is FALSE. Thus !4'b0101 is false.

References: parameters 4.5; $readmemh F.8; Verilog operators C; tasks 2.5.1; register specification E.1; memory specification E.2

3.5 **A Simple Pipelined Processor**

This section presents another example of a concurrent system. Here we will design a very simple pipelined processor based on the Mark-1 description started in chapter 2. Although the example is not indicative of the complexity of current-day processors, the basic approach suggests methods of modeling such processors.

3.5.1 **The Basic Processor**

The model for the processor, using the cycle-accurate style of specification, is shown in Example 3.9. An abstract level of modeling a processor allows the designer to understand what functionality will occur during each clock cycle, how that functionality is impacted by concurrent activity in other stages of the processor's pipeline, and what the performance of the machine will be, at least in terms of clock cycles.

This example is composed of two always blocks, one for each pipestage of this simple processor. The first always block models the first pipestage of the processor which fetches instructions. The second always block models the second pipestage which executes the instructions. Since each is described by an always block, we have modeled the concurrency found between pipestages of a processor.

Non-blocking assignment is used across the design to synchronize the updating of state to the clock edge **ck**. With non-blocking assignment, it is important to remember that all of the right-hand sides of the assignments across the whole design (the two always blocks here) are evaluated before any of the left-hand sides are updated. In this example, note that the instruction register (**ir**) is loaded in the first always block and it is accessed in the second. Since all accesses are implemented with non-blocking assignments, we know that the instruction fetch which loads the instruction register will not interfere with the instruction execution in the second always block — all right-hand sides in the second always block will be evaluated before **ir** is updated by the first always block.

```
module mark1Pipe;
      reg [15:0]   m [0:8191];   // 8192 x 16 bit memory
      reg [12:0]   pc;           // 13 bit program counter
      reg [15:0]   acc;          // 15 bit accumulator
      reg [15:0]   ir;           // 16 bit instruction register
      reg          ck;           // a clock signal

      always @(posedge ck) begin
            ir <= m [pc];
            pc <= pc + 1;
      end

      always @(posedge ck)
         case (ir [15:13])
            3'b000 :   pc <= m [ir [12:0]];
            3'b001 :   pc <= pc + m [ir [12:0]];
            3'b010 :   acc <= -m [ir [12:0]];
            3'b011 :   m [ir [12:0]] <= acc;
            3'b100,
            3'b101 :   acc <= acc - m [ir [12:0]];
            3'b110 :   if (acc < 0) pc <= pc + 1;
         endcase
endmodule
```

Example 3.9 A Pipelined Processor

However, the non-blocking assignments do not guard against all problems in synchronization. Note that when executing certain instructions, the **pc** is loaded in both always blocks — instruction 0 is such a case. The issue to consider is which update of the **pc** will occur first: the one in the first always block, or in the second? Of course, the order of updates is undefined so we need to alter this description to obtain correct operation.

3.5.2 **Synchronization Between Pipestages**

In the general case, having the same register written by two separate always blocks leads to indeterminate values being stored in the register. If a model can guarantee that the two always blocks never write the register at the same time (i.e., during the same state or clock time), then writing a register from two always blocks is a perfectly valid approach. However, in our case though, pc is written during every state by the fetch process and during some states by the execution process.

Example 3.10 corrects this problem by adding register **pctemp**. This register is written only by the execute stage while pc is written only by the fetch stage. In the case where a branch instruction is executed, **pctemp** is written with the branch target. At the same time, the next sequential instruction is fetched and the pc is incremented by the fetch stage. However, since a branch is being executed, this instruction and the incremented pc are not needed. A separate indicator register, **skip**, is set by the execution stage to indicate that a branch occurred and that the next instruction should be fetched from **m[pctemp]** rather than from **m[pc]**. Additionally, since the instruction after the branch was already fetched, **skip** also controls the execution stage to keep it from being executed.

In this example, all assignments are non-blocking except one. In the fetch process, pc is assigned with a blocking assignment so that it can be used on the following lines of the process.

There are alternate approaches to correcting this problem, including duplicating the **case(ir)** statement in the fetch stage so that pc is conditionally loaded with a branch target when a branch occurs. However, the execution stage will still need to skip the extra instruction.

3.6 **Disabling Named Blocks**

In Example 2.4, we showed how the *disable* statement could be used to break out of a loop or continue executing with the next iteration of the loop. The disable statement, using the same syntax, is also applicable in concurrent process situations. Essentially, the disable statement may be used to disable (or stop) the execution of any named begin-end block — execution will then continue with the next statement following the block. The block may or may not be within the process containing the disable statement. If the block being disabled is not within the local or upward scope, then hierarchical names are required.

To illustrate disabling a concurrent process we return to the scheduled behavior example in section 1.6 which has been expanded upon here in Example 3.11. A **reset** input has been added, along with an initial statement, and a wait statement in the

```
module mark1PipeStage;
     reg [15:0]   m [0:8191];     // 8192 x 16 bit memory
     reg [12:0]   pc, pctemp;     // 13 bit program counter and temporary
     reg [12:0]   acc;            // 13 bit accumulator
     reg [15:0]   ir;             // 16 bit instruction register
     reg          ck, skip;

     always @(posedge ck) begin        //fetch process
             if (skip)
                     pc = pctemp;
             ir <= m [pc];
             pc <= pc + 1;
     end


     always @(posedge ck) begin        //execute process
        if (skip)
             skip <= 0;
        else
             case (ir [15:13])
                  3'b000 :  begin
                                  pctemp <= m [ir [12:0]];
                                  skip <= 1;
                             end
                  3'b001 :  begin
                                  pctemp <= pc + m [ir [12:0]];
                                  skip <= 1;
                             end
                  3'b010 :  acc <= -m [ir [12:0]];
                  3'b011 :  m [ir [12:0]] <= acc;
                  3'b100,
                  3'b101 :  acc <= acc - m [ir [12:0]];
                  3'b110 :  if (acc < 0) begin
                                  pctemp <= pc + 1;
                                  skip <= 1;
                             end
             endcase
     end
endmodule
```

Example 3.10 Synchonization Between the Stages

always block. These additions provide an asynchronous, asserted-low, reset for this cycle-accurate specification.

Consider how the module works. At the start of time, both the initial and always block can begin executing. One stops to wait for a negative edge on **reset** while the other waits for **reset** to be TRUE. If we assume that **reset** is unasserted (1), then the always block will begin executing its cycle-accurate specification. At some time, **reset** is asserted (i.e., it becomes 0), and its negative edge activates the initial block. The initial block disables **main**, which is the name of the begin-end block in the always block. No matter where the **main** block was in its execution, it is exited, and the always block is restarted. The first statement at the start is a wait for **reset** to be TRUE — unasserted. Thus, when **reset** is asserted, the **main** block is stopped, and it does not restart at the beginning until **reset** becomes unasserted.

```
module simpleTutorialWithReset (clock, reset, y, x);
    input           clock, reset;
    output  [7:0]   x, y;
    reg     [7:0]   x, y, i;

    initial
        forever begin
            @(negedge reset)
                disable main;
        end

    always begin: main
        wait (reset);
        @(posedge clock) x <= 0;
        i = 0;
        while (i <= 10) begin
            @(posedge clock);
            x <= x + y;
            i = i + 1;
        end
        @(posedge clock);
        if (x < 0)
            y <= 0;
        else  x <= 0;
    end
endmodule
```

Example 3.11 Description Using Scheduled Behavioral Approach

A block is named as illustrated in the example. A block declaration is a statement and has the general form:

statement
     ::= seq_block
     | ...

seq_block
     ::= **begin** [: *block* _identifier {block_item_declaration}]
         { statement }
         end

block_item_declaration
     ::= parameter_declaration
     | reg_declaration
     | integer_declaration
     | real_declaration
     | time_declaration
     | realtime_declaration
     | event_declaration

Note that the introduction of a named block also allows for the optional block declarations. At this point, other parameters and registers may be defined for the scope of the block.

The action of the disable statement not only stops the named block, but also any functions or tasks that have been called from it. Also, any functions or tasks they have called are also stopped. Execution continues at the next statement after the block. If you disable the task (or function) you are in, then you return from the task (or function).

It is also interesting to point out what is not stopped by the disable statement. If the disabled named block has triggered an event control, by changing a value or by triggering a named event, the processes watching for these events will already have been triggered. They will not be stopped by the disable.

When we defined the term process, we emphasized that it referred to an independent thread of control. The implementation of the control was irrelevant; it could be as a microcoded controller, simple state machine, or in some other way. In the case of Example 3.11, if we assume that the first state of the controller implementing the always statement is encoded as state zero, then the initial block could be implemented as an asynchronous reset of the state register of the always' controller. That is, the initial statement would not look like a state machine, rather it would be some simple reset logic. The point is that regardless of the implementation of the two processes, there are two independent activities in the system capable of changing state. Each is active and operating independently of the other.

References: always 2.1; disable in loops 2.3.2; parallel blocks 3.9; hierarchical names 2.6; scope of identifiers 2.6

3.7 Intra-Assignment Control and Timing Events

Most of the control and timing events that we have used in examples have been specified to occur before the action or assignment occurs. We have written statements like:

    #25 a = b;

or

    @(posedge w) q = r;

The actions performed respectively are: delay 25 time units and then assign the value of **b** to **a**; and delay until there is a positive edge on **w** and then assign the value of **r** to **q**. What is common about these behavioral statements is the "delay" (either the # or the @) occurs before the assignment is performed. Indeed, the right-hand side of the statement is not evaluated until after the "delay" period. *Intra-assignment* timing controls allow for the "delay" to occur within the assignment — between when the right-hand side is evaluated and when the left-hand side is assigned. Conceptually, these assignments have a master-slave character; inputs are sampled, a delay occurs, and then later the outputs are assigned.

The assignments are written with the delay or event control specification in the middle of the assignment just following the "=". This makes intuitive sense when reading such an assignment. Given that the right-hand side of the equation is evaluated first and then assigned to the left-hand side, having the delay or event control in the middle of the assignment keys the reader that you must delay before completing the right-to-left assignment. Although all of our examples here are with blocking assignments, intra-assignment control and timing events can be used with non-blocking assignments as well. The intra-assignment timing control versions of the statements above are:

Table 3.1 Intra-Assignment Control and Timing Events

Statements using intra-assignment constructs	Equivalent statements without intra-assignments

a = #25 b;	begin
	  bTemp = b;
	  #25 a = bTemp;
	end

Table 3.1 Intra-Assignment Control and Timing Events

Statements using intra-assignment constructs	Equivalent statements without intra-assignments

q = @(posedge w) r;	begin
	   rTemp = r;
	   @(posedge w)
	      q = rTemp;
	end

w = repeat (2)
   @(posedge clock) t;
	begin
	   tTemp = t;
	   repeat (2)
	      @(posedge clock);
	   w = tTemp;
	end

The actions taken by the first two assignments are respectively: evaluate b and store the value in a temporary place, delay 25 time units, and then assign the stored value to a; and evaluate r and store the value in a temporary place, wait for the next positive edge on w, and then store the temporary value in q. These correspond to the illustrations above. The third entry shows the intra-assignment repeat which was not illustrated above. The right-hand side is calculated and assigned to a temporary place. When the delay is completed (in this case, waiting for two positive edges of **clock**), the value is assigned to w. Thus each of these statements stores a temporary copy of the right-hand-side value for assignment to the left-hand side at a later time.

The copy of the right-hand side is actually stored in the simulator event queue and is not accessible for any other purposes.

The three forms of the intra-assignment statement, for both blocking and non-blocking assignments, are described below:

statement
      ::= blocking_assignment ;
      | non_blocking assignment ;
      | ...

blocking assignment
      ::= reg_lvalue = [delay_or_event_control] expression

non-blocking assignment
      ::= reg_lvalue <= [delay_or_event_control] expression

delay_or_event_control
      ::= delay_control

```
        |    event_control
        |    repeat ( expression ) event_control

delay _control
        ::=  # delay_value
         |   # ( mintypmax_expression )

event_control
        ::=  @ event_identifier
         |   @ ( event expression )

event_expression
        ::=  expression
         |   event_identifier
         |   posedge_expression
         |   negedge_expression
         |   event_expression or event_expression
```

A use of intra-assignment timing controls is in the specification of a D flip flop. This approach uses the statement:

```
@(posedge clock) q = #10 d;
```

This statement provides a master-slave character to the behavior of the flip flop. This model samples the value of **d** at the clock edge and assigns it 10 time units later. However, the following does not accurately model a flip flop.

```
q = @(posedge clock) d;
```

This statement samples the value of **d** whenever the statement is executed. Then when the positive edge of the **clock** occurs, **q** is assigned that value. Given that the initial value of **d** could be sampled well before the time of the **clock** edge, the normal behavior of a flip flop is not captured.

References: non-determinism 5.3

3.8 Procedural Continuous Assignment

The continuous assignment statement presented in an earlier chapter, allows for the description of combinational logic whose output is to be computed anytime any one of the inputs change. There is a procedural version of the continuous assignment statement that allows for continuous assignments to be made to registers for certain specified periods of time. Since the assignment is not in force forever, as is true with the continuous assignment, we call this the *procedural continuous assignment* (these were called "quasi-continuous" in earlier versions of the manuals), While the procedural continuous assignment is in effect, the statement acts like a continuous assign.

Consider the example of a preset and clear on a register shown in Example 3.12. Note first that the difference between continuous and procedural continuous is immediately obvious from the context; the procedural continuous assignment is a procedural statement executed only when control passes to it. (The continuous assignment is always active, changing its outputs whenever its inputs change.) In this example, the first always statement describes a process that reacts to a change in either the **clear** or **preset** signals. If **clear** becomes zero, then we assign register **q** to be zero. If **preset** becomes zero, then we assign register **q** to be one. When a change occurs and neither are zero, then we *deassign* **q** (essentially undoing the previous procedural continuous assignment), and then **q** can be loaded with a value using the normal clock method described by the second always statement.

```
module dFlop (preset, clear, q, clock, d);
    input    preset, clear, clock, d;
    output   q;
    reg      q;

    always
        @(clear or preset)
            begin
                if (!clear)
                    #10    assign q = 0;
                else if (!preset)
                    #10    assign q = 1;
                else
                    #10    deassign q;
            end

    always
        @(negedge clock)
            q = #10 d;
endmodule
```

Example 3.12 Flip Flop With Procedural Continuous Assignment

The general form of the assignment is:

statement
    ::= procedural_continuous_assignments

procedural_continuous_assigmnent
    ::= **assign** reg_assignment ;
    | **deassign** reg_lvalue ;
    | ...

reg_assignment
    ::= reg_lvalue = expression

It is important to note that the procedural continuous assignment overrides a normal procedural assignment to a register. While the procedural continuous assignment is in effect, the reg_assignment acts like a continuous assignment. Thus, even if the negative edge of the clock occurred as watched for in the second always statement, the procedural assignment of d to q would not take effect. Further, if the value of the right-hand side of a procedural continuous assignment changes (it was not a constant as in the above example), then the left-hand side will follow it. The value procedural-continuously assigned remains in the register after the deassignment.

References: continuous assignment 4.4; procedural assignment 2.1; event control with or 3.2.1

3.9 **Sequential and Parallel Blocks**

The begin-end blocks that we have seen so far are examples of sequential blocks. Although their main use is to group multiple procedural statements into one compound statement, they also allow for the new definition of parameters, registers, and event declarations when the begin-end blocks are named. Thus new local variables may be specified and accessed within a named begin-end block.

An alternate version of the sequential begin-end block is the parallel or fork-join block shown below. Each statement in the fork-join block is a separate process that begins when control is passed to the fork. The join waits for all of the processes to complete before continuing with the next statement beyond the *fork-join* block.

This example illustrates the description of an asynchronous reset restarting a process. A **resetSequence** initializes registers and then begins the fork-join block named **mainWork**. The first statement of the fork is a forever loop that describes the main behavior of the microprocessor. The second statement is the process that watches for the positive edge of the **reset** signal. When the positive edge of the **reset** occurs, the **mainWork** block is disabled. As described previously, when a block is disabled, everything in the named block is disabled and execution continues with the next statement, in this case the next iteration of the always statement. Thus, no matter what was happening in the **fetch** and **execute** behavior of the system, the **reset** is able to asynchronously restart the whole system.

```
module microprocessor;
    always
        begin
            resetSequence;
            fork:    mainWork
                forever
                    fetchAndExecuteInstructions;
                @(posedge reset)
                    disable mainWork;
            join
        end
endmodule
```

Example 3.13 An Illustration of the Fork-Join Block

The general form for the parallel block is given below. Like the named (sequential) blocks previously described, naming the block allows for the optional block_declarations that can introduce new names for the scope of the block.

```
statement
    ::=  par_block
    |    ...
```

```
par_block
    ::=  fork [: block _identifier { block_item_declaration } ]
         { statement }
         join
```

```
block_item_declaration
    ::=  parameter_declaration
    |    reg_declaration
    |    integer_declaration
    |    real_declaration
    |    time_declaration
    |    realtime_declaration
    |    event_declaration
```

Example 3.14 shows a less abstract use of the fork-join block. Example 3.11 has been rewritten, this time with a single always that includes a fork-join.

Again, it is important to note that we consider each of the statements of the fork-join as a separate process. This example essentially replaced two always statements by one that has a fork-join. Comparing back to Example 3.11 serves to enforce further the notion that each statement in the fork-join should be considered, at least conceptually, a separate process.

```
module simpleTutorialWithReset (clock, reset, y, x);
    input              clock, reset;
    output  [7:0]   x, y;
    reg      [7:0]   x, y, i;

    always fork: main
        @(negedge reset)
                    disable main;
        begin
            wait (reset);
            @(posedge clock) x <= 0;
            i = 0;
            while (i <= 10) begin
                @(posedge clock);
                x <= x + y;
                i = i + 1;
            end
            @(posedge clock);
            if (x < 0)
                    y <= 0;
            else x <= 0;
        end
    join
endmodule
```

Example 3.14 Fork-Join Version of Simple Tutorial Example

References: named blocks 3.6

3.10 **Exercises**

3.1 Will the following two fragments of Verilog code result in the same behavior? Why or why not?

```
    ...                                         ...
    @(posedge exp)                    wait (exp)
            #1 statement1;                    #1 statement1;
    ...                                         ...
```

3.2 Rewrite the consumer and producer modules in Examples 3.6 at the behavioral level, such that a common clock signal controls the timing of the data transfer between the modules. On consecutive positive clock edges, the following is to happen: 1) the producer sets up the data on its output, 2) the consumer reads the data, 3) the producer sets up its next data value, and so on.

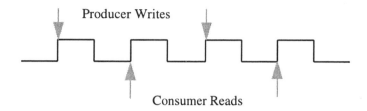

For the design to be valid there needs to be a suitable power-on initialization mechanism. Find a solution to this and include it in the model.

3.3 Extend Examples 3.6 to include internal processing between the consumer and producer parts that is a simple increment operation with a delay of 10 time units. Connect an instance of this module in a loop such that data can flow around the loop forever with data being incremented each time around. Add extra code to initialize the model for execution

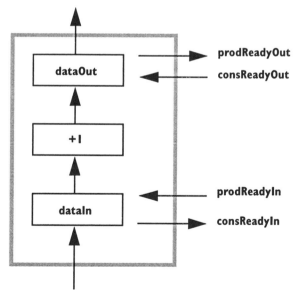

3.4 Consider four named events: e1, e2, e3, and e. Write a description to trigger event e after e1, e2, and e3 have occurred in a strict sequence Namely, if any event goes out of order the sequence is to be reset. Then, write a description to trigger event e after e1, e2, and e3 have each occurred three times in any order.

3.5   The following combinational logic block has three inputs and an output. The circuit was built in some screwy technology and then analyzed. We now want to insert the correct input-to-output timing information into the circuit (internal node timings need not be correct).

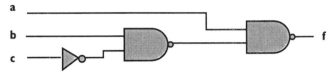

Here are the circuit timings that must be represented in the circuit.

- The delay of a rising or falling edge on **a** or **b** to output **f**: 15 time units

- The delay of a rising or falling edge on **c** to output **f**: 10 time units

Yes, those times are rather strange given the logic diagram. However, this is a screwy technology and the transistor implementation made for some strange, but actual, time delays.

Assume **a**, **b**, and **c** are outputs of synchronously clocked flip flops. Write the behavioral Verilog description that will be correct in functionality and timing.

3.6   For the pipeline processor in Example 3.10, add part of the instruction decode logic (i.e., like the case statement in the execute stage) into the fetch stage. Use it instead of the **skip** variable to determine how to load the **pc**.

3.7   For the **mark1PipeStage** module in Example 3.10, write an initial statement that will load the processor's memory and execute several instructions. Add a monitor statement and other initializations and clocking as needed. Write a program with the given machine instructions that will execute the following pseudo code:

```
if ((m[4] - m[5]) < 0)
        m[4] = 17;
else    m[4] = -10;
```

3.8   Add a third stage to the pipeline of Example 3.10. The second stage should only fetch operands; values read from memory should be put in a memory data register (mdr). The third stage will execute the instructions, loading the resulting values (mdr) in **acc**, **pctemp**, or **m**. Assume that the memory has multiple read and write ports. Handle any interstage conflicts that may arise.

4 | Logic Level Modeling

To this point, we have concentrated mostly on behavioral modeling of a digital system. Behavioral models are more concerned with describing the abstract functionality of a module, regardless of its actual implementation. Logic level modeling is used to model the logical structure of a module, specifying its ports, submodules, logical function, and interconnections in a way that directly corresponds to its implementation. This chapter presents the Verilog constructs that allow us to describe the logical function and structure of a system.

4.1 Introduction

There are several approaches to the logic level modeling of a digital system. Each of these approaches represents a sublevel of logic level modeling, and emphasizes different features of a module.

A *gate level* model of a circuit describes the circuit in terms of interconnections of logic primitives such as AND, OR, and XOR. Modeling at this level allows the designer to describe the actual logic implementation of a design in terms of elements found in a technology library or databook and thus be able to accurately analyze the design for such features as its timing and functional correctness. Since gate level modeling is so pervasive, the Verilog language provides *gate level primitives* for the standard logic functions.

A *structural model* of a digital system uses Verilog *module* definitions to describe arbitrarily complex elements composed of other modules and gate primitives. As we have seen in earlier examples, a structural module may contain behavioral modeling statements (an always statement), continuous assignment statements (an assign statement), module instantiations referencing other modules or gate level primitives, or any combination of these statements. By using module definitions to describe complex modules, the designer can better manage the complexity of a design. For instance, by enclosing the set of interconnected gate level primitives that implement an arithmetic-logic unit into a single module, the design description is considerably more easy to read and understand.

A more abstract means of describing the combinational logic of a design is provided by the *continuous assignment* statement. This approach allows for logic functions to be specified in a form similar to Boolean algebra. The continuous assignment statement typically describes the behavior of a combinational logic module, and not its implementation.

Finally, the Verilog language allows us to describe a circuit at the transistor switch level. At this level, the language provides abstractions of the underlying MOS and CMOS transistors, giving the designer access to some of the electrical characteristics of the logic implementation.

To help in reading and writing models at these levels, it is useful to understand how the simulator executes them. The basic data type in this style of modeling is the net which is driven by gate and continuous assign outputs. These nets then are inputs to other gates and continuous assigns, as well as to the right-hand side of procedural assignment statements. <u>Anytime</u> the input to a gate or continuous assign statement changes, its output is evaluated and any change to the output is propagated, possibly with a delay, via its output net to other inputs. We call this method of updating outputs when any input changes the *Verilog gate level timing model*; this is discussed further in Chapter 5.

In contrast, procedural assignment statements found in behavioral modeling only execute when control is passed to them. Thus just because a net on the right-hand side of a procedural assignment statement changes doesn't mean that the statement will execute. Rather, that input would have to have been to an event ("@") or wait statement which when triggered will cause the procedural statements in the behavioral model to execute.

The language provides different methods for the designer to describe a system, thus allowing the description to be at the level of detail appropriate to the designer's needs.

These different methods of describing the logic level function and structure of a system are presented in this and the next two chapters.

References: contrast to procedural assignment 2.1; gate level timing model 5.1

4.2 Logic Gates and Nets

We start with modeling a system at the logic gate level. Verilog provides a set of 26 *gate level primitives* that have been predefined in the language. From these primitives, we build larger functional modules by interconnecting the gates with nets and enclosing them into modules. When describing a circuit at the gate level, we try to maintain a close (some might say strict) correspondence to the actual gate level implementation.

4.2.1 Modeling Using Primitive Logic Gates

Example 4.1 shows a structural model of a full adder using some of Verilog's gate level primitives. This example was developed from a databook description of a CMOS one-

```
module fullAdder(cOut, sum, aIn, bIn, cIn);
        output   cOut, sum;
        input    aIn, bIn, cIn;

        wire     x2;

        nand     (x2, aIn, bIn),
                 (cOut, x2, x8);
        xnor     (x9, x5, x6);
        nor      (x5, x1, x3),
                 (x1, aIn, bIn);
        or       (x8, x1, x7);
        not      (sum, x9),
                 (x3, x2),
                 (x6, x4),
                 (x4, cIn),
                 (x7, x6);
endmodule
```

Example 4.1 A One-Bit Full Adder

bit full adder. Three single bit inputs and two single bit outputs provide connection to the outside world. Internal to the module description, we list the eleven primitive logic module instances that comprise the adder. Figure 4.1 shows a diagram of the adder with the internal connections labelled for ease of comparison. As a partial explanation, we see that there are two NAND gates, one with output **x2** (note that the first parameter of a gate level primitive is its output) and inputs **aIn** and **bIn**, and the other with output **cOut** and inputs **x2** and **x8**.

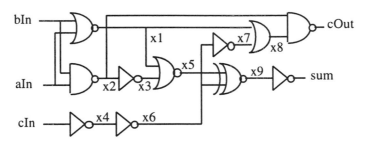

Figure 4.1 A One-Bit Full Adder

The general syntax for instantiating a gate is given by:

gate instantiation
        ::= n_input_gatetype [drive_strength] [delay2] n_input_gate_instance {,
        n_input_ gate_instance } ;
     | ...

n_input_gatetype
        ::= **and** | **nand** | **or** | **nor** | **xor** | **xnor**

n_input_gate_instance
        ::= [name_of_gate_instance] (output_terminal, input_ terminal {,
        input_terminal })

name_of_gate_instance
        ::= *gate_Instance*_identifier [range]

input_terminal
        ::= *scalar*_expression

output_terminal
        ::= *terminal*_identifier
     | *terminal* _identifier[constant_expression]

where the n_input_gatetype specifies one of the gate level primitives listed above, the optional drive_strength specifies the electrical characteristics of the gate's output, the optional delay specifies the simulation gate delay to be used with this instance, and the list of gate instances is a comma-separated list specifying the terminals of each gate instance and, optionally, names of each instance. The default strengths are strong0 and strong1. The default delay is 0. Further discussion of strengths is given in Chapter 9 and a further discussion of delay modeling is in sections 4.7 and 4.8.

Note that the above formal specification does not cover the NOT gate shown in Example 4.1. NOT and BUF gates may have any number of outputs (listed first) but only one input, as described formally below:

gate instantiation
        ::= n_output_gatetype [drive_strength] [delay2] n_output_gate_instance { ,
        n_output_gate_instance };
    | ...

n_output_gate_instance
        ::= [name_of_gate_instance] (output_terminal {, output_terminal },
        input_terminal)

n_output _gatetype
        ::= **buf | not**

In Example 4.1, we have not named any of the gate instances. However, we could name the NAND gates by changing the statement to:

      nand   John (x2, aIn, bIn),
              Holland (cOut, x2, x8);

Or, we could have specified a strong0 and strong1 drive, as well as a 3 unit gate delay for each of John and Holland.

      nand   (strong0, strong1) #3
              John (x2, aIn, bIn),
              Holland (cOut, x2, x8);

The drive strength and delay specifications qualify the gate instantiation(s). When one (or both) of these qualifiers is given, then it applies to all of the defined instances in the comma-separated list. To change one or both of these qualifiers, the gate instantiation list must be ended (with a ";") and restarted.

A complete list of predefined gate level primitives is given in Table 4.1. For the rest of the chapter, we will concern ourselves with the primitives in the first three columns. They represent logic abstractions of the transistors from which they are made. The other entries in the last three columns allow for modeling at the transistor switch level. These switch level elements will be discussed in Chapter 9.

The gate primitives in the first column of Table 4.1 implement the standard logic functions listed. In the second column, the **buf** gate is a non-inverting buffer, and the **not** gate is an inverter. In the third column, the **bufif** and **notif** gates provide the **buf** and **not** function with a tristate enable input. A **bufif0** drives its output if the enable is

0 and drives a high impedance if it is 1. The 4-level truth tables (using 0, 1, x, and z) for Verilog gates may be found in Appendix D.

Table 4.1 Gate and Switch Level Primitives

n_input gates	n_output gates	tristate gates	pull gates	MOS switches	bidirection-al switches
and	buf	bufif0	pullup	nmos	tran
nand	not	bufif1	pulldown	pmos	tranif0
nor		notif0		cmos	tranif1
or		notif1		rnmos	rtran
xor				rpmos	rtranif0
xnor				rcmos	rtranif1

For the gate level primitives in the first column, the first identifier in the gate instantiation is the single output or bidirectional port and all the other identifiers are the inputs. Any number of inputs may be listed. **Buf** and **not** gates may have any number of outputs; the single input is listed last.

Although the drive strength will be discussed further in Chapter 9, it is useful to point out that a strength may only be specified for the gates listed in the first three columns.

References: Verilog primitive gates D; four-level logic 4.2.2; strengths 9.2; delay specification 4.7; switch level gates 9; user-defined primitives 8

4.2.2 Four-Level Logic Values

The outputs of gates drive nets that connect to other gates and modules. The values that a gate may drive onto a net comes from the set:

  0   represents a logic zero, or FALSE condition
  1   represents a logic one, or TRUE condition
  x   represents an unknown logic value (any of 0, 1, z, or in a state of change)
  z   represents a high-impedance condition

The values 0 and 1 are logical complements of each other. The value x is interpreted as "either 0 or 1 or z or in a state of change". The z is a high-impedance condition. When the value z is present at the input of a gate or when it is encountered in an expression, the effect is usually the same as an x value. It should be reiterated that even the registers in the behavioral models store these four logic values on a bit-by-bit basis.

Each of the primitive gates are defined in terms of these four logic values. Table 4.2 shows the definition of an AND gate. Note that a zero on the input of an AND will force the output to a zero regardless of the other input — even if it is x or z.

Table 4.2 Four-Valued Definition of the AND Primitive

AND	0	1	x	z
0	0	0	0	0
1	0	1	x	x
x	0	x	x	x
z	0	x	x	x

References: four-level gate definitions D

4.2.3 **Nets**

Nets are a fundamental data type of the language, and are used to model an electrical connection. Except for the *trireg* net which models a wire as a capacitor that stores electrical charge, nets do not store values. Rather, they only transmit values that are driven on them by structural elements such as gate outputs and assign statements, and registers in a behavioral model.

In Example 4.1 we see a net of type wire named x2 being declared. We could have declared it to have a delay with the following statement

    wire   #3   x2;

meaning that any change of value driven on the wire from the first NAND gate instance is delayed by 3 before it is seen at the wire's terminations (which are the other NAND gate and the NOT gate). Further, the delay could include both rise and fall time specifications:

    wire   #(3,5)   x2;

meaning that the transition to 1 has a 3 unit delay and the fall to 0 has a 5 unit delay.

However, we also find many more wires *declared implicitly* in Example 4.1. For instance, net x9 which is the output of the XNOR gate has not been declared in the fullAdder module. If an identifier is used in a module instantiation and has not been previously declared, then the identifier is implicitly declared to be a scalar net of type wire. (By default, the type of an implicit declaration is type wire. However, this may be overridden by the *default_nettype typeOfNet* compiler directive where typeOfNet is any of the net types listed in Table 4.4 except the supply0 and supply1 types.)

Wire x2 need not have been declared separately here. It was only done so for illustration purposes.

Example 4.2 illustrates the use of a different type of net, the wired-AND, or *wand*. The wired-AND performs the AND function on the net. The only difference between the AND gate and the wand is that the wand will pass a z on its input whereas an AND gate will treat a z on its input as an x.

```
module andOfComplements (a, b, c, d);
      input    a, b;
      output   c, d;

      wand    c;
      wire    d;

      not (c, a);
      not (c, b);

      not (d, a);
      not (d, b);
endmodule
```

Example 4.2 Wire AND Example

Here we illustrate the differences between the normal wire and wand net types. d is declared to be a wire net, and c is declared to be a wand net. c is driven by two different NOT gates as is d. A net declared wand will implement the wired-AND function. The output c will be zero if any one of the inputs to the wand net is zero (meaning that one of the inputs, a or b, was one). The output c will be one if both of the inputs a and b are zero.

On the other hand, d is a wire net driven by two gates. Its value will be unknown (x) unless both gates drive it to the same value. Essentially the wand allows for several drivers on the net and will implement the wired-AND function between the drivers, while the wire net will show an unknown (x) when different values are driven on it. Table 4.3 shows the outputs for all possible inputs to Example 4.2 (The sixteen rows of the truth table are folded into two columns of eight rows).

The general form of the net declaration is:

```
net_declaration
      ::=   net_type [ vectored | scalared ] [range] [delay3] list_of_net_identifiers;
      |     trireg [ vectored | scalared ] [charge_strength] [range] [delay3]
            list_of_net_identifiers;
      |     net_type [ vectored | scalared ] [drive strength] [range] [delay3]
            list_of_net_decl_assignments;
```

Table 4.3 Wand and Wire Results From Example 4.2

a	b	c	d	a	b	c	d
0	0	1	1	x	0	x	x
0	1	0	x	x	1	0	x
0	x	x	x	x	x	x	x
0	z	x	x	x	z	x	x
1	0	0	x	z	0	x	x
1	1	0	0	z	1	0	x
1	x	0	x	z	x	x	x
1	z	0	x	z	z	x	x

net_type
    ::= **wire** | **tri** | **tri1** | **supply0** | **wand** | **triand** | **tri0** | **supply1** | **wor** | **trior**

list_of_net_identifiers
    ::= *net*_identifier {, *net*_identifier }

range
    ::= [*msb*_constant_expression: *lsb* _constant_expression]

We'll concentrate on the first net declaration in this section. net_type is one of the types (such as wire and wand) listed below in Table 4.4, range is the optional specifi cation of bit width (default is one bit), delay provides the option for the net to have its own delay (default is 0), and list_of_net_identifiers is a comma-separated list of nets that will all have the given range and delay properties. When a delay is specified on a net, the new value from any entity driving the net will be delayed by the specified time before it is propagated to any entities connected to the net.

The range of nets can optionally be declared as *vectored* or *scalared*. Scalared is the default case and indicates that the individual bits of a vector (i.e. a multibit net) may be accessed using bit- and part-selects. This allows individual bits and parts of a net to be driven by the outputs of gates, primitives, and modules, or to be on the left-hand side of a continuous assign. Essentially, when specified as scalared, a vector can be treated as a collection of **n** scalars. The vectored specification prevents such access and only allows access to the vector net as an indivisible entity.

References: trireg 9.1; charge storage properties 9.2.2; delay 4.7; continuous assign to nets 4.4.2; primitives 8; bit- and part-selects E.1; scope of identifiers 2.6

Table 4.4 Net Types and Their Modeling Usage

Net Type	Modeling Usage
wire and tri	Used to model connections with no logic function. Only difference is in the name. Use appropriate name for readability.
wand, wor, triand, trior	Used to model the wired logic functions. Only difference between wire and tri version of the same logic function is in the name.
tri0, tri1	Used to model connections with a resistive pull to the given supply
supply0, supply1	Used to model the connection to a power supply
trireg	Used to model charge storage on a net. See Chapter 9.

4.2.4 Module Instantiation and Port Specifications

A port of a module can be viewed as providing a link or connection between two items, one internal to the module instance and one external to it. We have seen numerous examples of the specification of module ports.

An input port specifies the internal name for a vector or scalar that is driven by an external entity. An output port specifies the internal name for a vector or scalar which is driven by an internal entity and is available external to the module. An inout port specifies the internal name for a vector or scalar that can be driven either by an internal or external entity.

It is useful to recap some of the do's and don't's in their specification. First, an input or inout port cannot be declared to be of type register. Either of these port types may be read into a register using a procedural assignment statement, used on the right-hand side of a continuous assignment, or used as input to instantiated modules or gates. An inout port may only be driven through a gate with high impedance capabilities such as a bufif0 gate.

Secondly, each port connection is a continuous assignment of source to sink where one connected item is the signal source and the other is a signal sink. The output ports of a module are implicitly connected to signal source entities such as nets, registers, gate outputs, instantiated module outputs, and the left-hand side of continuous assignments internal to the module. Input ports are connected to gate inputs, instantiated module inputs, and the right-hand side of continuous and procedural assignments. Inout ports of a module are connected internally to gate outputs or inputs. Externally, only nets may be connected to a module's outputs.

Finally, a module's ports are normally connected at the instantiation site in the order in which they are defined. However, we may connect to a module's ports by naming the port and giving its connection. Given the definition of **andOfComplements** in Example 4.2, we can instantiate it into another module and connect its ports by name as shown below.

```
module ace;
    wire    r, t;
    reg     q, s;
        // other declarations

    andOfComplements   m1 (.b(s), .a(q), .c(r), .d(t));
endmodule
```

In this example, we have specified that port **b** of instance **m1** of module **andOfComplements** will be connected to the output of register s, port **a** to the output of register q, port **c** to wire r, and port **d** to wire t. Note that a period (".") introduces the port name as defined in the module's definition, and that the connections may be listed in any order. If a port is to be left unconnected, no value is specified in the parentheses — thus .d() would indicate that no connection is to be made to port **d** of instance **m1** of module **andOfComplements** within module **ace**.

At this point we can formally specify the syntax needed to instantiate modules and connect their ports. Note that the following syntax specification includes both means of listing the module connections: ordered-port and named-port specifications.

module instantiation
        ::= *module*_identifier [parameter_value_assignment] module_instance {, module_instance };

parameter_value_assignment
        ::= **#** (expression {, expression })

module_instance
        ::= name_of_instance ([list_of_module_connections])

name_of_instance
        ::= module_instance_identifier [range]

list_of_module_connections
        ::= ordered_port_connection {, ordered_port_connection }
        | named_port_connection {, named_port_connection }

ordered_port_connection
        ::= [expression]

named_port_connection
        ::= .*port*_identifier ([expression])

References: parameter specifications 4.5

4.2.5 **A Logic Level Example**

As an example of logic level modeling, this section presents a system implementing a Hamming encoding and decoding function. Hamming encoding is used when there is a possibility of noise entering a system and data being corrupted. For instance, data in a memory might be stored in an encoded form. The example presented here will encode eight bits of data, pass the encoded data through a noisy channel, and then regenerate the original data, correcting a single bit error if necessary. Detailed derivation and presentation of the technique can be found in most introductory logic design texts.

The error detection and correction is implemented by adding extra bits to the message to be encoded. The basic encoding is shown in Figure 4.2. Here we see eight original bits (Dx) on the left being encoded into twelve bits on the right. The original data bits are interleaved with four Hamming bits (Hx) as shown in the center column. The four bits are determined by xoring certain of the original bits. The interleaved ordering of the bits is important as the final decoding of the bits will indicate which of the bits (including the Hamming bits) is incorrect by specifying its bit position. The bit numbering of the encoded data is shown on the right.

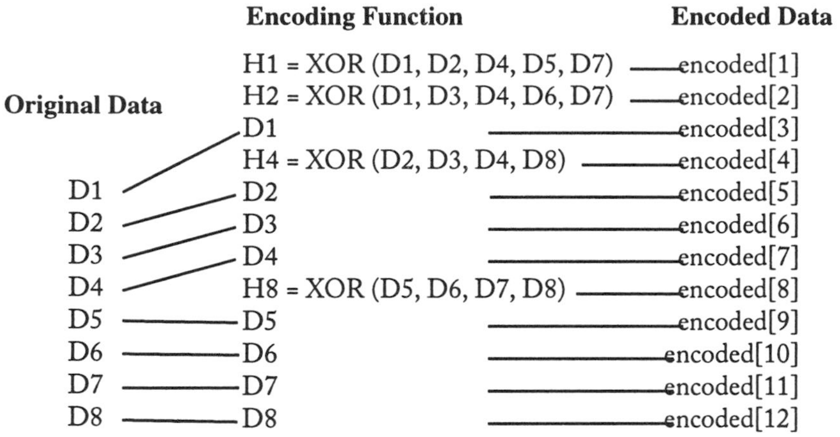

<pre>
                         Encoding Function   Encoded Data

                         H1 = XOR (D1, D2, D4, D5, D7) ——encoded[1]
    Original Data   H2 = XOR (D1, D3, D4, D6, D7) ——encoded[2]
                        ╱ D1   ——————encoded[3]
                       ╱ H4 = XOR (D2, D3, D4, D8) ——encoded[4]
    D1 ╱   ╱ D2   ——————encoded[5]
    D2 ─╳╳─————— D3   ——————encoded[6]
    D3 ─╳╳─————— D4   ——————encoded[7]
    D4 ╱   H8 = XOR (D5, D6, D7, D8) ——encoded[8]
    D5 ——————— D5   ——————encoded[9]
    D6 ——————— D6   ——————encoded[10]
    D7 ——————— D7   ——————encoded[11]
    D8 ——————— D8   ——————encoded[12]
</pre>

Figure 4.2 The Basic Hamming Encoding

The whole picture of our example, which includes this encoding function, is shown in Figure 4.3. We will have one module, **testHam**, which instantiates all of the other modules and provides test vectors to it. Submodules to **testHam** include **hamEncode**, which implements the function in Figure 4.2, and **hamDecode**, which itself has several submodules. There is also an assign statement shown in gray in the center of the figure that will insert a single error into the data after it is encoded. The **hamDecode** module regenerates the original eight-bit message by correcting any single bit errors. A simulation trace of the whole system is presented in Figure 4.4, illustrating the values passed between the major subentities of **testHam** (namely, **original**, **encoded**, **messedUp**, and **regenerated**).

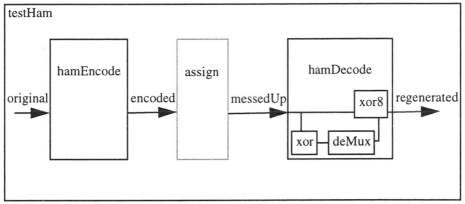

Figure 4.3 The Hamming Encoder and Decoder with Noisy Channel

The Hamming code example is shown in Example 4.3. Module **hamEncode** generates the twelve-bit encoding (**valueOut**) of **vIn**. The encoding is implemented with four instantiated XOR gates implementing the encoding functions shown in Figure 4.2. The outputs of these gates are connected to wires (**h1**, **h2**, **h4**, and **h8**) and the wires are concatenated together with the data bits in the assign statement. Concatenation is indicated by the "{}" construct. The comma separated list of wires and part-selects of wires is combined into the output **valueOut**. Note that the order in which the values are concatenated matches that given in Figure 4.2. It is also interesting to note that the module is completely structural in nature; there are no procedural statements or registers.

Module **hamDecode** takes the 12-bit input **vIn** and produces the 8-bit output **valueOut**. Internally, **hamDecode** needs to determine which of the bits (if any) is incorrect, and then correct it. The four XOR gates producing outputs on **c1**, **c2**, **c4**, and **c8** indicate if a bit is incorrect. Consider the c's to be the separate bits of a vector; **c8** has place-value 8, and so on. If the value of the c's taken together is 0, then there is no correction to be made. However, if the c's take on a non-zero value, that value encodes the bit number of the bit that is incorrect. This bit needs to be inverted. The c bits are input to the **deMux** module which decodes them to one of eight possible data bits. These bits, assigned to the 8-wire vector **bitFlippers**, correspond to the bit position that needs to be inverted (a one indicates invert, and a zero indicates no inversion). The individual bits of **bitFlippers** are then inputs to eight XOR gates in **xor8**. The other input of the XOR gates is the data bits to be corrected. A one on a **bitFlipper** bit will invert (correct) the corresponding data bit. The output of **xor8** is the corrected data and is the output of the **hamDecode** module.

Looking more closely at module **deMux**, we see four select inputs (**a** - **d**) and an **enable**. Input **d** corresponds to the 8's place-value and **a** corresponds to the 1's place. The purpose of this module is to generate an 8-bit vector that has at most one bit set. That one bit corresponds to the encoded bit that needs to be corrected. Since we are only going to correct the data bits, only the necessary minterms of bits **a-d** are generated. These are: 3, 5, 6, 7, 9, 10, 11, and 12, which correspond to the encoded bit positions of the data in Figure 4.2. The AND gates generate the minterms and the assign statement concatenates these minterms together into **outVector**.

BitFlippers, the output of **deMux**, is input to **xor8**. These input bits (input **xin1**) along with bits 3, 5, 6, 7, 9, 10, 11, and 12 of the encoded data (input **xin2**) are inputs to eight XOR gates. Thus, an incorrect input bit, indicated by a one in one of the bits of **xin1**, will cause that bit to be inverted by the XOR gates. The output of **xor8** is also the output of **hamDecode**.

Returning to module **hamTest**, we see that **original** is the input to **hamEncode** and that **encoded** is its output. **Encoded** is then the input to the assign statement which produces **messedUp**. The purpose of the assign statement is to simulate a noisy channel where one of the input bits gets inverted. In this case bit 7 is inverted. The output of the assign (**messedUp**) is input to **hamDecode** which corrects this inversion and produces the original data on **regenerated**.

The only procedural statements in the whole example are in the initial statement of this module. Their purpose is to run test vectors through the system. To do this, we use the $random system task to produce random numbers. Here, we set the seed value for $random to 1 and enter a forever loop. **Original** is loaded with the result of $random. The output of **original** drives the **hamEncode** module. None of the gate primitives or wires have delays associated with them, so **regenerated** is produced in zero simulation time. Our forever loop delays 1 time unit to insure **regenerated** is produced and then displays all of the inter-module values as shown in Figure 4.4. Consider the first row of the figure. The original data is 00 which is encoded as 000. The assign statement inverts bit 7 producing 020. (In this example, the bits are counted from the left starting with 1 and the $display task specifies hexadecimal.) The bit is then corrected producing the original data.

There are several features to note in this example:

- **Seed** is declared to be an integer. Integers are often used for ancillary calculations in a simulation model. In a real design, this value would not exist as it is only there for testing purposes. Registers should be used when modeling real parts of hardware. See Appendix E for more discussion on integers.

```
module testHam();
      reg      [1:8]    original;
      wire     [1:8]    regenerated;
      wire     [1:12]   encoded,
                        messedUp;
      integer           seed;

      initial begin
         seed = 1;
         forever begin
               original = $random (seed);
               #1
               $display ("original=%h, encoded=%h, messed=%h,regen=%h",
                         original, encoded, messedUp, regenerated);
         end
      end

      hamEncode       hIn (original, encoded);
      hamDecode       hOut (messedUp, regenerated);

      assign messedUp = encoded ^ 12'b 0000_0010_0000;
endmodule


module hamEncode (vIn, valueOut);
      input    [1:8]    vIn;
      output   [1:12]   valueOut;

      wire     h1, h2, h4, h8;

      xor      (h1, vIn[1], vIn[2], vIn[4], vIn[5], vIn[7]),
               (h2, vIn[1], vIn[3], vIn[4], vIn[6], vIn[7]),
               (h4, vIn[2], vIn[3], vIn[4], vIn[8]),
               (h8, vIn[5], vIn[6], vIn[7], vIn[8]);

      assign valueOut = {h1, h2, vIn[1], h4, vIn[2:4], h8, vIn[5:8]};

endmodule
```

```
module hamDecode (vIn, valueOut);
    input    [1:12]  vIn;
    output   [1:8]   valueOut;
    wire             c1, c2, c4, c8;
    wire     [1:8]   bitFlippers;
    xor      (c1, vIn[1], vIn[3], vIn[5], vIn[7], vIn[9], vIn[11]),
             (c2, vIn[2], vIn[3], vIn[6], vIn[7], vIn[10], vIn[11]),
             (c4, vIn[4], vIn[5], vIn[6], vIn[7], vIn[12]),
             (c8, vIn[8], vIn[9], vIn[10], vIn[11], vIn[12]);

    deMux mux1 (bitFlippers, c1, c2, c4, c8, 1'b1);
    xor8 x1 (valueOut, bitFlippers, {vIn[3], vIn[5], vIn[6], vIn[7], vIn[9],
                            vIn[10], vIn[11], vIn[12]});
endmodule

module deMux (outVector, A, B, C, D, enable);
    output   [1:8]   outVector;
    input            A, B, C, D, enable;
    and      v (m12, D, C, ~B, ~A, enable),
             h (m11, D, ~C, B, A, enable),
             d (m10, D, ~C, B, ~A, enable),
             l (m9, D, ~C, ~B, A, enable),
             s (m7, ~D, C, B, A, enable),
             u (m6, ~D, C, B, ~A, enable),
             c (m5, ~D, C, ~B, A, enable),
             ks (m3, ~D, ~C, B, A, enable);

    assign outVector = {m3, m5, m6, m7, m9, m10, m11, m12};
endmodule

module xor8 (xout, xin1, xin2);
    output   [1:8]   xout;
    input    [1:8]   xin1, xin2;
    xor      (xout[8], xin1[8], xin2[8]),
             (xout[7], xin1[7], xin2[7]),
             (xout[6], xin1[6], xin2[6]),
             (xout[5], xin1[5], xin2[5]),
             (xout[4], xin1[4], xin2[4]),
             (xout[3], xin1[3], xin2[3]),
             (xout[2], xin1[2], xin2[2]),
             (xout[1], xin1[1], xin2[1]);
endmodule
```

Example 4.3 The Hamming Encode/Decode Example

- This use of the $display system task requests printing in hexadecimal with the "%h" printing control. See Appendix F for more discussion of the $display task.

- The assign statement in testHam shows a useful way of writing large numbers. The underline ("_") character can arbitrarily be inserted in a number specification.

- The bit numbering is different compared with other examples. In this case the bits were numbered from the left as is done in the classic presentation of the algorithm. Bits may be numbered in either direction and can include negative indices.

```
original=00, encoded=000, messed =020, regen=00
original=38, encoded=078, messed =058, regen=38
original=86, encoded=606, messed =626, regen=86
original=5c, encoded=8ac, messed =88c, regen=5c
original=ce, encoded=79e, messed =7be, regen=ce
original=c7, encoded=e97, messed =eb7, regen=c7
original=c6, encoded=f86, messed =fa6, regen=c6
original=f3, encoded=2e3, messed =2c3, regen=f3
original=c3, encoded=a83, messed =aa3, regen=c3
```

Figure 4.4 Simulation Results of Example 4.3

References: $display F.1; $random F.7

4.3 **Arrays of Instances**

The definition of the **xor8** module in Example 4.3 was rather tedious because each XOR instance had to be individually numbered with the appropriate bit. Verilog has a shorthand method of specifying an array of instances where the bit numbering of each successive instance differ in a controlled way. Example 4.4 shows the equivalent redefinition of module **xor8** on the left using arrays of instances. On the right is the expanded version; this is equivalent to the original module **xor8** in Example 4.3.

The array of instances specification uses the optional range specifier to provide the numbering of the instance names. The module in Example 4.4 will have eight XOR gates instantiated in it. The range specifier is defined to be:

range
       ::= [*msb*_constant_expression : *lsb*_constant_expression]

There are no requirements on msb or lsb regarding their absolute values or their relationship — both must be integers and one is not required to be larger than the other. Indeed, they can be equal in which case only one instance will be generated. Given msb and lsb, 1 + abs(msb-lsb) instances will be generated.

```
module xor8 (xout, xin1, xin2);          module xor8 (xout, xin1, xin2);
output  [1:8]    xout;                    output  [1:8]     xout;
input   [1:8]    xin1, xin2;              input   [1:8]     xin1, xin2;
                                            xor (xout[1], xin1[1], xin2[1]),
      xor a[1:8] (xout, xin1, xin2);             (xout[2], xin1[2], xin2[2]),
endmodule                                        (xout[3], xin1[3], xin2[3]),
                                                 (xout[4], xin1[4], xin2[4]),
                                                 (xout[5], xin1[5], xin2[5]),
                                                 (xout[6], xin1[6], xin2[6]),
                                                 (xout[7], xin1[7], xin2[7]),
                                                 (xout[8], xin1[8], xin2[8]);
                                          endmodule
```

Example 4.4 Equivalent xor8 Using Array of Instances

The above example showed the case where each instance was connected to a bit-select of the outputs and inputs. When the instances are generated and the connections are made, there must be an equal number of bits provided by the terminals (ports, wires, registers) and needed by the instances. In the above case, eight instances needed eight bits in each of the output and input ports. (It is an error if the numbers are not equal.) However, instances are not limited to bit-select connections. When the instance counts are known, it might be the case that each instance will receive two (or more) bits from each terminal. In this case, part-selects are created for each connection. Again, there cannot be any bits left over. If a terminal has only one bit but there are n instances, then each instance will be connected to the one-bit terminal.

```
module reggae (Q, D, clock, clear);
      output  [7:0]   Q;
      input   [7:0]   D;
      input           clock, clear;

      dff     r[7:0]  (Q, D, clear, clock);
endmodule
```

Example 4.5 Creating a Register Using Arrays of Instances

Example 4.5 shows D flip flops connected to form a register. The equivalent module with the instances expanded is shown in Example 4.6. Note that **clock** and **clear**, being one-bit terminals, are connected to each instance. Now, let's consider the situation where **dff** is not a one-bit flip flop but rather a two-bit flip flop. Then the array of instance specification would be twoBitDff   r[3:0] (Q, D, clear, clock);

and the first instance of the expansion would be

        twoBitDff   r[3]   (Q[7:6], D[7:6], clear, clock),

        module regExpanded (Q, D, clock, clear);
            output   [7:0]   Q;
            input   [7:0]   D;
            input   clock, clear;

            dff   r7   (Q[7], D[7], clear, clock),
                     r6   (Q[6], D[6], clear, clock),
                     r5   (Q[5], D[5], clear, clock),
                     r4   (Q[4], D[4], clear, clock),
                     r3   (Q[3], D[3], clear, clock),
                     r2   (Q[2], D[2], clear, clock),
                     r1   (Q[1], D[1], clear, clock),
                     r0   (Q[0], D[0], clear, clock);
        endmodule

Example 4.6 Expanded Equivalent of Example 4.5

All the connections to an instance need not come from the same terminal. Example 4.7 shows how the inputs to our register module can come from two places but still be connected correctly. In this example, **busHigh** and **busLow** are concate-

        module regFromTwoBusses (Q, busHigh, busLow, clock, clear);
            output   [7:0]   Q;
            input   [3:0]   busHigh, busLow;
            input   clock, clear;

            dff   r[7:0]   (Q, {busHigh, busLow}, clear, clock);
        endmodule

Example 4.7 Concatenating Ports With Instance Arrays

nated together in the array-of-instance specification. Together these eight bits will be connected to the eight instances as shown below:

```
        dff    r7     (Q[7], busHigh[3], clear, clock),
               r6     (Q[6], busHigh[2], clear, clock),
               r5     (Q[5], busHigh[1], clear, clock),
               r4     (Q[4], busHigh[0], clear, clock),
               r3     (Q[3], busLow[3], clear, clock),
               r2     (Q[2], busLow[2], clear, clock),
               r1     (Q[1], busLow[1], clear, clock),
               r0     (Q[0], busLow[0], clear, clock);
```

The above examples have shown the specification of one-dimensional structures using arrays of instances — a register was constructed out of flip flops. Multidimensional structures may be specified by instantiating one-dimensional structures in another array of instances. Thus a shift register could be made by instantiating register **reggae** from Example 4.5 using an array of instances as shown in Example 4.8.

```
        module shiftRegister (in, out, clock, clear);
        input    [7:0]    in;
        output   [7:0]    out;
        input             clock, clear;
        wire     [15:0]   w;


            reggae    stage[2:0]  ({out, w}, {w, in}, clock, clear);
        endmodule
```

Example 4.8 A Shift Register

The expanded instantiations would be

```
        reggae    stage2    (out7:0], w[15:8], clock, clear),
                  stage1    (w[15:8], w[7:0], clock, clear),
                  stage0    (w[7:0], in[7:0], clock, clear);
```

4.4 Continuous Assignment

Continuous assignments provide a means to abstractly model combinational hardware driving values onto nets. An alternate version of the one-bit full adder in the previous section is shown using continuous assignments in Example 4.9. Here we show the two outputs **sum** and **cOut** being described with an assign statement. The first (**sum**) is the exclusive-or of the three inputs, and the second is the majority function of the three inputs.

```
module oneBitFullAdder(cOut, sum, aIn, bIn, cIn);
    output  cOut, sum;
    input   aIn, bIn, cIn;

    assign      sum = aIn ^ bIn ^ cIn,
                cOut = (aIn & bIn) | (bIn & cIn) | (aIn & cIn);

endmodule
```

Example 4.9 Illustration of Continuous Assignment

The continuous assignment is different from the procedural assignment presented in the chapters on behavioral modeling. The continuous assignment is always active (driving a 0, 1, x, or z), regardless of any state sequence in the circuit. If <u>any</u> input to the assign statement changes at <u>any</u> time, the assign statement will be reevaluated and the output will be propagated. This is a characteristic of combinational logic and also of the Verilog gate level timing model.

The general form of the assign statement is:

continuous_assign
     ::= **assign** [drive_strength] [delay3] list_of_net_assignments ;

list_of_net_assignments
     ::= net_assignment {, net_assignment }

net_assigmnent
     ::= net_lvalue = expression

where *assign* is a keyword, the *drive_strength* and *delay3* specifications are optional parts, and the *list_of_net_assignments* takes the form of a comma-separated list as shown in Example 4.9. The drive strength of a continuous assign defaults to strong0 and strong1 and can be specified for assignments to scalar nets of any type except type supply0 and supply1. The delay defaults to 0. For instance, the above assign could have been written as shown below:

```
assign  (strong0, strong1)
            sum = aIn ^ bIn ^ cIn,
            cOut = (aIn & bIn) | (bIn & cIn) | (aIn & cIn);
```

Here we specify that both of the continuous assignments have the default drive strength.

References: delay modeling 4.7 and 4.8; strength modeling 9; timing models 5.1

4.4.1 **Behavioral Modeling of Combinational Circuits**

The continuous assign provides a means of abstracting from a gate level model of a circuit. In this sense, the continuous assign is a form of behavioral modeling for combinational circuits. That is, we only need specify the Boolean algebra of the logic function, not its actual gate level implementation. The final gate level implementation is then left to a logic synthesis program or further designer effort.

The right-hand side expression in the assign statement may contain a function call to a Verilog function. Recall that within a function, we may have procedural statements such as case and looping statements, but not wait, @event, or #delay. Thus we may use procedural statements to describe a complex combinational logic function. For instance, in Example 4.10 a description of a multiplexor illustrates a function call in an assign.

```
module multiplexor(a, b, c, d, select, e);
    input        a, b, c, d;
    input    [1:0]select;
    output       e;

    assign   e = mux (a, b, c, d, select);

function mux;
    input        a, b, c, d;
    input    [1:0]select;

    case (select)
        2'b00:    mux = a;
        2'b01:    mux = b;
        2'b10:    mux = c;
        2'b11:    mux = d;
        default:  mux = 'bx;
    endcase
endfunction
endmodule
```

Example 4.10 Function Call From Continuous Assignment

In this example, module multiplexor has a continuous assignment which calls function **mux**. The function uses the procedural case statement to describe the behavior of the combinational multiplexing function. If one of the case expressions match the controlling expression, then **mux** is assigned the appropriate value. If none of the first four match (e.g. there is an x or z on a **select** input), then by default, **mux** is assigned to carry the unknown value x.

Although the assign statement provides access to an assortment of procedural statements for behaviorally describing combinational hardware, we must be cognizant of different levels of abstraction in behavioral modeling. At a high level of abstraction we have the *process* that models sequential activity as described in Chapters 2 and 3. At that level, we are describing a situation which involves a separate thread of control and the implementation will typically have its own internal state machine watching for changes on its inputs. To model this, we would define a module with an always statement and communicate with it through module ports and with the interprocess wait and event statements. Clearly, this is not the modeling situation of Example 4.10 where we are only describing a combinational multiplexor which gates one of its inputs to its output without the need for an internal state machine to control it.

Rather, at this lower level of abstraction we model combinational behavior which does not contain its own internal state. Instead of using Boolean algebra to describe a multiplexor, Example 4.10 used procedural statements. The use of procedural statements in a function called from an assign merely gives us another method of describing the combinational behavior. Modeling in this way does not imply the use of a sequential state machine for implementation and should not be used when sequential activity is to be modeled.

References: functions 2.5.2

4.4.2 **Net and Continuous Assign Declarations**

Continuous assign statements specify a value to be driven onto a net. A shorthand way to describe this situation combines the net and assign definition statements as shown in Example 4.11.

```
module modXor (AXorB, a, b);
     output  [7:0]   AXorB;
     input   [7:0]   a, b;

     wire    [7:0]   #5 AXorB = a ^ b;
endmodule
```

Example 4.11 Combined Net and Continuous Assignment

Here we have defined a vector wire with eight bits and an eight-bit exclusive-or of inputs **a** and **b** which drive them. The delay specifies the delay involved in the exclusive-or, not in the wire drivers.

If we had declared the wire and exclusive-or separately as

```
wire    [7:0]      AXorB;
assign  #5         AXorB = a ^ b;
```

we could have assigned a separate delay of 10 to the wire drivers by substituting the statement:

```
wire    [7:0]      #10 AXorB;
```

When a delay is given in a net declaration as shown, the delay is added to any driver that drives the net. For example, consider the module in Example 4.12. We have defined a wand net with delay of 10 and two assign statements that both drive the net. One assign statement has delay 5 and the other has delay 3. When input **a** changes, there will be a delay of fifteen before its change is reflected at the inputs that c connects to. When input **b** changes, there will be a delay of thirteen.

```
module wandOfAssigns (a, b, c);
    input    a, b;
    output   c;

    wand    #10    c;

    assign  #5   c = ~a;
    assign  #3   c = ~b;
endmodule
```

Example 4.12 Net and Continuous Assignment Delays

The combined use of a net specification and continuous assign is formally specified with the third entry in net_declaration: (Recall that the first is used to declare nets. The second will be covered in Chapter 9.)

net_declaration
      ::= net_type [**vectored** | **scalared**] [range] [delay3] list_of_net_identifiers;
      | trireg [**vectored** | **scalared**] [charge_strength] [range] [delay3]
           list_of_net_identifiers;
      | net_type [**vectored** | **scalared**] [drive strength] [range] [delay3]
           list_of_net_decl_assignrnents;

net_type
      ::= **wire** | **tri** | **tri1** | **supply0** | **wand** | **triand** | **tri0** | **supply1** | **wor** | **trior**

list_of_net_decl_assignments
      ::= net_decl_assigmnent {, net_decl_assignment}
```
```

net_decl_assignment
     ::=   *net_*identifier = expression

The difference compared to the first entry is that strengths can be specified, and that there is a list of assignments associated with a strength-range-delay combination.

Continuous assignment statements may also be used to drive an inout port. Example 4.13 shows an example of a buffer-driver.

```
module bufferDriver (busLine, bufferedVal, bufInput, busEnable);
    inout    busLine;
    input    bufInput, busEnable;
    output   bufferedVal;

    assign   bufferedVal = busLine,
             busLine = (busEnable) ? bufInput : 1'bz;
endmodule
```

Example 4.13 Continuous Assignment to an Inout

Here we see **busEnable** being used to select between **bufInput** driving the **busLine** and a high impedance driving the line. However, no matter what the state of **busEnable**, **bufferedVal** always follows the value of **busLine**. Thus **busLine** may be driven in an external module when **busEnable** is zero and **bufferedVal** will show its value.

A typical use of tristate drivers is in a memory module designed to attach to a processor bus. Example 4.14 illustrates a 64K byte memory. The **dataBus** port is defined to be an inout, allowing it be driven in the module's assign statement and also be used as the source when writing memory. Writing the memory is a synchronous activity controlled by the positive edge of the **clock**. A new value is read from the memory when read enable (**re**) first becomes asserted (i.e., the negative edge), or when there is a change on the address lines (**addrBus**). The value read is stored in temporary register **out** which drives the **dataBus** when **re** is asserted. If **re** is unasserted, **dataBus** is tristated.

References: nets, vectored/scalared 4.2.3

```
module Memory_64Kx8 (dataBus, addrBus, we, re, clock);
    input    [15:0]  addrBus;
    inout    [7:0]   dataBus;
    input            we, re, clock;
    reg      [7:0]   out;
    reg      [7:0]   Mem [65535:0];

    assign dataBus = (~re)? out: 16'bz;      /* drive the tristate output */

    always @(negedge re or addrBus)
        out = Mem[addrBus];

    always @(posedge clock)
        if (we == 0)
            Mem[addrBus] <= dataBus;
endmodule
```

Example 4.14 Memory Module With Tristate Drivers

4.5 Parameterized Definitions

Parameters allow us to define a generic module that can be parameterized for use in different situations. Not only does this allow us to reuse the same module definition in more situations, but it allows us to define generic information about the module that can be overridden when the module is instantiated.

In Example 4.11, we defined an 8-bit XOR module using a continuous assign statement. In this section we develop a parameterized version of this module. Example 4.15 is an excerpt from Example 4.3, showing only the xor8 module definition. First, we replace the eight XOR gate instantiations with a single assign statement of the form:

assign xout = xin1 ^ xin2;

where **xout, xin1,** and **xin2** are as defined in Examples 4.3 and 4.15.

We then make this module more generally useful with the definition shown in Example 4.16. Here we specify the general form of the **xorx** module by specifying two parameters, the width of the module (4) and its delay (10). Parameter specification is part of module definition as seen in the following syntax specification:

```
module xor8 (xout, xin1, xin2);
output   [1:8]      xout;
input    [1:8]      xin1, xin2;

    xor        (xout[8], xin1[8], xin2[8]),
               (xout[7], xin1[7], xin2[7]),
               (xout[6], xin1[6], xin2[6]),
               (xout[5], xin1[5], xin2[5]),
               (xout[4], xin1[4], xin2[4]),
               (xout[3], xin1[3], xin2[3]),
               (xout[2], xin1[2], xin2[2]),
               (xout[1], xin1[1], xin2[1]);
endmodule
```

Example 4.15 The xor8 Module From Example 4.3

module declaration
    ::= module_keyword *module*_identifier [list_of_ports] ;
        { module_item }
        endmodule

module_item
    ::= module_item_declaration
    | ...

module_item_declaration
    ::= parameter_declaration
    | ...

parameter_declaration
    ::= **parameter** list_of_pararn_assignments;

list_of_pararn_assignments
    ::= param_assignment {, param_assignment }

param_assigmnent
    ::= *parameter*_identifier = constant_expression

The values specified in the parameter declaration are those that are used in a *generic* instantiation of the module. This module could then be instantiated into Example 4.3 with the statement

```
xorx    #(8, 0) x1(valueOut, bitFlippers,
                {vIn[3], vIn[5], vIn[6], vIn[7], vIn[9], vIn[10], vIn[11], vIn[12]});
```

The main change in instantiating this module versus module **xor8** is the parameter specification given above. The "#(8, 0)" specifies that the value of the first parameter (width) is 8 for this instantiation, and the value of the second (delay) is 0. This of course matches the needs of Example 4.3. If the "#(8, 0)" was omitted, then the values specified in the module definition would be used instead. That is, we are able to override the parameter values on a per-module-instance basis.

The general form of specifying parameter values at instantiation time is seen in the following syntax specification:

module instantiation
      ::= *module*_identifier [parameter_value_assignment] module_instance { ,
      module_instance };

parameter_value_assignment
      # (expression {, expression } **)**

```
module xorx (xout, xin1, xin2);
    parameter    width = 4,
                 delay = 10;
    output   [1:width]  xout;
    input    [1:width]  xin1, xin2;

    assign #(delay) xout = xin1 ^ xin2;
endmodule
```

Example 4.16 A Parameterized Module Specification

The order of the overriding values follows the order of the parameter specification in the module's definition. It is not possible to skip over some parameters in a module definition and respecify the rest; either the one to be skipped over should be respecified as the default, or the parameter list should be reordered to have the parameter to be skipped over at the end of the list. For instance, we could have specified instance **x1** of **xorx** to have width 8 (an override) and delay 10 (the default) with the statement:

```
xorx    #(8) x1(valueOut, bitFlippers, {vIn[3], vIn[5], vIn[6], vIn[7],
                vIn[9],vIn[10], vIn[11], vIn[12]});
```

But, to give it the default width (four) and a different delay (20) would require us to respecify the size too.

        xorx   #(4,20) x1(valueOut, bitFlippers, {vIn[3], vIn[5], vIn[6], vIn[7], vIn[9],
                                    vIn[10], vIn[11], vIn[12]});

Another approach to overriding the parameters in a module definition is to use the *defparam* statement and the hierarchical naming conventions of Verilog. This approach is shown in Example 4.17.

```
module xorsAreUs (a1, a2);
    output   [3:0]   a1, a2;
    reg[3:0]         b1, c1, b2, c2;

    xorx     a(a1, b1, c1),
             b(a2, b2, c2);
endmodule

module xorx (xout, xin1, xin2);
    parameter   width = 4,
                delay = 10;
    output   [1:width]  xout;
    input    [1:width]  xin1, xin2;

    assign #delay xout = xin1 ^ xin2;
endmodule

module annotate;
    defparam
        xorsAreUs.b.delay = 5;
endmodule
```

Example 4.17 Overriding Parameter Specification With defparam

Using the *defparam* statement, all of the respecifications of parameters can be grouped into one place within the description. In this example, the delay parameter of instance **b** of module **xorx** instantiated within module **xorsAreUs** has been changed so that its delay is five. Thus, the parameters may be respecified on an individual basis. The general form of the defparam statement is:

parameter_override
        ::= **defparam** list_of_param_assignments ;

list_of_param_assignments
        ::= param_assigmnent {, param_assignment }

The choice of using the defparam or module instance method of modifying parameters is a matter of personal style and modeling needs. Using the module instance method makes it clear at the instantiation site that new values are overriding defaults. Using the defparam method allows for grouping the respecifications in specific locations. Indeed, the defparams can be collected in a separate file and compiled with the rest of the simulation model. The system can be changed by compiling with a different defparam file rather than by re-editing the entire description. Further, a separate program could generate the defparam file for back annotation of delays.

References: module instantiation and port specification 4.2.4; hierarchical names 2.6

4.6 A Mixed Behavioral/Structural Example

Example 3.8 presented an example of a synchronous bus. In this section we will alter the description by modeling the bus lines using wires rather than registers, and parameterizing the modules to make them more generically useful. The new model is shown in Example 4.18. The bus protocol and the organization of the Verilog description are the same as in the earlier example. The reader is referred to the earlier presentation in section 3.4 as background for this section.

Again we have a bus master process communicating with a bus slave process. In contrast to the previous example, the communication in Example 4.18 is carried out over wires defined in the **sbus** module. Here we see wires **rw**, **addr**, and **data** being the only means of communication between the instantiated **master** and **slave** modules. The **rw** and **addr** lines are driven only by the bus **master**. However, the **data** lines must be driven during a write cycle by the **master**, and during a read cycle by the **slave**. Thus we need to develop a means of synchronizing the driving of the data lines. Of course, the **rw** line produced by the **master** is the global indicator of whether a bus read or write is in progress. Both the **master** and **slave** modules include a register called **enable** which is used internally to enable the bus drivers at the appropriate times.

Module **busDriver** is defined in a manner similar to the bus driver in Example 4.13. The main difference being that the module does not also act as a bus receiver. The module is parameterizable to the bus size, and will drive the bus with **valueToGo** if **driveEnable** is TRUE. Otherwise it drives a z. This module is instantiated into both the **master** and **slave** modules.

In the **slave** module, the **enable** register has been added to control the bus driver. **Enable** is set to 0 during initialization which causes the bus line to be at z. **Enable** is then set to 1 during the second clock cycle of the read cycle. This is the time when the value being read is driven on the bus by the **slave**. In the **master** module a separate **enable** has been added to control the bus driver. Again **enable** is set to 0 during initialization. The **master** sets **enable** to 1 during the write cycle as it is during this time that the **master** drives the data bus.

The **sbus** module has been set up so that it can be instantiated with parameters of clock period, address and data bus size, and memory size. Thus it can be used in a number of modeling situations.

```
`define READ 0
`define WRITE 1

module sbus;
      parameter
          Tclock = 20,
          Asize = 4,
          Dsize = 15,
          Msize = 31;

      reg clock;

      wire              rw;
      wire    [Asize:0]  addr;
      wire    [Dsize:0]  data;

      master  #(Asize, Dsize)      m1  (rw, addr, data, clock);
      slave   #(Asize, Dsize, Msize)s1   (rw, addr, data, clock);

      initial
         begin
              clock = 0;
              $monitor ("rw=%d, data=%d, addr=%d at time %d",
                               rw, data, addr, $time);
         end

      always
          #Tclock clock = !clock;
endmodule

module busDriver(busLine, valueToGo, driveEnable);
      parameter    Bsize = 15;
      inout    [Bsize:0]  busLine;
      input    [Bsize:0]  valueToGo;
      input              driveEnable;

      assign busLine = (driveEnable) ? valueToGo: 'bz;
endmodule
```

```
module slave (rw, addressLines, dataLines, clock);
    parameter
        Asize = 4,
        Dsize = 15,
        Msize = 31;
    input    rw, clock;
    input    [Asize:0]  addressLines;
    inout    [Dsize:0]  dataLines;

    reg      [Dsize:0]  m[0:Msize];
    reg      [Dsize:0]  internalData;
    reg      enable;

    busDriver    #(Dsize)   bSlave (dataLines, internalData, enable);

    initial
        begin
            $readmemh ("memory.data", m);
            enable = 0;
        end

    always    // bus slave end
        begin
            @(negedge clock);
            if (~rw) begin //read
                internalData <= m[addressLines];
                enable <= 1;
                @(negedge clock);
                enable <= 0;
            end
            else    //write
                m[addressLines] <= dataLines;
        end
endmodule

module master (rw, addressLines, dataLines, clock);
    parameter
        Asize = 4,
        Dsize = 15;
    input                clock;
    output               rw;
    output   [Asize:0]   addressLines;
    inout    [Dsize:0]   dataLines;
```

```
        reg                 rw, enable;
        reg     [Dsize:0] internalData;
        reg     [Asize:0] addressLines;

        busDriver #(Dsize) bMaster (dataLines, internalData, enable);

        initial   enable = 0;

        always   // bus master end
            begin
                #1
                wiggleBusLines (`READ, 2, 0);
                wiggleBusLines (`READ, 3, 0);
                wiggleBusLines (`WRITE, 2, 5);
                wiggleBusLines (`WRITE, 3, 7);
                wiggleBusLines (`READ, 2, 0);
                wiggleBusLines (`READ, 3, 0);
                $finish;
            end

task wiggleBusLines;
        input               readWrite;
        input   [Asize:0]  addr;
        input   [Dsize:0]  data;

        begin
            rw <= readWrite;
            if (readWrite) begin// write value
                addressLines <= addr;
                internalData <= data;
                enable <= 1;
            end
            else begin      //read value
                addressLines <= addr;
                @ (negedge clock);
            end
            @(negedge clock);
            enable <= 0;
        end
endtask
endmodule
```

Example 4.18 A Synchronous Bus Using Behavioral and Structural Constructs

Results of simulating Example 4.18 are shown in Figure 4.5. It differs from the previous simulation run (Figure 3.3) only in the fact that the data lines are z during the first clock cycle of a read bus cycle. Other than that, the two models produce identical results.

rw=x, data=	z, addr= x at time	0
rw=0, data=	z, addr= 2 at time	1
rw=0, data=	29, addr= 2 at time	40
rw=0, data=	z, addr= 3 at time	80
rw=0, data=	28, addr= 3 at time	120
rw=1, data=	5, addr= 2 at time	160
rw=1, data=	7, addr= 3 at time	200
rw=0, data=	z, addr= 2 at time	240
rw=0, data=	5, addr= 2 at time	280
rw=0, data=	z, addr= 3 at time	320
rw=0, data=	7, addr= 3 at time	360

Figure 4.5 Results of Simulating Example 4.18

4.7 **Logic Delay Modeling**

Gate level modeling is used at the point in the design process when it is important to consider the timing and functionality of the actual gate level implementation. Thus, at this point the gate and net delays are modeled, possibly reflecting the actual placement and routing of the gates and nets. In this section, we will concentrate on the logic gate primitives and specifying their timing properties for simulation.

4.7.1 **A Gate Level Modeling Example**

The tristate NAND latch shown in Example 4.19 illustrates the use of the bufif1 gate and detailed timing information. A diagram of the circuit is also shown in Figure 4.6. This latch drives its **qOut** and **nQOut** ports, which are defined as tristate nets, when the **enable** input is one. The bufif1 gate models the tristate functionality. As shown in Table 4.5, when the control input is 1, then the output is driven to follow the input. Note that a z on the **data** input is propagated as an unknown on the data output. When the control input is 0, the output is high impedance (z).

module triStateLatch (qOut, nQOut, clock, data, enable);
    output   qOut, nQOut;
    input   clock, data, enable;
    tri   qOut, nQOut;

    not   #5   (ndata, data);
    nand   #(3,5)   d(wa, data, clock),
                       nd(wb, ndata, clock);
    nand   #(12, 15)   qQ(q, nq, wa),
                       nQ(nq, q, wb);
    bufif1 #(3, 7, 13) qDrive (qOut, q, enable),
                       nQDrive(nQOut, nq, enable);
endmodule

Example 4.19 A Tristate Latch

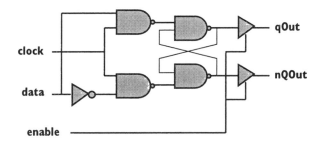

Figure 4.6 Illustration of the Tristate Latch

Table 4.5 BUFIF1 Gate Function

			Control Input		
	Bufif1	0	1	x	z
D	0	z	0	L	L
A	1	z	1	H	H
T	x	z	x	x	x
A	z	z	x	x	x

In the case where the control input is either x or z, the data output is modeled with L and H. L indicates the output is either a 0 or a z, and H indicates either a 1 or a z.

Other tristate modeling primitives include bufif0 which reverses the sense of the control input from bufif1, notif1 which inverts the data input and drives the output when the control input is one, and notif0 which inverts the data input and drives the output when the control input is zero. Truth tables for these gates may be found in Appendix D.

The functionality of Example 4.19 may now be described. The basic latch function is implemented by the cross-connected NAND gates qQ and nQ. When the clock is low, the outputs of d and nd are held high and the latch pair hold their value. When the clock is high, then the d and nd values propagate through and change the latch value. The qQ and nQ NAND gates follow the data input as long as the clock is high. The two bufif1 gates are driven by the output of the NAND latch gates and the input enable signal. As per the definition of the bufif1 gate, when enable is high, the output will be driven. When enable is low, the output will be z.

References: Verilog gates D; nets 4.2; delays across a module 4.8

4.7.2 **Gate and Net Delays**

Gate, continuous assign, and net delays provide a means of accurately describing the delays through a circuit. The gate delays describe the delay from when the inputs of a gate change until when the output of the gate is changed and propagated. Continuous assign delays describe the delay from when a value on the right-side changes to when the left-hand side is changed and propagated. Net delays describe the delay from when any of the net's driving gates or assign statements change to when the value is propagated. The default delay for gates, nets, and assign statements is zero. If one delay parameter is specified, then the value is used for all propagation delays associated with the gate, net, or assign.

The following gate instantiations are excerpts from Example 4.19 and will be used to illustrate the different propagation situations.

```
not      #5         (ndata, data);
nand     #(12, 15)  qQ(q, nq, wa),
                    nQ(nq, q, wb);
bufif1   #(3, 7, 13) qDrive (qOut, q, enable),
                    nQDrive(nQOut, nq, enable);
```

Propagation delays are specified in terms of the transition to 1, the transition to 0, and the transition to z (turn-off delay). The NOT gate has been specified with a delay of 5. Since only this one value is given, the delay will pertain to both the transition to 1 and the transition to 0. The NAND gate instances have a rising delay of 12 and a falling delay of 15. Finally, the bufif1 gates have a rising delay of 3, falling delay of 7, and a delay to the high impedance value of 13. Note that if the gate is in the high impedance condition, then when the enable becomes 1, it will take 3 time units (i.e. the rising delay) for the output to change to 1.

Generally speaking, the delay specifications takes the form of

#(d1, d2)

or

#(d1, d2, d3)

where d1 is the rising delay, d2 the falling delay, and d3 the delay to the high impedance value. The reason for the two-specification form is that some gates allow only two times to be specified and some allow three. A special case of the meaning of d3 is when it is used with the trireg net; d3 is then the decay time at which point the wire's value becomes x. Delay specification may be summarized in the following syntax:

delay2
    ::= # delay_value
    | # (delay_value [, delay_value])

delay3
    ::= # delay_value
    | # (delay_value [, delay_value [, delay_value]])

delay_value
    ::= unsigned_number
    | parameter_identifier
    | constant_mintypmax_expression

constant_mintypmax_expression
    ::= constant_expression
    | constant_expression : constant_expression : constant_expression

(Note that the second form of mintypmax_expression will be discussed in section 4.7.1.) Table 4.6 summarizes the from-to propagation delay used by the simulator for the two and three delay specifications. Again, if no delay specification is made, zero is the default. If only one value is given, then all of the propagations are assumed to take that time.

A shorthand for remembering some of the delays is that a rising delay (d1) is from 0 to x, x to 1, or z to 1. Likewise, a falling delay is from 1 to x, x to 0, or z to 0.

The tri net defined in Example 4.19 does not include its own delay parameters. However, it could have been defined as:

Table 4.6 Delay Values Used In Simulation

From value	To value	2 Delays specified	3 Delays specified
0	1	d1	d1
0	x	min(d1, d2)	min(d1, d2, d3)
0	z	min(d1, d2)	d3
1	0	d2	d2
1	x	min(d1, d2)	min(d1, d2, d3)
1	z	min(d1, d2)	d3
x	0	d2	d2
x	1	d1	d1
x	z	min(d1, d2)	d3
z	0	d2	d2
z	1	d1	d1
z	x	min(d1, d2)	min(d1, d2, d3)

```
tri    #(2, 3, 5)      qOut, nQOut;
```

In this case, any driver that drives either of these nets would incur a rising delay of 2, a falling delay of 3, and a delay to z of 5 before its output would be propagated. Thus in Example 4.19 with the bufif1 **qDrive** gate instance driving the **qOut** net, the rising delay from when an input to gate **qDrive** changes to when the result is propagated on the **qOut** net is 5 (2 + 3), the falling delay is 10, and the delay to z is 18.

If the case of a continuous assign where the left-hand side is a vector, then multiple delays are handled by testing the value of the right-hand side. If the value was non-zero and becomes zero, then the falling delay is used. If the value becomes z, then the turn-off delay is used. Otherwise, the rising delay is used.

References: delays across a module 4.8

4.7.3 **Specifying Time Units**

Our examples have used the # delay operator to introduce time into the simulation models of hardware components. However, time units for the delay values have not been specified. The `timescale compiler directive is used to make these specifications.

The form of the compiler directive is:

`timescale   <time_unit> / <time_precision>

This directive sets the time units and precision for the modules that follow it. Multiple `timescale directives may be included in a description.

Table 4.7 Arguments for `timescale compiler directive

Unit of Measurement	Abbreviation
seconds	s
milliseconds	ms
microseconds	us
nanoseconds	ns
picoseconds	ps
femtoseconds	fs

The <time_unit> and <time_precision> entries are an integer followed by a unit of time measure. The integer may be one of 1, 10, or 100. The time measure abbreviations are shown in Table 4.7. Thus a module following a `timescale directive of:

`timescale   10 ns / 1 ns

maintains time to the precision of 1 nanosecond. The values specified in delays though are multiples of 10 nanoseconds. That is, #27 means delay 270 nanoseconds. Table 4.8 shows several examples of delay specifications and the actual time delayed for a given `timescale directive. The simulation times are determined by rounding to the appropriate number of decimal places, and then multiplying by the time unit.

Table 4.8 Time delay / precision specifications

Unit / precision	Delay specification	Time delayed	Comments
10 ns / 1 ns	#7	70 ns	The delay is 7 * time_unit, or 70 ns
10 ns / 1 ns	#7.748	77 ns	7.748 is rounded to one decimal place (due to the difference between 10 ns and 1 ns) and multiplied by the time_unit
10 ns / 100 ps	#7.748	77.5 ns	7.748 is rounded to two decimal places and multiplied by the time_unit
10 ns / 1 ns	#7.5	75	7.5 is rounded to one decimal place and multiplied by 10
10 ns / 10 ns	#7.5	80	7.5 is rounded to the nearest integer (no decimal places) and multiplied by 10

4.7.1 **Minimum, Typical, and Maximum Delays**

Verilog allows for three values to be specified for each of the rising, falling, and turn-off delays. These values are the minimum delay, the typical delay, and the maximum delay.

```
module IOBuffer (bus, in, out, dir);
    inout    bus;
    input    in, dir;
    output   out;

    parameter
        R_Min = 3, R_Typ = 4, R_Max = 5,
        F_Min = 3, F_Typ = 5, F_Max = 7,
        Z_Min = 12, Z_Typ = 15, Z_Max = 17;

    bufif1   #(R_Min: R_Typ: R_Max,
                F_Min: F_Typ: F_Max,
                Z_Min: Z_Typ: Z_Max)
             (bus, out, dir);

    buf      #(R_Min: R_Typ: R_Max,
                F_Min: F_Typ: F_Max)
             (in, bus);
endmodule
```

Example 4.20 Illustration of Min, Typical, and Max Delays.

Example 4.20 shows the use of the minimum, typical, and maximum delays being separated by colons, and the rising, falling, and turn-off delays being separated by commas. Generally, the delay specification form

   #(d1, d2, d3)

is expanded to:

   #(d1_min: d1_typ: d1_max, d2_min: d2_typ: d2_max, d3_min: d3_typ: d3_max)

This is the second form of mintypmax_expression shown in the formal syntax specifi cation of the previous section.

Min/Typ/Max delays may be used on gate primitives, nets, continuous assignments, and procedural assignments.

4.8 Delay Paths Across a Module

It is often useful to specify delays to paths across a module (i.e. from pin to pin), apart from any gate level or other internal delays specified inside the module. The *specify block* allows for timing specifications to be made between a module's inputs and outputs. Example 4.21 illustrates the use of a specify block.

```
module dEdgeFF (clock, d, clear, preset, q);
     input    clock, d, clear, preset;
     output   q;

     specify
        // specify parameters
        specparam    tRiseClkQ= 100,
                     tFallClkQ= 120,
                     tRiseCtlQ = 50,
                     tFallCtlQ = 60;

        // module path declarations
        (clock => q) = (tRiseClkQ, tFallClkQ);
        (clear, preset *> q) = (tRiseCtlQ, tFallCtlQ);
     endspecify

     // description of module's internals
endmodule
```

Example 4.21 Delay Path Specifications.

A specify block is opened with the *specify* keyword and ended with the *endspecify* keyword. Within the block, specparams are declared and module paths are declared. The *specparams* name constants that will be used in the module path declarations. The module path declarations list paths from the module's inputs and inouts (also called the path's *source*), to its inouts and outputs (also called the path's *destination*). The timing specified will be used for all instances of the module.

In this example, the first module path declaration specifies that the rising delay time from the **clock** input to the **q** output will be 100 time units and that the fall time will be 120. The second module path declaration specifies the delays from both **clear** and **preset** to q. Delay paths are not typically mixed with delay (#) operators in a module description. However, if they are, then the maximum of the two delays will be used for simulation.

Two methods are used to describe the module paths, one using "=>" and the other using "*>". The "=>" establishes a *parallel connection* between source input bits and destination output bits. The inputs and outputs must have the same number of bits. Each bit in the source connects to its corresponding bit in the destination.

The "*>" establishes a *full connection* between source inputs and destination outputs. Each bit in the source has a path to every bit in the destination. The source and destination need not have the same number of bits. In Example 4.21, we specify that **clear** and **preset** have a path to the **q** output. Multiple outputs may be specified. So, for instance, we could state:

(a, b *> c, d) = 10;

This statement is equivalent to:

(a => c) = 10;
(a => d) = 10;
(b => c) = 10;
(b => d) = 10;

Here, we assume that **a**, **b**, **c**, and **d** are single bit entities. We could also state:

(e => f) = 10;

If **e** and **f** were both 2-bit entities, then this statement would be equivalent to:

(e[1] => f[1]) = 10;
(e[0] => f[0]) = 10;

Module paths may connect any combination of vectors and scalars, but there are some restrictions. First, the module path source must be declared as a module input or inout. Secondly, the module path destination must be declared as an output or inout, and be driven by a gate level primitive other than a bidirectional transfer gate.

The delays for each path can be specified as described in the previous section, including the capability of specifying rising, falling, and turn-off delays, as well as specifying minimum, typical, and maximum delays. Alternately, six delay values may be given. Their order of specification is 0 to 1, 1 to 0, 0 to z, z to 1, 1 to z, z to 0. In addition, minimum, typical, and maximum delays may be specified for each of these.

The formal syntax for specify blocks can be found in Appendix G.8. A set of system tasks, described in the simulator reference manual, allow for certain timing checks to be made. These include, setup, hold, and pulse-width checks, and are listed within the specify block.

4.9 **Summary**

This chapter has covered the basics in logic level modeling using the Verilog language. We have seen how to define gates and nets and interconnect them into more complex modules. The use of delays and strengths have been illustrated, and we have shown how module definitions can be parameterized.

4.10 **Exercises**

4.1 Write a module with the structure:

    module progBidirect (ioA, ioB, selectA, selectB, enable);
        inout   [3:0]   ioA, ioB;
        input   [1:0]   selectA, selectB;
        input   enable;
        ...
    endmodule

such that **selectA** controls the driving of **ioA** in the following way:

selectA	ioA
0	no drive
1	drive all 0's
2	drive all 1's
3	drive ioB

and **selectB** controls the driving of **ioB** in the same way. The drivers are only to be in effect if **enable** is 1. If **enable** is 0 the state of the **ioA** and **ioB** drivers must be high impedance.

A. Write this module using gate level primitives only.

B. Write this module using continuous assignments only.

4.2 Change the Hamming encoder/decoder in Example 4.3 so that random individual bits are set for each data item passed through the noisy channel.

4.3 The Hamming encoder/decoder in Example 4.3 detected and corrected one error bit. By adding a thirteenth bit which is the exclusive-OR of the other twelve bits, double bit errors can be detected (but not corrected). Add this feature to the example and modify the noisy channel so that sometimes two bits are in error. Change the $display statement to indicate the double error.

4.4 Change the memory in Example 4.18 to use the double bit detector/single bit corrector circuit from the previous problem. Change the system data size to be 8 bits. When a word is written to memory, it should be stored in encoded form.

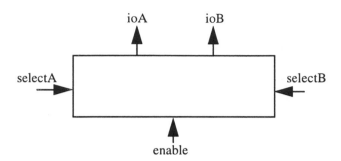

When it is read, it should be decoded and corrected. Add a bus line driven by the **slave** and read by the **master** that indicates when a double error has occurred. Devise a means for the data in the memory to become corrupted, and a means of displaying when a double error has occurred.

4.5 Use the array-of-instances construct to specify a multi-bit full adder. The module header is:
module fullAdder (cOut, sum, a, b, cIn);

A. Describe this as an 8-bit adder where **sum**, **a**, and **b** are 8-bit elements and **cOut** and **cIn** are one-bit inputs.

B. Parameterize the bit-width of elements **sum**, **a**, and **b** of module **fullAdder**.

4.6 The following combinational logic block has three inputs and an output. The circuit was built in some screwy technology and then analyzed. We now want to insert the correct input-to-output timing information into the circuit (internal node timings need not be correct).

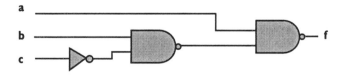

Here are the circuit timings that must be represented in the circuit.

• The delay of a rising or falling edge on **a** or **b** to output **f**: 15 time units

• The delay of a rising or falling edge on **c** to output **f**: 10 time units

Yes, those times are rather strange given the logic diagram. However, this is a screwy technology and the transistor implementation made for some strange, but actual, time delays.

Assume **a**, **b**, and **c** are outputs of synchronously clocked flip flops. Write the structural Verilog description that will be correct in functionality and timing.

5 | Advanced Timing

The previous chapters were based on a relatively straight-forward understanding of how the Verilog simulator schedules and executes events. This chapter develops a more detailed model of the simulator, including the processing of a number of the more subtle timing semantics of the language. Topics include the simulator scheduling algorithm, non-deterministic aspects of the language, and non-blocking assignments.

The material in this chapter is meant to explain conceptually how Verilog simulators are expected to work. However, the presentation may not match any particular implementation. There are plenty of short-cuts, tricks, and go-fasts that are or could be implemented. Their mileage and software-engineering appropriateness may vary and are not the topic of the chapter.

5.1 Verilog Timing Models

A hardware description language is used to model both the function and timing of digital systems. The simulation of these models is organized around events. An *event* is a change in a value in the simulation model at a specific time. The semantics of the language specify how an event causes other events to occur in time. Through this sequence of events, simulation models are executed, and simulation time is advanced.

A *timing model* is a model of how simulation time is advanced — it is tied closely to the semantics of the hardware description language. So far, we have seen two timing models used by the Verilog language. These timing models are illustrated by gate level and behavioral level descriptions.

A *simulation model* should not be confused with a *timing model.* The first is a model of digital hardware: e.g., an ALU or register file. The latter is a model of how time is advanced by the simulator. In this section, we will discuss these timing models and how the simulator advances time.

Example 5.1 shows a simple NAND latch. By the semantics of the language we know that when a change occurs on one of the gate inputs, that gate will evaluate its

```
module nandLatch (q, qBar, set, reset);
    output   q, qBar;
    input    set, reset;

    nand #2
        (q, qBar, set),
        (qBar, q, reset);
endmodule
```

Example 5.1 A NAND Latch

inputs and determine if its output is to change. If it is, then after the specified gate delay (#2), the output will change and be propagated. The gate instance is *sensitive* to its inputs — a change on any of these inputs will cause the model of the gate instance to be executed.

A simulation model has a *sensitivity list* — a list of inputs to the simulation model that, when a change occurs on one or more of them, will cause the model to be executed. The sensitivity list is a different view of a fanout list. The fanout list is organized around the element producing a new value — it tells us which elements need to be evaluated when an event occurs. The sensitivity list is organized around the element receiving new values — it tells us which of the inputs are to cause the model to be executed when a change occurs.

Example 5.1 illustrates the Verilog *gate level timing model.* When *any* input changes at *any* time, the gate instance will execute to evaluate its output, and create a new event, possibly in the future, if the output changes. All inputs are always sensitive to a change; the change will cause the evaluation of the simulation model. The gate level timing model applies to all the gate primitives, user defined primitives, continuous assignment statements, and procedural continuous assignment statements. A continuous assignment statement is sensitive to any change at any time on its right-hand side. The change will cause the expression to be evaluated and assigned to the left-hand side, possibly at a future time.

Another characteristic of the gate level timing model pertains to the scheduling of new events. Consider the situation where an event for a particular element exhibiting the gate level timing model has previously been scheduled but has not occurred. If a new event is generated for the output of that element, the previously scheduled event is cancelled and the new one is scheduled. Thus, if a pulse that is shorter than the propagation time of a gate appears on the gate's input, the output of the gate will not change. An *inertial delay* is the minimum time a set of inputs must be present for a change in the output to be seen. Verilog gate models have inertial delays just greater than their propagation delay. That is, a pulse on a gate's input will not be seen on the output unless its width is greater than the propagation delay of the gate. As we will see, if the input pulse is equal to the propagation delay, it is indeterminate whether it affects the output. This is true for all elements exhibiting the gate level timing model.

Now consider the behavioral model of a D flip flop shown in Example 5.2. The semantics of the language tell us that the always statement will begin executing and will wait for a positive edge on the **clock** input. When a positive edge occurs, the model will delay five time units, set **q** equal to the value on the **d** input at that time, and then wait for the next positive edge on **clock**. In contrast to the gate level timing model, this example illustrates a different timing model.

```
module DFF(q, d, clock);
     output   q;
     input    d, clock;
     reg      q;

     always
          @ (posedge clock)
               #5 q = d;
endmodule
```

Example 5.2 A Behavioral Model of a D Flip Flop

The always statement can be thought of as having two inputs (**clock** and **d**) and one output (**q**). The always statement is not sensitive to *any* change at *any* time as the gate level timing model was. Rather, its sensitivities are control context dependent. For instance, during the time the always is delaying for five time units, another positive edge on the **clock** input will have no effect. Indeed that second positive edge will not be seen by the simulation model since when the 5 time units are up, the model will then wait for the next clock edge. It will only be sensitive to positive clock edges that are greater than 5 time units apart. Thus the always statement is only sensitive to **clock** when execution of the model is stopped at the "@". Further, the always statement is never sensitive to the **d** input — a change on **d** will not cause the always statement to do any processing.

This example illustrates the Verilog *procedural timing model* which occurs in the behavioral blocks contained in initial and always statements. In general, the initial and always statements are only sensitive to a subset of their inputs, and this sensitivity changes over time with the execution of the model. Thus the sensitivities are dependent on what part of the behavioral model is currently being executed.

Another characteristic of the procedural timing model pertains to how events are scheduled. Assume that an update event for a register has already been scheduled. If another update event for the same register is scheduled, even for the same time, the previous event is not cancelled. Thus there can be multiple events in the event list for an entity such as a register. If there are several update events for the same time, the order of there execution is indeterminate. This is in contrast to the gate level timing model where new update events for an output will cancel previously scheduled events for that output.

There is an overlap in the simulation models that can be built using the two Verilog timing models. Indeed, in terms of input sensitivities, the procedural timing model can be used to model a super set of what a gate level timing model can. To see this, consider the behavioral NAND gate model shown in Example 5.3. This model uses the or construct with the control event ("@") to mimic the input sensitivities of the gate level timing model. If there is a change on **in1**, **in2**, or **in3**, the output will be evaluated. Thus, the procedural timing model can be used mimic the input sensitivities of the gate level timing model. However, as shown above, the procedural timing model can have other timing sensitivities, making it more flexible.

```
module behavioralNand (out, in1, in2, in3);
        output      out;
        input       in1, in2, in3;
        reg         out;
        parameter   delay = 5;

        always
            @ (in1 or in2 or in3)
                    #delay out = ~(in1 & in2 & in3);
endmodule
```

Example 5.3 Overlap in Timing Models

There are several subtle differences between Example 5.3 and a three-input NAND-gate instantiation. First, the procedural assignment makes the behavioral model insensitive to the inputs during the propagation delay of the gate. Second, if the inputs of a gate level timing model change and there is already a new output scheduled for a future time, the previously scheduled update will be cancelled and a new event will be scheduled.

In summary, elements of a Verilog description follow either the gate level or procedural timing model. These timing models define two broad classes of elements in the language, specifying how they are sensitive to changes on their inputs. Further, these specify two methods for how events are scheduled for future action.

5.2 Basic Model of a Simulator

In this section, we will develop a model for the inner workings of an event-driven simulator — specifically how a simulator deals with the execution of simulation models that create events, and with the propagation of events that cause other simulation models to execute. Timing models are important to understand because each model requires different actions by the simulation algorithm.

5.2.1 Gate Level Simulation

Consider first the basic operation of a simulator as it simulates the gate level model shown in Figure 5.1. Assume each gate has d units of delay. At the initial point of our example, the logic gates have the stable values shown in Figure 5.1a. An event occurs on line A at time t, changing it to logic 1 as shown by the arrow in Figure 5.1b. At time t, gate g1 is evaluated to see if there is a change on its output B. Since B will change to a 0, this event is scheduled for a gate delay of d time units in the future.

At time t+d, gate g1's output (B) will be set to 0 as indicated by the arrow in Figure 5.1c and this new value will be propagated to the gates on g1's fanout. Since g1's output is connected to gates g2 and g3, each of these gate models are evaluated to see if there will be an event on their outputs due to the event on B. As can be seen, only gate g2 (output C) will change. This event (C = 1) will be scheduled to change d more time units in the future. Figure 5.1d shows the results after this event at time t+2d. At this point, the new value on C will be propagated to the gates on the fanout of gate g2. These gates will be evaluated and new events will be scheduled, and so on.

5.2.2 Towards a More General Model

Clearly, a gate level event-driven simulator needs to keep track of the output values of all the gate instances, the future times at which new events will occur, and a fanout list for each of the gate instances in the simulation model. The events are stored in a list of *event lists*. The first list is ordered by times in the future. For each future time, there is a list of events; all events for a specific time are kept together. A *simulator scheduler*

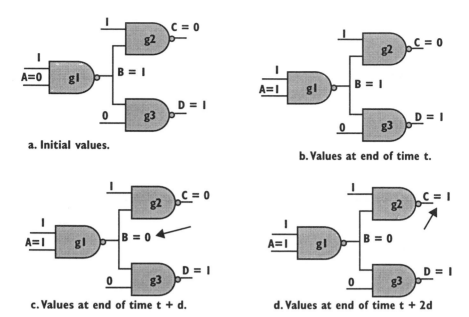

Figure 5.1 Simulation of a Gate Level Circuit

keeps track of the new events occurring and maintains the event list. The scheduler can *schedule* an event at a future time by inserting the event into the event list. The scheduler can also *unschedule* an event by removing it from the list.

To this point, we have defined an event to be a change of a value at a specified time. From here on, we will distinguish between two types of events: *update events*, and *evaluation events*. An *update event* causes a value to be updated at a specified time. An *evaluation event* causes a gate (or as we will see later, a behavioral model) to be evaluated, possibly producing a new output. Indeed, update events cause evaluation events, and evaluation events may cause update events.

Figure 5.2 illustrates the interconnection of the major elements of an event-driven simulator. The simulation scheduler is shown here as being the major actor in the system. Each of the arrows connecting to it has a label attached describing the actions taken by the scheduler. From the last section, we remember that current update events (new values) are removed from the event list and gate output values are updated. These update events cause the scheduler to look at the fanout list and determine which gates need to be evaluated. These gates are evaluated and any resulting output changes will cause an update event to be scheduled, possibly for a future time.

Figure 5.3 shows an algorithm specification for a simulator scheduler. Here we see the typical flow of an event-driven simulator. Each iteration around the outer (while) loop is called a *simulation cycle*. Since the event lists are maintained in time order, it is

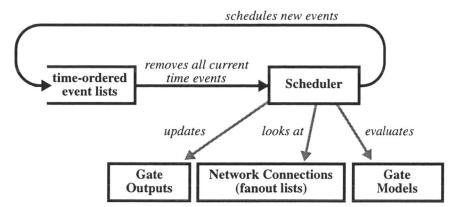

Figure 5.2 Organization of an Event-Driven Simulator

easy to find the next time and the events to execute at that time; they are first in the list. If there are no more events for the current time, **currentTime** is updated to that of the next chronological event. All the events for the **currentTime** are removed from the event list. These are then selected for processing in an arbitrary order by the "For each" statement.

If the event selected is an update event, the assignment is made and the fanout list is followed, building a list of gates to evaluate. These gates are evaluated and any resulting output changes are scheduled as update events. If there are behaviors on the fanout, evaluation events is scheduled for them. If the event selected is an evaluation event, the gate or behavioral model is executed. Any output change causes an update event for the output. Note that the new update event may be for the current time (e.g., a gate of zero delay was executed). This event is still inserted into the event list and will be removed at the next cycle of the outer loop. Thus, there may be several simulation cycles at the current time.

Let's follow this simulation algorithm, seeing how the event list develops over time. Figure 5.4a shows the initial event list for the example of Figure 5.1. The unprocessed entries in the list are shown in bold, and the processed (old) entries are shown in gray to illustrate the progression of time. (In a simulator, the processed entries would be removed from the list.) Specifically, when update event A = 1 is removed from the list, gate **g1** evaluated. Since its output changes, an update for B = 0 is scheduled for t+d. This event is inserted into the event list as shown in Figure 5.4b. The next iteration of the simulation cycle is started and time is updated to t+d. At that time, update event B = 0 is executed causing gates **g2** and **g3** to be evaluated. Only gate **g2** changes, so an update event is scheduled for C = 1 at time t+2d as shown in Figure 5.4c. In the next simulation cycle update event C = 1 is executed.

The discussion so far has centered around simulating gate level simulation models exhibiting the gate level timing model. That is, when an event occurs on a gate out-

```
while (there are events in the event list) {
    if (there are no events for the current time)
        advance currentTime to the next event time
    Unschedule (remove) all the events scheduled for currentTime
    For each of these events, in arbitrary order {
        if (this is an update event) {
            Update the value specified
            Evaluate gates on the fanout of this value and Schedule update
            events for gate outputs that change
            Schedule evaluation events for behaviors waiting for this value
        }
        else {      // it's an evaluation event
            Evaluate the model
            Schedule any update events resulting from the evaluation
        }
    }
}
```

Figure 5.3 A Simulation Cycle for a Two-Pass Event-Driven Simulator

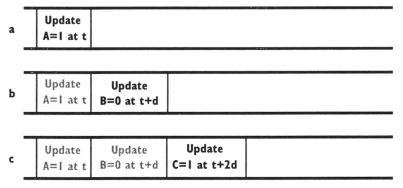

Figure 5.4 An Event List Example

put, all other gates on the fanout of that gate are evaluated to see if their outputs change. The next section will extend our understanding of a simulator to be able to handle behavioral models.

5.2.3 **Scheduling Behavioral Models**

Behavioral models in Verilog follow the procedural timing model. Thus, these simulation models are sensitive only to a subset of their inputs, and these sensitivities may change over the execution of the model. In this section we will consider the various aspects of simulating behavior models, including handling fanout lists, and register updates.

Consider Example 5.4, a behavioral model of a master-slave latch. The operation of the latch is dependent on the two clock phases **phi1** and **phi2**. First the latch waits for the positive edge of **phi1**. When this occurs, the value of **d** is saved internally and then the always waits for the positive edge of **phi2**. When it occurs, the output **q** is set to the **qInternal** value and the always loop repeats.

```
module twoPhiLatch (phi1, phi2, q, d);
    input    phi1, phi2, d;
    output   q;
    reg      q, qInternal;

    always begin
        @ (posedge phi1)
            qInternal = d;
        @ (posedge phi2)
            q = qInternal;
    end
endmodule
```

Example 5.4 A Master-Slave Latch

The important point to realize is that over the execution of this behavioral model, it is alternately sensitive to the positive edges of **phi1** and **phi2**, and is never sensitive to input **d**. A behavioral model has a *sensitivity list* — a list that specifies which of its inputs the always or initial statement is currently sensitive to. Thus, we can examine any always or initial statement and determine, as a function of time, what update events can cause it to be evaluated.

To simulate elements using the procedural timing model within the framework of Section 5.2.2, we need to be able to alter the fanout lists as the execution of the simulation models proceed. That is, because the sensitivity lists change, the fanout lists need to change. For instance, at the start of simulation in Example 5.4, the control event ("@") is executed and the process statement (i.e., the always) containing the control event is put on the fanout list of **phi1**. When there is an update event on **phi1**, an evaluation event for the process is scheduled. When this evaluation event is executed, the process determines if there is a positive edge. If there isn't, then the always block continues waiting — the fanout lists are not changed. If there is, the process is removed from the fanout list of **phi1**, and the behavioral statements resume their execution (in this case with "qInternal = d;"). When the next control event is executed, the process is placed on the fanout list of **phi2**. Now, any change on **phi2** will cause an evaluation event to be scheduled for the process. When the evaluation event is executed and the positive edge found to have occurred, the process is removed from the fanout list of **phi2**, execution of the behavioral statements proceeds, and at the next control event the process is placed on the fanout list of **phi1**.

In general, execution of a control event or a wait statement with a FALSE condition will cause the current process statement (an always or an initial) to be suspended and placed on the fanout lists of the elements in the event or conditional expression. When an event occurs on one of the elements, an evaluation event is scheduled for the process to determines whether the event or wait condition has been satisfied. When the condition has been satisfied, the process statement is removed from the fanout lists.

Not only is the process statement placed on the fanout list, but also an indicator as to where to resume executing the process is maintained. This is analogous to a software program trying to read from an input device. The operating system will suspend execution of the program until the input has arrived. Once input has arrived, the program continues executing from the point where it was suspended. In like manner, a suspended Verilog process resumes executing from where it was suspended.

Now consider an altered version of Example 5.4 shown in Example 5.5. The only difference here is that there is a delay of two time units before each of the procedural assignments. The action taken by the simulator when a delay is executed is to suspend the process statement and schedule an evaluation event for its resumption at the appropriate time in the future. The process' sensitivity list is not changed. Thus, instead of the statement "qInternal = d" being executed right after a positive edge is seen on **phi1**, an evaluation event for the process is scheduled two time units later. At that point, the process resumes executing by assigning to **qInternal**.

Registers are assigned new values as a result of executing behavioral models. The values are assigned immediately without need for creating update events. Thus if a register is assigned to on the left-hand side of a procedural expression, and immediately used in the next statement on the right-hand side, its new value is used. In addition, registers that are outputs of the process will also create update events. So, if a register is used as a source in a continuous assignment, or in a wire, or if another behavioral process is waiting (with @ or wait) for a change in the register, the update event will cause evaluation events to be scheduled.

Behavioral models, exhibiting the procedural timing model, can be simulated using the algorithm of Figure 5.3 if we allow for fanout lists to be changed during execution of the models, and if register values are updated so they are available for the next behavioral statements.

```
module twoPhiLatchWithDelay (phi1, phi2, q, d);
    input    phi1, phi2, d;
    output   q;
    reg      q, qInternal;

    always begin
        @ (posedge phi1)
            #2 qInternal = d;
        @ (posedge phi2)
            #2 q = qInternal;
    end
endmodule
```

Example 5.5 Delay in a Behavioral Model

5.3 Non-Deterministic Behavior of the Simulation Algorithm

Verilog is a concurrent language, allowing for the specification of actions that occur at the same time. Executing these actions requires their serialization because the computer being used is not as parallel as the hardware being modeled. There are two sources of non-deterministic behavior in the Verilog language: arbitrary execution order in zero time, and arbitrary interleaving of statements from other processes; these will be discussed in this section. Although one simulator will always produce the same results given the same simulation model and inputs, a different simulator version or a different supplier's simulator may choose to execute these same events in a different order. Thus, we say that the results are not deterministic.

5.3.1 Near a Black Hole

A simulator executes events scheduled for the same time in a group. It may take several simulation cycles to execute all of these events because some events may create other events for the current time. We speak of executing events for the same time as executing them in *zero-time*. It is not that these take no time to execute. Rather all of the events occur without the passage of simulation time. They occur in zero-time.

The "For each" statement in the scheduling algorithm of Figure 5.3 removes one or more events from the event list for execution during the current simulation time. Further, it specifies that the order in which these events are executed is arbitrary. The arbitrary execution order of events in zero-time is a source of non-determinism in the simulation language. When writing models, one needs to be sensitive to the fact that the ordering of events in zero-time is unspecified.

A contrived illustration of non-determinism is shown in Example 5.6. The example has three behavioral processes (one initial and two always statements), and one gate model. Assume at some time q = 0, f = qBar = b = 1, and a = 0. Later, a changes to 1. a changing to one will create a positive edge that will cause the first always statement to begin executing. The always statement will delay ten time units, set q equal to b (which is 1), and then wait for the next positive edge on a. Setting q to a new value will cause evaluation events for the two elements that are on q's fanout — the second always statement and the not gate. In the next simulation cycle, these will be removed from the event list and executed in arbitrary order. Note however that depending on the order, a different value for output f will be obtained. If the always statement is executed first, f will remain 1. If the not gate is executed first, f will be set to 0.

```
module stupidVerilogTricks (f, a, b);
    input    a, b;
    output   f;
    reg      f, q;

    initial
        f = 0;

    always
        @ (posedge a)
            #10 q = b;

    not      (qBar, q);

    always
        @ q
            f = qBar;
endmodule
```

Example 5.6 Problems in Zero-Time

Which answer is correct? Based on the semantics of the language, either one is correct. They are both correct because the simulator is allowed to take events out of the event list for the current time and execute them in whatever order it pleases. If you think that q and qBar (and thus f) should always appear to have complementary values, then you need to change the simulation model. For example, one change is to combine the second always statement and the not gate instantiation, leaving only the always statement shown in Example 5.7. This solution will maintain the timing. Also, placing a "#1" before "f = qBar" in Example 5.6 will ensure the "correct" value is

```
always
   begin
      @ q
         qBar = ~q;
         f = qBar;
   end
```

Example 5.7 One Correction to Example 5.6

loaded into **f** — however, the timing characteristics of the module would be changed too. A solution that maintains the timing uses "#0" instead of the "#1" in the "f = qBar" statement. This solution will be discussed further in section 5.4.

Although the above example was contrived, be assured that non-determinism surfaces in uncontrived examples. Consider the ripple counter in Example 5.8. Here two D flip flops are connected together in a counter configuration; the low order flip flop (instance **a**) is connected in a toggle mode. The higher order bit (**b**) has the low order bit as its input. We would expect the counter to increment through the states 00, 01, 10, 11, 00, ... at the positive edge of the clock. However, on closer inspection we see that the "q = d" statement of both instances of the **dff** is scheduled to continue executing three time units into the future. At that time, the scheduler will take both of these evaluation events off of the event list and execute them in arbitrary order. Of course, the order does matter. Executing instance **a** first will lead to an incorrect counting sequence (00, 11, 00, ...). Executing instance **b** first will produce intended order.

This problem can be corrected by using the intra-assignment delay statement "q = #3 d;" in the **dff** module. This statement will cause all of the **d** inputs of the **dff** instances to be sampled and stored as update events in the event list before any of the updates are made to the instances of **q**. Thus, the instances can be executed in any order and the behavior is deterministic. The problem can also be corrected by using non-blocking assignment: "q <= d;" in the **dff** module. Here the non-blocking assignment works with the **clock** edge to separate the reading of all of the **d**'s from the updating of the **q**'s.

The fact that events in zero-time can be executed in arbitrary order is part of the basic definition of the language. Non-deterministic behavior in a design reflects either poor usage of the modeling constructs, or a real race condition. Non-determinism is allowed in the language both for efficiency reasons and because it happens in real life ... "non-determinism happens". Care must be exercised when writing models without races so that the results will be deterministic given any ordering of execution in zero-time.

```
module goesBothWays (Q, clock);
    input              clock;
    output   [2:1]    Q;

    wire     q1, q2;
    assign   Q = {q2, q1};

    dff      a (q1, ~q1, clock),
             b (q2, q1, clock);
endmodule

module dff (q, d, clock);
    input    d, clock;
    output   q;
    reg      q;

    always
        @(posedge clock)
            #3 q = d;
endmodule
```

Example 5.8 Non-Determinism in a Flip Flop Model

5.3.2 It's a Concurrent Language

The second source of non-determinism in Verilog stems from potential interleaving of the statements in different behavioral processes. By behavioral process models, we mean the behavioral statements found in always and initial statements. Update events and all evaluation events except for the execution of behavioral process models are *atomic* actions; these events are guaranteed to be executed in their entirety before another event is executed. The behavioral process models found in initial and always statements live by a different set of rules.

Consider first a software programming environment. In a normal programming language such as C, a single process is described that starts and ends with the "main" function. As it executes, we expect the statements to be executed in the order written and for the values calculated and stored in a variable on one line to have the same value when used as sources on succeeding lines. Indeed, this is the case as long as there is only one process. However, if there is more than one process and these processes share information — they store their variables in the same memory locations — then it is possible that the value in a variable will change from one line to the next because some other software process overwrote it.

Continuing with the software analogy, consider the excerpts from two processes shown in Figure 5.5 executing in a parallel programming environment. Each process is its own thread of control, executing at its own rate. But the two processes share a variable — in this case the variable a in both processes refers to the same memory words. If these processes were being executed on one processor, then process A might execute for a while, then process B would execute, and then A again, and so on. The operating system scheduler would be charged with giving time to each of the processes in a fair manner, stopping one when its time is up and then starting the other. Of course, there could be a problem if process A is stopped right after the "a = b + c" statement and process B is started; process B will change the value of a seen by process A and the result calculated for q when process A is finally resumed will be different than if process A executed the two shown statements without interruption.

Alternatively, these two processes could be executed on two parallel processors with the variable a in a shared memory. In this case, it is possible that process B will execute its "a = a + 3" statement between process A's two statements and change the value of a. Again, the result of q is not deterministic.

What is the chance of this happening? Murphy's law states that the probability is greater than zero!

Process A	**Process B**
...	...
a = b + c;	a = a + 3
q = a + 1;	...
...	

Figure 5.5 Non-Determinism Between Two Concurrent Processes

In a software parallel programming environment, we are guaranteed that the statements in any process will be executed in the order written. However, between the statements of one process, statements from other processes may be *interleaved*. Given the parallel programming environments suggested here, there could be many different interleavings. We will call any specific interleaving of statements in one process by those of other processes a *scenario*. The two following scenarios give rise to the two differing values for q described above.

Scenario 1	**Scenario 2**
A: a = b + c	A: a = b + c
B: a = a + 3	A: q = a + 1
A: q = a + 1	B: a = a + 3

Which of these two scenarios is correct? According to the normal understanding of a parallel programming environment, both interpretations are correct! If the writer wanted Scenario 2 to be the correct way for q to be determined, then the writer would have to change the description to insure that this is the only way q can be calculated. In a parallel programming environment, any access to **a** would be considered a *critical section*. When program code is in a critical section, the operating system must make sure that only one process is executing in the critical section at a time. Given that the statements shown in process A and process B in Figure 5.5 would be in a critical section to protect the shared variable **a**, scenario 1 would be impossible. That is, the operating system would not allow process B to execute "a = a + 3" because process A is still in the critical section.

The above discussion of parallel software programing environments is exactly the environment that Verilog processes execute in. Specifically, the execution rules for behavioral processes are:

- the statements in a begin-end block in a Verilog process (i.e., the statements within an always or initial statement) are guaranteed to execute in the order written.

- the statements in a Verilog process may be interleaved by statements from other Verilog processes.

- registers and wires whose names resolve through the scope rules to the same entity, are the same. These shared entities can be changed by one process while another process is using them.

Thus, many scenarios are possible. Indeed, be aware that the processes may call functions and tasks which do not have their own copies of variables — they too are shared. It is the designer's role to make sure that only correct scenarios are possible. Generally, the culprits in these situations are the shared registers or wires. Any register or wire that can be written from more than one process can give rise to interleaving problems.

Sometimes you want the current process to stop executing long enough for other values to propagate. Consider Example 5.9. The result printed for **b** is indeterminate — the value could be x or 1. If the initial process is executed straight through, **b** will have the value x. However, given the semantics described above, it is possible that when **a** is set to 1, the behavioral process can be suspended and the value of **b** could then be updated. When the behavioral process is restarted, the display statement would show **b** set to 1.Changing the display statement to start with a "#0" will cause the initial process to be suspended, **b** to be updated, and when the display statement resumes it will show **b** as 1.

Interestingly, in concurrent software languages, high level methods are provided to synchronize multiple processes when they try to share information. P and V semaphores are one approach; critical sections are another. To make these methods work, there are instructions (such as "test and set") that are atomic — they cannot be interrupted by another process. These instructions, acting in "zero-time," provide the basis for the higher level synchronization primitives. In hardware, synchronization between processes is maintained by clock edges, interlocked handshake signals, and in some cases timing constraints.

```
module suspend;
    reg     a;
    wire    b = a;

    initial begin
        a = 1;
        $display ("a = %b, b = %b", a, b);
    end
endmodule
```

Example 5.9 Suspending the Current Process

5.4 Non-Blocking Procedural Assignments

A procedural assignment statement serves two purposes: one is to assign a value to the left-hand side of a behavioral statement, the second is to control the scheduling of when the assignment actually occurs. Verilog's two types of procedural assignment statements, blocking and non-blocking, do both of these functions differently.

5.4.1 Contrasting Blocking and Non-Blocking Assignments

The non-blocking assignment is indicated by the "<=" operator instead of the "=" operator used for blocking assignments. The <= operator is allowed anywhere the = is allowed in procedural assignment statements. The non-blocking assignment operator cannot be used in a continuous assignment statement. Although <= is also used for the less-than-or-equal operator, the context of usage determines whether it is part of an expression and thus a less-than-or-equal operator, or whether it is part of a procedural assignment and thus a non-blocking assignment.

Consider the two statements: "a = b;" and "a <= b;". In isolation, these two statements will perform the same function — they will assign the value currently in b to the register a. Indeed, if b had the value 75 when each statement was encountered, a would receive the value 75. The same is true for the paired statements:

- "#3 a = b;" and "#3 a <= b;" , and
- "a = #4 b;" and "a <= #4 b;"

In each of these paired cases, the resulting values stored in a are equal. The differences between these statements pertain to how the assignment is actually made and what ramifications the approach has on other assignments.

Let's consider the differences between "a = #4 b;" and "a <= #4 b;". The first calculates the value b (which could have been an expression), stores that value in an internal temporary register, and delays for 4 time units by scheduling itself as an update event for a 4 time units in the future. When this update event is executed, the internal temporary register is loaded into a and the process continues. This could have been written:

```
bTemp = b;              combined, these are the same as a = #4 b;
#4 a = bTemp;
```

The statement ("a <= #4 b;") calculates the value b, schedules an update event at 4 time units in the future for a with the calculated value of b, and continues executing the process in the current time. That is, it does not block or suspend the behavioral process — thus the name *non-blocking*. Note that in both cases, the value assigned to a is the value of b when the statement first started executing. However, the new value will not be assigned until 4 time units hence. Thus if the next statement uses a as a source register, it will see the old value of a, not the new one just calculated.

The two Verilog fragments shown below contrast these two forms of assignment. The blocking assignments on the left will cause the value of b to be assigned to c four time units after the begin-end block starts. In the non-blocking assignments on the right, the first statement schedules a to get the value b two time units into the future. Because this statement is non-blocking, execution continues during the current time and c is scheduled to get the value a two time units into the future. Thus, c will be different in these two situations.

```
begin                          begin
    a = #2 b;                      a <= #2 b;
    c = #2 a;                      c <= #2 a;
end                            end
```

Beyond the definition of blocking versus non-blocking, there is another important distinction between blocking and non-blocking assignments; the distinction is when in the simulation scheduler algorithm the update events are handled. In section 5.2.3 we only discussed how the results of blocking assignments are updated; they are updated immediately so that the following behavioral statements will use the new value. If they are also process outputs, they are also put in the event list for the current time, in which case they will be propagated during the next simulation cycle. Non-blocking assignment statements produce update events that are stored in a separate part of the event list. These update events are not executed until all of the currently scheduled update and evaluation events for the current time have been executed — including the events generated by these for the current time. That is, when the only events for the current time are non-blocking update commands, then they are handled. Of course the non-blocking updates may cause other evaluation events to be scheduled in the event list for the current time.

5.4.2 Prevalent Usage of the Non-Blocking Assignment

As presented in Chapter 1, the main use of non-blocking assignment is with an edge specifier as shown in Example 5.10, which is revised from Example 1.7. The non-blocking assignment serves to separate the values existing before the clock edge from those generated by the clock edge. Here, the values on the right-hand side of the non-blocking assignment are values before the clock edge; those on the left-hand side are generated by the clock edge.

Using non-blocking assignments causes these two assignments to be concurrent — to appear to happen at the same time. The first statement in the always block is executed and a non-blocking update for cS1 is scheduled for the current time. However, the update is not made immediately and execution continues with the second line. Here a non-blocking update for cS0 is scheduled for the current time. This update is not made immediately and execution continues with the always block waiting for the next posedge **clock**. Thus, the cS1 calculated on the first line is not the same value used on the right-hand side of next statement.

When will the values of cS1 and cS0 be updated? They will be updated only after all blocking updates for the current time are executed. This includes any blocking updates or evaluation events generated from them. Thus all right-hand sides will be evaluated before any of the left-hand sides are updated. The effect is that all non-blocking assignments appear to happen concurrently across the whole design. The order of the two statements for cS1 and cS0 could be switched in the description with no change in the resulting value.

The powerful feature of the non-blocking assignment is that not only are the two statements in this module concurrent, but *all* non-blocking assignments waiting on the same edge in *any* of the always or initial statements in the whole design are concurrent.

5.4.3 Extending the Event-Driven Scheduling Algorithm

An expanded version of the simulator scheduler algorithm (previously shown in Figure 5.3) is shown in Figure 5.6. Several elements have changed. First, the term *regular event* has been used to include all events other than the non-blocking update events. Thus regular events include blocking assignment updates and evaluation events for behavioral processes and gate models. Secondly, the then clause of the second if has been changed to look for non-blocking update events when all regular

```
module fsm (cS1, cS0, in, clock);
    output          cS1, cS0;
    input           in, clock;
    reg             cS1, cS0;

    always @(posedge clock) begin
        cS1 <= in & cS0;
        cS0 <= in | cS1;
    end
endmodule
```

Example 5.10 Illustrating the Non-Blocking Assignment

events have been executed. Conceptually, the non-blocking update events are changed to regular events so that the rest of the scheduler algorithm can handle them directly. Finally, monitor events are handled after all of the above events have been executed.

```
while (there are events in the event list) {
    if (there are no events for the current time)
        advance currentTime to the next event time
    if (there are no regular events for the current time)
        if (there are non-blocking assignment update events)
            turn these into regular events for the current time
    else
        if (there are any monitor events)
            turn these into regular events for the current time
    Unschedule (remove) all the regular events scheduled for currentTime
    For each of these events, in arbitrary order {
        if (this is an update event) {
            Update the value specified
            Evaluate gates on the fanout of this value and Schedule update
            events for gate outputs that change
            Schedule evaluation events for behaviors waiting for this value
        }
        else {      // it's an evaluation event
            Evaluate the model
            Schedule any update events resulting from the evaluation
        }
    }
}
```

Figure 5.6 Event Driven Scheduler Including Non-Blocking Events

The event list can be thought of as having separate horizontal layers as shown in Figure 5.7. For any given time τ in the event list, there are three separate layers: the regular events, the non-blocking events, and the monitor events. The scheduler algorithm removes the regular events from the list and executes them, possibly causing other events to be scheduled in this and other time slots. Regular events for time τ are put in the list in the regular event section; these will be removed during the next simulation cycle. Other events will be scheduled into their respective sections or into event lists for future times.

When we get to the next simulation cycle and there are more regular events, these are handled as just described. When there are no more regular events for the current time, events from the non-blocking layer are moved to the regular event layer and executed. These in turn may cause other regular events and non-blocking events which are scheduled into their respective sections. The event scheduling algorithm continues repeatedly executing all of the regular events for the current time, followed by the non-blocking events for the current time until no more events (regular or non-blocking) exist for the current time. At this point, the scheduler handles monitor events. These are inserted in the monitor events layer when the input to a monitor statement changes. These are the last to be handled before time is advanced. They cause no further events.

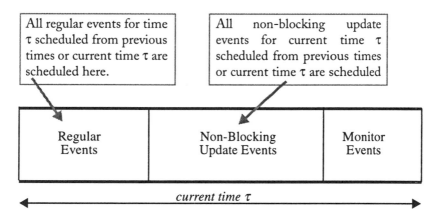

Figure 5.7 The Stratified Event List for the Current Time

Given this background, here is a list of how the different procedural assignments are handled by the simulation scheduler:

- "a = b;"   b is calculated and used immediately to update a. Note that the next statement in the behavioral process that uses a as a source will use this new value. If a is an output of the process, elements on a's fanout list are scheduled in the current time as a regular evaluation events.

- "a <= b;"   b is calculated and a non-blocking update event is scheduled for a during the current time. Execution of the process continues. This new value for a will not be seen by other elements (not even the currently executing behavioral process) until the non-blocking update events are executed.

- "a = #0 b;"   b is calculated and an update event for a is scheduled as a regular event in the current time. The current process will be blocked until the next simulation cycle when the update of a will occur and the process will continue executing.

- "a <= #0 b;"   b is calculated and a non-blocking update event is scheduled for the current time. The current process will continue executing. The update event will be executed after all regular events for the current time are executed. The same as "a <= b;".

- "a = #4 b;"   This is like "a = #0 b;" except that the update event and the continuation of the process is scheduled 4 time units into the future.

- "a <= #4 b;"   This is like "a <= #0 b;" except that a will not be updated (using a non-blocking update event) until 4 time units into the future.

- "#3 a = b;"   Wait 3 time units before doing the action for "a = b;" specified above. The value assigned to a will be the value of b 3 time units hence.

- "#3 a <= b;"   Wait 3 time units before doing the action for "a <= b;" specified above. The value assigned to a will be the value of b 3 time units hence.

Note that in the above situations the value assigned to a is the same. (Well okay, the value of b in the last two examples could change in the next three time units. But for those two cases, the value assigned to a would be the same.) The differences lie in what part of the event list the update is scheduled in, whether the value is available in the next behavioral statement, and whether the current process is blocked because of the #.

5.4.4 **Illustrating Non-Blocking Assignments**

As presented in the previous section, the non-blocking assignment allows us to schedule events to occur at the end of a time step, either the current one or a future one. Further, they allow the process to continue executing. As with blocking assignments, event control and repeat constructs can be specified within the assignment statement. The general form for the non-blocking assignment is shown below:

non-blocking assignment
      ::= reg_lvalue <= [delay_or event_control] expression

delay_or_event_control
      ::= delay_control
      | event_control
      | **repeat** (expression) event_control

delay _control
      ::= # delay_value
      | # (mintypmax_expression)

event_control
      ::= @ *event*_identifier
      | @ (event expression)

event_expression
      ::= expression
      | *event*_identifier
      | **posedge**_expression
      | **negedge**_expression
      | event_expression **or** event_expression

We have already illustrated the optional delay control. This section will discuss the event control and repeat constructs.

A differentiating feature of the non-blocking assignment is the fact that it schedules an assignment but does not block the current process from executing further. Consider the behavioral model of a NAND gate, shown in Example 5.11, that changes the inertial delay of a gate to zero. Any change on **lisa** or **michael** will cause an update event for **doneIt** to be scheduled **pDelay** time units in the future. A non-blocking assignment is necessary here because it allows the behavioral model to remain sensitive to its inputs; a change one time unit later will cause another update event on **doneIt**. If a blocking assignment had been used, the behavioral model would be delaying and the input change one time unit later would have been missed until after the delay.

Figure 5.8 shows the output waveforms for the NAND gate of Example 5.11 (**iDelay** = 0) as compared to an instantiated NAND gate. The instantiated NAND gate's output

```
module inertialNand (doneIt, lisa, michael);
     output      doneIt;
     input       lisa,
                 michael;
     reg         doneIt;
     parameter   pDelay = 5;

     always
        @(lisa or michael)
             doneIt <= #pDelay ~(lisa & michael);
endmodule
```

Example 5.11 Illustration of Non-Blocking Assignment

only responds to a set of inputs when they have been supporting the new output for the propagation time. Thus the output does not see the pulses on the inputs and twice an output update event is cancelled (see "*"). With the inertial delay equal to 0, the input pulses show up a propagation time (**pDelay**) later. Note at the right that an input "pulse" can be generated from two different inputs changing. Because of the 0 inertial delay, this pulse is seen on the output at the right of the figure.

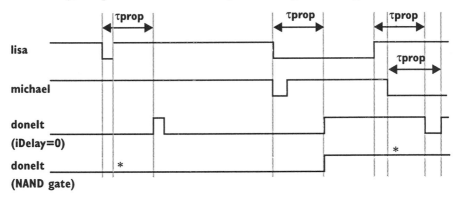

Figure 5.8 Waveforms for Differing Inertial Delays

Consider a behavioral model of a pipelined multiplier shown in Example 5.12. The latency for the multiplier is four clock periods and it can accept a new set of inputs each clock period. A positive edge on **go** is the signal to start a multiply. At that time, the inputs are multiplied together and **product** is scheduled to be updated on the fourth positive edge of **clock**. Since this is a non-blocking assignment, the calculated **product** is stored internally in the event list and the always can then wait for the next **go** signal which will start another, possibly overlapping, multiply. In this situation, **go** must be synchronous with respect to **clock** because we cannot have more than one multiply started for each **clock** edge. However, we can have one multiply started each clock period. The example further illustrates that the event list can be used to store multiple events for the same name and from the same assignment.

```
module pipeMult (product, mPlier, mCand, go, clock);
    input           go, clock;
    input   [9:0]   mPlier, mCand;
    output  [19:0]  product;
    reg     [19:0]  product;

    always
        @(posedge go)
            product <= repeat (4) @(posedge clock) mPlier * mCand;
endmodule
```

Example 5.12 A Pipelined Multiplier

An interesting contrast between gate level timing models and procedural timing models is illustrated here. If an update is generated for the output of an element using the Verilog gate level timing model, update events already scheduled in the event list for that element will be removed and the new update will be scheduled. This is not the case with elements using the procedural timing model. As we have seen in this example, multiple update events for **product** are scheduled without changing any of the already scheduled update events.

References: intra-assignment repeat 3.7

5.5 **Summary**

Timing models have been introduced as a means of separating simulation models into two broad classes characterized by how they advance simulation time. Algorithms for a simulator scheduler that handles these models was presented. Detailed timing issues, including non-determinism in the language and the contrast between blocking and non-blocking procedural assignments were covered.

5.6 **Exercises**

5.1 Below is a circuit and two Verilog models, one written as a structural model and the other as a behavioral model. Note that the models are not equivalent. Current logic levels are shown in the circuit. Assume there are no events in the event list except for those specified below.

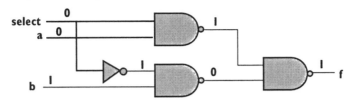

module sMux (f, a, b, select);   module bMux (f, a, b, select);
    input   a, b, select;   input   a, b, select;
    output   f;   output   f;
                                                 reg   f;

    nand   #8   always
        (f, aSelect, bSelect),   @select
        (aSelect, select, a),   #8 f = (select) ? a : b;
        (bSelect, notSelect, b);   endmodule
    not
        (notSelect, select);
endmodule

A. Simulate only module **sMux** and show all events that will eventually appear in the event list. The initial event in the event list is the update event "b = 0 at time 35". Separately simulate it with the initial update event as "select = 1 at time 50".

B. Simulate only module **bMux** and show all events that will eventually appear in the event list. The initial event in the event list is the update event "b = 0 at time 35". Separately simulate it with the initial update event as "select = 1 at time 50".

C. As mentioned, the models are not equivalent. Briefly explain why the models are not equivalent. Change the **bMux** model to make it equivalent to **sMux** in function and timing by rewriting the always statement. Aspects you may or may not want to consider: functionality only, input sensitivity, and/or timing with respect to inertial delay. Explain your changes.

D. As a function of time, what is the input sensitivity list of the always process statement in **bMux**?

5.2 Fill in the following table by simulating module **nbSchedule** for 25 time units. Each line of the table represents a simulation cycle. You do not need to turn in the event lists and how they change over tim. However, keeping the lists would probably help you keep track of what you should put in the table.

Current Time	Simulation Cycle (This is just a number (1 — n) to name them).	Events removed from list (indicate whether blocking or non-blocking)	New events (update and evaluation) scheduled as a result of the events removed (indicate which events caused the new event, whether the new ones are blocking or non-blocking, and new event time)
...	...	...	...

5.3 Start executing the following description at time = 0 and stop at time = 40.

```
module beenThere;
    reg      [15:0]  q;
    wire             h;
    wire     [15:0]  addit;

    doneThat  dT (q, h, addit);
    initial q = 20;

    always begin
        @ (posedge h);
        if (addit == 1)
            q = q + 5;
        else  q = q - 3;
    end
endmodule
```

```
module doneThat(que, f, add);
    input    [15:0]  que;
    output           f;
    reg              f;
    output   [15:0]  add;
    reg      [15:0]  add;
    always
        #10 f = ~ f;

    initial begin
        f = 0;
        add = 0;
        #14 add = que + 1;
        #14 add = 0;
    end
endmodule
```

Fill in the trace below (adding more lines), giving the time a register changes, the register name, and the new value assigned. List these in time order.

at time = _____; _____ = _____

5.4 Write and execute a test module for Example 5.12. The **clock** should have a 100 ns. period. Several test vectors (numbers to multiply) should be loaded into **mPlier** and **mCand** and then **go** should be pulsed high for 10 ns. (Test module? See Chapter 1.)

A. Show that your test module along with **pipeMult** produce correct answers.

B. Trace the update and evaluation events in the event list.

```
module nbSchedule (q2);
    wire    q1;
    output  q2;
    reg     c, a;

    xor     (d, a, q1),
            (clk, 1'b1, c);
            // holy doodoo, Batman, a gated clock!
    dff     s1 (q1, d, clk),
            s2 (q2, q1, clk);

    initial begin
        c = 1;
        a = 0;
        #8 a = 1;
    end

    always
        #20 c = ~c;
endmodule

module dff (q, d, c);
    input   d, c;
    output  q;
    reg     q;

    initial q = 0;

    always
        @(posedge c) q <= d;
endmodule
```

5.5 Here's a skeleton of two modules (**interleave** and **huh**) that could have non-determinism problems due to interleaving with other behavioral processes. Where might a problem be encountered. Explain how to correct the problem.

5.6 Remembering that there is some non-determinism built into the simulator, explain how different results can be obtained by simulating this circuit. Suggest two different corrections to the description that remove the problem.

```
module interleave;
    reg      [7:0]   a;
    huh      h ();
    ...
endmodule

module huh;
    reg      [7:0]   b, c, q, r;

    always begin
        ...
        a = b + c;
        q = a + r;
        ...
    end
endmodule

module ouch (select, muxOut, a, b);
    input      a, b;
    input      select;
    output     muxOut;
    reg        muxOut;

    always begin
        @select
            muxOut = (a & select) | (b & notSelect);

    not
        (notSelect, select);
endmodule
```

5.7 Assuming that all registers are single-bit initially with the value x, contrast the two following situations. At what times will the registers change?

```
initial begin                    initial begin
    q = #15  1;                      q <= #15  1;
    r = #25  0;                      r <= #25  0;
    s = #13  1;                      s <= #13  1;
end                              end
```

5.8 Change the **pipeMult** module in Example 5.12 so that it can only take new values every two clock periods. That is, the pipeline latency is still 4 clock periods, but the initiation rate is every two clock periods. Test the new module.

5.9 Write a behavioral description that swaps the values in two registers without using a temporary register. The new values should appear #2 after the positive edge. Complete the following module.

```
module swapIt (doIt);
    reg      [15:0]  george, georgette;
    input            doIt;

    always
        @(posedge doIt)
            //do it
endmodule
```

5.10 Rewrite **twoPhiLatch** in Example 5.4 using a non-blocking assignment.

5.11 Write a model for a simple component that <u>requires</u> the use of "<=" rather than "=" somewhere in the model. Example 5.12 was one such example; come up with another.

5.12 A student once asked if they could use blocking assignments rather than non-blocking assignments in their finite state machine descriptions. As it turns out, they could have but I would have pryed off their fingernails. Keeping in mind the differences between "may" and "can", …

A. Show an example where they *can* and it doesn't matter. Explain why. What assumptions are required?

B. Explain why they *may* not do this — briefly.

6 | Logic Synthesis

Our view of the language so far has been toward modeling and simulating logic hardware. We have presented language constructs that can be used to specify the intricate functionality and timing of a circuit. Using this approach, we can simulate a design using timing parameters based on circuits that have been placed and routed, giving great confidence in the results of the simulation. In this chapter, we consider an alternate view of the language: synthesis. When using the language as an input specification for synthesis, the concern is specifying a functionally correct system while allowing a synthesis CAD tool to design the final gate level structure of the system. These views of the language are complementary. However, care must be taken in writing a description that will be used in both simulation and synthesis.

6.1 Overview of Synthesis

The predominate synthesis technology in use today is *logic synthesis*. A system is specified at the register-transfer level of design, and, by using logic synthesis tools, a gate level implementation of the system can be obtained. The synthesis tools are capable of optimizing a design with respect to various constraints, including timing and/or area. They use a technology library file to specify the components to be used in the design. Writing Verilog specifications for logic synthesis tools will be discussed in this chapter.

6.1.1 **Register-Transfer Level Systems**

A register-transfer level description may contain different features; parts of the description may be purely combinational while others may specify sequential elements such as latches and flip flops. There may also be a finite state machine description, specifying a state transition graph.

A logic synthesis tool compiles a register-transfer level design using two main phases. The first is a technology independent phase where the design is read in and manipulated without regard to the final implementation technology. In this phase, major simplifications in the combinational logic may be made. The second phase is technology mapping where the design is transformed to match the components in a component library. If there are only two-input gates in the library, the design is transformed so that each logic function is implementable by a component in the library. Indeed, synthesis tools can transform one gate level description into another, providing the capability of redesigning a circuit when a new technology library is used.

The attraction of a logic synthesis CAD tool is that it aids in a fairly complex design process. (After all, did your logic design professor ever tell you what to do when the Karnaugh map had more than five or six variables!) These tools target large combinational design and different technology libraries, providing implementation trade-offs in time and area. Further, they promise functional equivalence of the initial specification and its resulting implementation. Given the complexity of this level of design, these tools improve the productivity of designers in many common design situations.

To obtain this increased productivity, we must specify our design in a way that it can be simulated for functional correctness and then synthesized. Whereas the earlier parts of this book focussed on the semantics of the full language and how it can be used to model intricate timing and behavior, this chapter discusses methods of describing register-transfer level systems for input to logic synthesis tools.

6.1.2 **Disclaimer**

The first part of this chapter defines what a *synthesizable description* for logic synthesis is. There are behaviors that we can describe but that common logic synthesis tools will not be able to design. (Or they may design something you'd want your competitor to implement!) Since synthesis technology is still young, and the task of mapping an arbitrary behavior on to a set of library components is complex, arbitrary behavior specifications are not allowed as inputs to logic synthesis tools. Thus, only a subset of the language may be used for logic synthesis, and the style of writing a description using that subset is restricted. The first part of this chapter describes the subset and restrictions commonly found in logic synthesis specification today. As logic synthesis technology matures, the set of allowable constructs will probably expand and the style restrictions will probably lessen; they both have evolved over the last several years.

Logic synthesis tools are available from several CAD tool vendors. Their language subsets and restrictions vary. Our discussion of logic synthesis is based on experience using tools from Synopsys, Inc and from Synplicity, Inc. If you use others, your mileage may vary. Read the synthesis tool manual closely.

6.2 Combinational Logic Using Gates and Continuous Assign

Using gate primitives and continuous assignment statements to specify a logic function for logic synthesis is quite straightforward. Examples 6.1 and 6.2 illustrate two synthesizable descriptions in this style. Both of the examples implement the same combinational function; the standard sum-of-products specification is:

$$f(a, b, c) = \Sigma\, m(a, b, c) = \Sigma\, m(1, 2, 3, 4, 7).$$

Essentially, logic synthesis tools read the logic functionality of the specification and try to optimize the final gate level design with respect to design constraints and library elements. Even though Example 6.1 specifies a gate level design, a logic synthesis tool is free, and possibly constrained, to implement the functionality using different gate primitives. The example shows a different, but functionally equivalent, gate level design. Here, the technology library only contained two-input gates; the synthesis tool transformed the design to the implementation on the right of the example. Other designs are possible with alternate libraries and performance constraints.

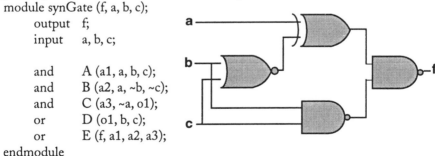

```
module synGate (f, a, b, c);
    output   f;
    input    a, b, c;

    and      A (a1, a, b, c);
    and      B (a2, a, ~b, ~c);
    and      C (a3, ~a, o1);
    or       D (o1, b, c);
    or       E (f, a1, a2, a3);
endmodule
```

Example 6.1 A Description and Its Synthesized Implementation

The example does not contain delay (#) information, illustrating one of the key differences between writing Verilog descriptions for simulation and synthesis. In simulation, we normally provide detailed timing information to the simulator to help the designer with the task of timing verification. A logic synthesis tool will ignore these timing specifications, using only the functional specification provided in the description. Because timing specifications are ignored, having them in a description could give rise to differences in simulating a design being input to a logic synthesis tool versus simulating the resulting implementation.

Consider gate instance A in Example 6.1. If it had been specified as:

and   #5   A (a1, a, b, c);

then simulation of the description would have shown a 5 time unit delay between changes on the input to changes on the output of this gate. The implementation shown in Example 6.1 does not have a gate corresponding to A. Thus, the timing of the simulation of that implementation would be different. Logic synthesis does not try to meet such timing specifications. Rather, synthesis tools provide means of specifying timing requirements such as the clock period. The tool will then try to design the logic so that all set-up times are met within that clock period. In this example, probably what is important is that Boolean function f is generated in time for input to a flip flop.

```
module synAssign (f, a, b, c);
    output  f;
    input   a, b, c;

    assign  f = (a & b & c) | (a & ~b & ~c) | (~a & (b | c));
endmodule
```

Example 6.2 A Synthesizable Description Using Continuous Assign

Using a continuous assign statement, as shown in Example 6.2, is similar to specifying logic in Boolean algebra, except Verilog has far more operators to use in the specification. In this example, the same sum of products functionality from Example 6.1 is used but the assign statement is written combining products 1, 2, and 3 into the last product term. Of note is the fact that a continuous assign may call a function which contains procedural assignment statements. The use of procedural assignment statements to describe combinational logic will be discussed in section 6.3; thus we will limit the discussion here to continuous assigns without function calls.

Continuous assign statements are often used for describing datapath elements. These modules tend to have one-line specifications as compared to the logic specifications for next state and output logic in a finite state machine. In Example 6.3 both an adder and a multiplexor are described with continuous assign. The **addWithAssign** module is parameterized with the width of the words being added and include carry in (**Cin**) and carry out (**carry**) ports. Note that the sum generated on the right-hand side of the assign generates a result larger than output **sum**. The concatenation operator specifies that the top-most bit (the carry out) will drive the **carry** output and the rest of the bits will drive the **sum** output. The multiplexor is described using the conditional operator.

```
module addWithAssign (carry, sum, A, B, Cin);
    parameter WIDTH = 4;
    output  [WIDTH:0]  sum;
    input   [WIDTH:0]  A, B;
    input              Cin;
    output             carry;

    assign  {carry, sum} = A + B + Cin;
endmodule

module muxWithAssign (out, A, B, sel);
    output     out;
    input      A, B, sel;

    assign  out = (sel) ? A: B;
endmodule
```

Example 6.3 Datapath Elements Described With Continuous Assign

There are limits on the operators that may be used as well as the ways in which unknowns (**x**) are used. An unknown may be used in a synthesizable description but only in certain situations. The following fragment is not synthesizable because it compares a value to an unknown.

```
assign   y = (a === 1'bx)? c : 1 ;
```

An unknown used in this manner is a data type in a simulator; it is useful in determining if the value of **a** has become unknown. But we don't build digital hardware to compare with unknowns and thus this construct is not synthesizable. However, the following fragment, using an unknown in a non-comparison fashion, is allowable:

```
assign   y = (a == b) ? 1'bx : c ;
```

In this case, we are specifying a don't-care situation to the logic synthesizer. That is, when **a** equals **b**, we don't care what value is assigned to **y**. If they are not equal, the value c is assigned. In the hardware synthesized from this assign statement, either 1 or 0 will be assigned to **y** (after all, there are no unknowns in real hardware). A don't-care specification used in this manner allows the synthesizer additional freedom in optimizing a logic circuit. The best implementation of this specification is just y = c.

References: assign 4.4; primitive gates 4.2.

6.3 Procedural Statements to Specify Combinational Logic

In addition to using continuous assign statements and primitive gate instantiations to specify combinational logic, procedural statements may be used. The procedural statements are specified in an always statement, within a task called from an always statement, or within a function called from an always statement or a continuous assign. In spite of the fact that a description using procedural statements appears "sequential", combinational logic may be specified with them. Section 1.2 introduced this approach to specifying combinational logic. This section covers the topic in more detail.

6.3.1 The Basics

The basic form of a procedural description of combinational logic is shown in Example 6.4. It includes an always statement with an event statement containing all of the input variables to the combinational function. The example shows a multiplexor described procedurally. In this case, input **a** selects between passing inputs **b** or **c** to output **f**. Even though **f** is defined to be a register, a synthesis tool will treat this module as a specification of combinational logic.

```
module synCombinationalAlways (f, a, b, c);
     output   f;
     input    a, b, c;
     reg      f;

     always @ (a or b or c)
       if (a == 1)
               f = b;
       else
               f = c;
endmodule
```

Example 6.4 Combinational Logic Described With Procedural Statements

A few definitions will clarify the rules on how to read and write such descriptions. Let's define the *input set* of the always block to be the set of all registers, wires, and inputs used on the right-hand side of the procedural statements in the always block. In Example 6.4, the input set contains **a**, **b**, and **c**. Further, let's define the *sensitivity list* of an always block to be the list of names appearing in the event statement ("@"). In this example, the sensitivity list contains **a**, **b**, and **c**. When describing combinational logic using procedural statements, every element of the always block's input set must appear in the sensitivity list of the always statement. This follows from the very definition of combinational logic — a change of an input value may have an immediate effect on the resulting output. If an element of the input set is not in the sensitivity list, then it cannot have an immediate effect. Rather, it must always wait for some other input to change; this is not true of combinational circuits.

Considering Example 6.4 further, we note that the combinational output f is assigned in every branch of the always block. A *control path* is defined to be a sequence of operations performed when executing an always loop. There may be many different control paths in an always block due to the fact that conditional statements (e.g. case and if) may be used. The output of the combinational function must be assigned in each and every one of the possible control paths. Thus, for every conceivable input change, the combinational output will be calculated anew; this is a characteristic of combinational logic.

The above example and discussion essentially outline the rules for specifying combinational hardware using procedural statements: the sensitivity list must be the input set, and the combinational output(s) must be assigned to in every control path. Another one that we'll see later is that the sensitivity list may not contain any edge-sensitive specifications — these are reserved for specifying flip flops.

References: always 2.1; sensitivity list 5.1; @ 3.2; edge specifications 3.2; input set 7.2.1

6.3.2 **Complications — Inferred Latches**

If there exists a control path that does not assign to the output, then the previous output value needs to be remembered. This is not a characteristic of combinational hardware. Rather it is indicative of a sequential system where the previous state is remembered in a latch and gated to the output when the inputs specify this control path. A logic synthesis tool will recognize this situation and infer that a latch is needed in the circuit. Assuming that we are trying to describe combinational hardware, we want to insure that this *inferred* latch is not added to our design. Assigning to the combinational output in every control path will insure this.

An example of a situation that infers a latch is shown in Example 6.5. If we follow the control paths in this example, we see that if a is equal to one, then f is assigned the value of b & c. However, if a is equal to zero, then f is not assigned to in the execution of the always block. Thus, there is a control path in which f is not assigned to. In this case a latch is inferred and the circuit shown on the right of the example is synthesized. The latch is actually a gated latch — a level-sensitive device that passes the value on its input D when the latch's gate input (G which is connected to a) is one, and holds the value when the latch's gate input is zero.

Example 6.6 illustrates using a case statement to specify a combinational function in a truth table form. (This example specifies the same logic function as Examples 6.1 and 6.2.) The example illustrates and follows the rules for specifying combinational logic using procedural statements: all members of the always' input set are contained

```
module synInferredLatch (f, a, b, c);
    output   f;
    input    a, b, c;
    reg      f;

    always @(a or b or c)
        if (a == 1)
            f = b & c;
endmodule
```

Example 6.5 An Inferred Latch

in the always' sensitivity list, the combinational output is assigned to in every control path, and there are no edge specifications in the sensitivity list.

```
module synCase (f, a, b, c);
    output   f;
    input    a, b, c;
    reg      f;

    always @(a or b or c)
        case ({a, b, c})
            3'b000:    f = 1'b0;
            3'b001:    f = 1'b1;
            3'b010:    f = 1'b1;
            3'b011:    f = 1'b1;
            3'b100:    f = 1'b1;
            3'b101:    f = 1'b0;
            3'b110:    f = 1'b0;
            3'b111:    f = 1'b1;
        endcase
endmodule
```

Example 6.6 Combinational Logic Specified With a Case Statement

Of course, when using a case statement it is possible to incompletely specify the case. If there are n bits in the case's controlling expression, then there are 2^n possible control paths through the case. If we don't specify all of them, then there will be a control path in which the output is not assigned to; a latch will be inferred. The default case item can be used to define the remaining unspecified case items. Thus Example 6.6 could also be written as shown in Example 6.7. Here, we explicitly list all of the zeros of the function using separate case items. If the input does not match one of these items, then by default f is assigned the value one.

```
module synCaseWithDefault (f, a, b, c);
    output   f;
    input    a, b, c;
    reg      f;

    always @(a or b or c)
        case ({a, b, c})
            3'b000:    f = 1'b0;
            3'b101:    f = 1'b0;
            3'b110:    f = 1'b0;
            default:   f = 1'b1;
        endcase
endmodule
```

Example 6.7 Using Default to Fully Specify a Case Statement

A case statement in which all of the control paths are specified (either explicitly or by using a default) is called a *full* case. A full case statement helps avoid inferred latches by providing a means for specifying the output in every possibly control path. Some synthesis tools provide a compiler directive allowing you to specify that a case is to be considered full even though all case items are not specified. In this situation, a latch is not inferred and the value assigned to the output in the unspecified case items is considered to be undefined for logic optimization.

Another situation arises when there is overlap within the specification of the case items. A *parallel* case is a case statement where there is no overlap among the case items. That is, if more than one of the case items could be true for a given value of the controlling expression, then the case is not parallel. If the case is parallel (and full), it can be regarded as a sum-of-products specification which helps logic optimization. If the case is not parallel, meaning there is overlap, then the logic function can be far more complex.

References: case 2.4.

6.3.3 **Specifying Don't Care Situations**

Logic synthesis tools make great use of logical don't care situations to optimize a logic circuit. Example 6.8 illustrates specifying a logic function that contains a don't care. Often these can be specified in the default statement of a case. As shown, assigning the value **x** to the output is interpreted in this example as specifying input cases 3'b000 and 3'b101 to be don't cares. The optimized implementation of this function is shown on the right; only the single zero of the function (input case 3'b110) is implemented and inverted. In general, specifying an input to be **x** allows the synthesis tool to treat it as a logic don't care specification.

```
module synCaseWithDC (f, a, b, c);
    output  f;
    input   a, b, c;
    reg     f;

    always @(a or b or c)
        case ({a, b, c})
            3'b001:   f = 1'b1;
            3'b010:   f = 1'b1;
            3'b011:   f = 1'b1;
            3'b100:   f = 1'b1;
            3'b110:   f = 1'b0;
            3'b111:   f = 1'b1;
            default:  f = 1'bx;
        endcase
endmodule
```

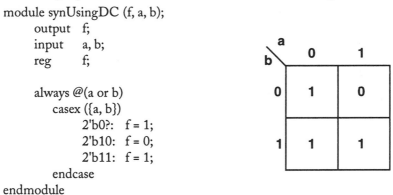

Example 6.8 A Logic Function With a Don't Care

A casex statement may use logical don't cares in a specification. Recall that a casex statement allows for the use of x, z, or ? in the controlling expression or in a case-item expression. In synthesis, they may only be used in the case-item expression and not in the controlling expression. Consider the module shown in Example 6.9.

```
module synUsingDC (f, a, b);
    output  f;
    input   a, b;
    reg     f;

    always @(a or b)
        casex ({a, b})
            2'b0?:  f = 1;
            2'b10:  f = 0;
            2'b11:  f = 1;
        endcase
endmodule
```

Example 6.9 Specifying a Logical Function Using a Don't Care

The first case item specifies that if a is zero, then the output f is one. The use of the ? in this statement specifies that the value of b does not matter in this situation. Note that the function does not contain a don't care. Rather, the way we chose to specify the function was made simpler and more compact using the ?. Since this first case item covers two of the four possible case-items, it along with the other two case-items make this a full casex. In this example, ? was used to specify the logical don't care. x or z could also have been used.

The casez statement can also be used to specify logical don't cares. In this situation, only z or ? are used for the don't care in the case-item expression.

Care should be taken when using don't cares in a specification because they give rise to differences between simulation and synthesis. In a simulator, an x is one of the four defined logic values. Comparing to an x makes sense in a simulation but not in synthesis. To reduce the differences between simulation and synthesis, a synthesizable description does not compare with x or z. Further, an x is only assigned to a combinational output as already illustrated in Example 6.8, and later in Example 6.15.

References: casex and casez 2.4.

6.3.4 **Procedural Loop Constructs**

A reading of the above examples might suggest that the only means to specify logic functions is through if and case statements. Of special interest are the looping statements: for, while, repeat, forever. Of these, only repeat is not allowed in synthesizable specifications.

For loops allow for a repetitive calculation to be specified such as in Example 6.10, which is Example 4.4 rewritten. In this example, each iteration of the loop specifies a different logic element which is indexed by the loop variable i. Here, eight xor gates are connected between the inputs and the outputs. Since this is a specification of combinational logic, i does not appear as a register in the final implementation.

```
module synXor8 (xout, xin1, xin2);
    output  [1:8]   xout;
    input   [1:8]   xin1, xin2;
    reg     [1:8]   xout, i;

    always @(xin1 or xin2)
        for (i = 1; i <= 8; i = i + 1)
            xout[i] = xin1[i] ^ xin2[i];
endmodule
```

Example 6.10 Using for to Specify an Array of xors

The example illustrates several points about using for statements for specifying logic. The for statement will have an index i that must either start with a low limit and step up to a high limit, or start with a high limit and step down to a low limit. The comparison for end of loop may be <, >, <=, or >=, and the step size need not be one. The general form shown below illustrates the count down version:

> for (i = highLimit; i >= lowLimit; i = i - step);
>   ...

The for loop is highly structured, clearly specifying the step variable and its limits. While and forever loops are not nearly so structured and there are limits on their usage. Each control path through a while or forever loop must have an edge specifier for a clock. Thus, while and forever loops cannot be used to specify combinational logic.

References: Unallowed constructs 6.7

6.4 **Inferring Sequential Elements**

Sequential elements are the latches and flip flops that make up the storage elements of a register-transfer level system. Although they are a fundamental component of a digital system, they are difficult to describe to a synthesis tool; the main reason being that their behavior can be quite intricate. As we will see, the form of the description of some of these elements (especially flip flops) are almost prescribed so that the synthesis tool will know which library element to map the behavior on to. These prescriptions save the synthesis tool from trying to match an arbitrary behavior specification to the behavior specification of each of the library elements.

6.4.1 **Latch Inferences**

Latches are *level sensitive* storage devices. Typically, their behavior is controlled by a system wide clock that is connected to a gate input (G). While the gate is asserted (either high or low), the output Q of the latch follows the input D — it is a combinational function of D. When the gate is unasserted, the output Q remembers the last value of the D input. Sometimes these devices have asynchronous set and/or reset inputs. As we have seen in section 6.3.2, latches are not explicitly specified. Rather, they arise by inference from the way in which a description is written. We say that latches are *inferred*. One example of an inferred latch was shown in Example 6.5.

Latches are inferred using the always statement as a basis. Within an always statement, we define a *control path* to be a sequence of operations performed when executing an always loop. There may be many different control paths in an always block due to the fact that conditional statements (e.g. case and if) may be used. To produce a combinational circuit using procedural statements, the output of the combinational function must be assigned in each and every one of the different control paths. Thus, for every conceivable input change, the combinational output will be calculated anew.

To infer a latch, two situations must exist in the always statement: at least one control path must exist that does not assign to an output, and the sensitivity list must not contain any edge-sensitive specifications. The first gives rise to the fact that the previous output value needs to be remembered. The second leads to the use of level-sensitive latches (as opposed to edge-sensitive flip flops). The requirement for memory is indicative of a sequential element where the previous state is remembered in a latch and gated to the output when the inputs specify this control path. A logic synthesis tool will recognize this situation and infer that a latch is needed in the circuit. Assuming that we are trying to describe a sequential element, leaving the output variable unassigned in at least one path will cause a latch to be inferred.

Example 6.11 shows a latch with a reset input. Although we have specified output Q to be a register, that alone does not cause a latch to be inferred. To see how the latch inference arises, note that in the control flow of the always statement, not all of the possible input combinations of **g** and **reset** are specified. The specification says that if there is a change on either **g, d** or **reset**, the always loop is executed. If **reset** is zero, then Q is set to zero. If that is not the case, then if **g** is one, then Q is set to the **d** input. However, because there is no specification for what happens when **reset** is one and **g** is zero, a latch is needed to remember the previous value of Q in this situation. This is, in fact, the behavior of a level sensitive latch with reset. The latch behavior could also have been inferred using a case statement.

```
module synLatchReset (Q, g, d, reset);
     output   Q;
     input    g, d, reset;
     reg      Q;

     always @(g or d or reset)
        if (~reset)
              Q = 0;
        else if (g)
              Q = d;
endmodule
```

Example 6.11 Latch With Reset

6.4.2 Flip Flop Inferences

Flip flops are *edge-triggered* storage devices. Typically, their behavior is controlled by a positive or negative edge that occurs on a special input, called the clock. When the edge event occurs, the input d is remembered and gated to the output Q. They often have set and/or reset inputs that may change the flip flop state either synchronously or asynchronously with respect to the clock. At no time is the output Q a combinational function of the input d. These flip flops are not explicitly specified. Rather, they are inferred from the behavior. Since some of their behavior can be rather complex, there is essentially a template for how to specify it. Indeed some synthesis tools provide special compiler directives for specifying the flip flop type.

Example 6.12 shows a synthesizable model of a flip flop. The main characteristic of a flip flop description is that the event expression on the always statement specifies an edge. It is this edge event that infers a flip flop in the final design (as opposed to a level sensitive latch). As we will see, an always block with an edge-triggered event expression will cause flip flops to be inferred for all of the registers assigned to in procedural assignments in the always block. (Thus, an always block with an edge-triggered event expression cannot be used to define a fully combinational function.)

```
module synDFF (q, d, clock);
    output  q;
    input   clock, d;
    reg     q;

    always @(negedge clock)
        q <= d;
endmodule
```

Example 6.12 A Synthesizable D Flip Flop

Typically flip flops include reset signals to initialize their state at system start-up. The means for specifying these signals is very stylized so that the synthesis tool can determine the behavior of the device to synthesize. Example 6.13 shows a D flip flop with asynchronous set and reset capabilities. In this example, the **reset** signal is asserted low, the **set** signal is asserted high, and the clock event occurs on the positive edge of **clock**.

```
module synDFFwithSetReset (q, d, reset, set, clock);
    input   d, reset, set, clock;
    output  q;
    reg     q;

    always @(posedge clock or negedge reset or posedge set) begin
        if (~reset)
            q <= 0;
        else if (set)
            q <= 1;
        else   q <= d;
    end
endmodule
```

Example 6.13 A Synthesizable D Flip Flop With Set and Reset

Examples 6.12 and 6.13 both use non-blocking assignments in their specification. This specification allows for correct simulation if multiple instances of these modules are connected together.

Although the Example 6.13 appears straight-forward, the format is quite strict and semantic meaning is inferred from the order of the statements and the expressions within the statements. The form of the description must follow these rules:

- The always statement must specify the edges for each signal. Even though asynchronous reset and set signals are not edge triggered they must be specified this way. (They are not edge triggered because **q** will be held at zero as long as **reset** is zero — not just when the negative edge occurs.)

- The first statement following the always must be an if.

- The tests for the set and reset conditions are done first in the always statement using else-if constructs. The expressions for set and reset cannot be indexed; they must be one-bit variables. The tests for their value must be simple and must be done in the order specified in the event expression.

- If a negative edge was specified as in **reset** above, then the test should be:
  if (!reset) ...

  or
  if (reset == 1'b0) ...

  or
  if (~reset) ...

- If a positive edge was specified as in **set** above, then the test should be:
  if (set) ...

  or
  if (set == 1'b1) ...

- After all of the set and resets are specified, the final statement specifies the action that occurs on the clock edge. In the above example, **q** is loaded with input **d**. Thus, "clock" is not a reserved word. Rather, the synthesis tools infer the special clock input from assignment's position in the control path; it is the action that occurs when none of the set or reset actions occur.

- All procedural assignments in an always block must either be blocking or non-blocking assignments. They cannot be mixed within an always block. Non-blocking assignments ("<=") are the assignment operator of choice when specifying the edge-sensitive behavior of a circuit. The "<=" states that all the transfers in the whole system that are specified to occur on the edge in the sensitivity list should occur concurrently. Although descriptions using the regular "=" will synthesize properly, they may not simulate properly. Since both simulation and synthesis are generally of importance, use "<=" for edge sensitive circuits.

- The sensitivity list of the always block includes only the edges for the clock, reset and preset conditions.

These are the only inputs that can cause a state change. For instance, if we are describing a D flip flop, a change on D will not change the flip flop state. So the D input is not included in the sensitivity list.

• Any register assigned to in the sequential always block will be implemented using flip flops in the resulting synthesized circuit. Thus you cannot describe purely combinational logic in the same always block where you describe sequential logic. You can write a combinational expression, but the result of that expression will be evaluated at a clock edge and loaded into a register. Example 1.7 had an example of this.

References: non-blocking versus blocking assignment 5.4.

6.4.3 Summary

Latches and flip flops are fundamental components of register-transfer level systems. Their complex behavior requires that a strict format be used in their specification. We have only covered the basics of their specification. Most synthesis tools provide compiler directives to aid in making sure the proper library element is selected to implement the specified behavior. Read the synthesis tool manual closely.

6.5 Inferring Tri-State Devices

Tri-state devices are combinational logic circuits that have three output values: one, zero, and high impedance (z). Having special, non-typical capabilities, these devices must be inferred from the description. Example 6.14 illustrates a tri-state inference.

```
module synTriState (bus, in, driveEnable);
    input    in, driveEnable;
    output   bus;
    reg      bus;

    always @(in or driveEnable)
        if (driveEnable)
            bus = in;
        else  bus = 1'bz;
endmodule
```

Example 6.14 Inferring a Tri-State Device

The always statement in this module follows the form for describing a combinational logic function. The special situation here is that a condition (in this case, driveEnable) specifies a case where the output will be high impedance. Synthesis tools infer that this condition will be the tri-state enable in the final implementation.

6.6 Describing Finite State Machines

We have seen how to specify combinational logic and sequential elements to a synthesis tool. In this section we will combine these into the specification of a finite state machine. The standard form of a finite state machine is shown in Figure 6.1. The machine has inputs x_i, outputs z_i, and flip flops Q_i holding the current state. The outputs can either be a function solely of the current state, in which case this is a Moore machine. Or, they can be a function of the current state and input, in which case this is a Mealy machine. The input to the flip flops is the next state; this is a combinational function of the current state and inputs.

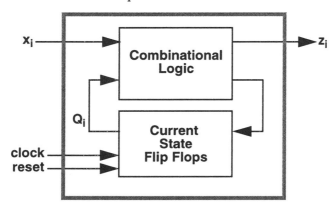

Figure 6.1 Standard Model of a Finite State Machine

   The Verilog description of a finite state machine (FSM) follows this model closely. The outer box of Figure 6.1 will be the FSM module. The two inner boxes will be two separate always statements. One will describe the combinational logic functions of the next state and output. The other will describe the state register.

6.6.1 An Example of a Finite State Machine

An example of an FSM description will be presented, using the *explicit* style of FSM description. In this style, a case statement is used to specify the actions in each of the machine's states and the transitions between states. Consider the state transition diagram shown in Figure 6.2. Six states and their state transitions are shown with one input and three output bits specified. Example 6.15 is the Verilog description of this FSM.

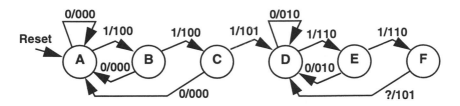

Figure 6.2 State Transition Diagram for Example 6.15

The first always statement is a description of the combinational output (**out**) and next state (**nextState**) functions. The input set for these functions contains the input **i** and the register **currentState**. Any change on either of these will cause the always statement to be re-evaluated. The single statement within the always is a case statement indicating the actions to be performed in each state. The controlling expression for the case is the state variable (**currentState**). Thus, depending on what state the machine is in, only the specified actions occur. Note that in each case item, the two combinational functions being computed (**out** and **nextState**) are assigned to. In addition, a default case item is listed representing the remaining unassigned states. The default sends the machine to state **A** which is equivalent to a reset. By arbitrary choice, **out** is set to don't care in the unassigned states.

This always statement will result in combinational logic because: the sensitivity list contains all of the input set, there are no edge specifiers in the sensitivity list, and for every control path, both of the combinational outputs have been assigned to. This includes every possible case item. Thus, there will be no inferred latches.

The second always statement infers the state register with its reset condition. In this case, **reset** is asserted low and will cause the machine to go into state **A**. If **reset** is not asserted, then the normal action of the always will be to load **currentState** with the value of **nextState**, changing the state of the FSM on the positive edge of **clock**.

Notice that **currentState** is assigned to in every control path of the always — so why is a flip flop inferred? The reason is that the edge specifications in the event expression cause <u>any</u> register assigned to in the block to be implemented using flip flops. You cannot specify combinational logic in an always block with edge triggers in the sensitivity list. This is why we need two always blocks to specify an FSM: one for the state register, and the other for the combinational logic.

The parameter statement defines the state assignment for the FSM. By overriding the parameter specifications, alternate state assignments can be explored.

Together, these two always statements work together to implement the functionality of a finite state machine. The output of the second always is the current state of the

```
module fsm (i, clock, reset, out);
    input              i, clock, reset;
    output  [2:0]      out;
    reg     [2:0]      out;

    reg     [2:0]      currentState, nextState;

    parameter [2:0] A = 0,      // The state labels and their assignments
                    B = 1,
                    C = 2,
                    D = 3,
                    E = 4,
                    F = 5;

    always @(i or currentState) // The combinational logic
        case (currentState)
            A:  begin
                    nextState = (i == 0) ? A : B;
                    out = (i == 0) ? 3'b000 : 3'b100;
                end
            B:  begin
                    nextState = (i == 0) ? A : C;
                    out = (i == 0) ? 3'b000 : 3'b100;
                end
            C:  begin
                    nextState = (i == 0) ? A : D;
                    out = (i == 0) ? 3'b000 : 3'b101;
                end
            D:  begin
                    nextState = (i == 0) ? D : E;
                    out = (i == 0) ? 3'b010 : 3'b110;
                end
            E:  begin
                    nextState = (i == 0) ? D : F;
                    out = (i == 0) ? 3'b010 : 3'b110;
                end
            F:  begin
                    nextState = D;
                    out = (i == 0) ? 3'b000 : 3'b101;
                end
            default: begin // oops, undefined states. Go to state A
                    nextState = A;
                    out = (i == 0) ? 3'bxxx : 3'bxxx;
                end
        endcase
```

```
always @(posedge clock or negedge reset) // The state register
    if (~reset)
            currentState <= A;
    else
            currentState <= nextState;
endmodule
```

Example 6.15 A Simple Finite State Machine

FSM and it is in the input set of the first always statement. The first always statement is a description of combinational logic that produces the output and the next state functions.

References: parameters 4.5; non-blocking assignment 5.4; implicit style 6.6.2.

6.6.2 **An Alternate Approach to FSM Specification**

The above explicit approach for specifying FSMs is quite general, allowing for arbitrary state machines to be specified. If an FSM is a single loop without any conditional next states, an *implicit* style of specification may be used.

The basic form of an implicit FSM specification is illustrated in Example 6.16. The single always statement lists several clock events, all based on the same edge (positive or negative). Since the always specifies a sequential loop, each state is executed in order and the loop executes continuously. Thus, there is no next state function to be specified.

In this particular example, a flow of data is described. Each state computes an output (**temp** and **dataOut**) that is used in later states. The output of the final state (**dataOut**) is the output of the FSM. Thus, a new result is produced every third clock period in **dataOut**.

Another example of a flow of data is a pipeline, illustrated in Example 6.17 using a slightly different calculation. Here a result is produced every clock period in **dataOut**. In this case, three FSMs are specified; one for each stage of the pipe. At every clock event, each stage computes a new output (**stageOne**, **stageTwo**, and **dataOut**). Since these variables are used on the left-hand side of a procedural statement in an always block with an edge specifier, there are implemented with registers. The non-blocking assignment (<=) must be used here so that the simulation results will be correct. Figure 6.3 shows a simplified form of the implementation of module **synPipe**.

References: explicit style 6.6.1

```
module synImplicit (dataIn, dataOut, c1, c2, clock);
    input    [7:0]    dataIn, c1, c2;
    input             clock;
    output   [7:0]    dataOut;
    reg      [7:0]    dataOut, temp;

    always begin
        @ (posedge clock)
            temp = dataIn + c1;
        @ (posedge clock)
            temp = temp & c2;
        @ (posedge clock)
            dataOut = temp - c1;
    end
endmodule
```

Example 6.16 An Implicit FSM

```
module synPipe (dataIn, dataOut, c1, c2, clock);
    input    [7:0]    dataIn, c1, c2;
    input             clock;
    output   [7:0]    dataOut;
    reg      [7:0]    dataOut;

    reg      [7:0]    stageOne;
    reg      [7:0]    stageTwo;

    always   @ (posedge clock)
        stageOne <= dataIn + c1;

    always   @ (posedge clock)
        stageTwo <= stageOne & c2;

    always   @ (posedge clock)
        dataOut <= stageTwo + stageOne;
endmodule
```

Example 6.17 A Pipeline

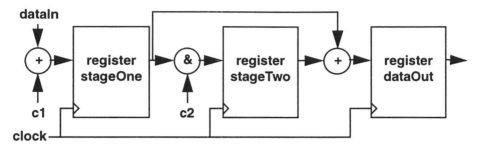

Figure 6.3 The Data Path of Example 6.17

6.7 **Summary on Logic Synthesis**

We have seen that descriptions used for logic synthesis are very stylized and that some of the constructs are overloaded with semantic meaning for synthesis. In addition, there are several constructs that are not allowed in a synthesizable description. Because these vary greatly by vendor and version of the tool, we chose not to include a table of such constructs. Consult the user manual for the synthesis tool you are using.

Table 6.1 summarizes some of the basic rules of using procedural statements to describe combinational logic and how to infer sequential elements in a description.

Table 6.1 Basic Rules for Using Procedural Statements in Logic Synthesis

Type of Logic	Output Assigned To	Edge Specifiers in Sensitivity List
Combinational	An output must be assigned to in all control paths.	Not allowed. The whole input set must be in the sensitivity list.
Inferred latch	There must exist at least one control path where an output is not assigned to. From this "omission," the tool infers a latch.	Not allowed.
Inferred flip flop	No affect	Required — from the presence of an edge specifier, the tool infers a flip flop. All registers in the always block are clocked by the specified edge.

6.8 **Exercises**

6.1   In section 6.2 on page 191, we state that a synthesis tool is capable, and possibly constrained, to implement the functionality using different gate primitives. Explain why it might be "constrained" to produce an alternate implementation.

6.2   Alter the description of Example 6.5 so that there is no longer an inferred latch. When **a** is not one, **b** and **c** should be or-d together to produce the output.

6.3   Alter the description of Example 6.11. Use a case statement to infer the latch.

6.4   Why can't while and forever loops be used to specify combinational hardware?

6.5   Rewrite Example 6.15 as a Moore machine. An extra state will have to be added.

6.6   Rewrite Example 6.15 using a one-hot state encoding. Change the description to be fully parameterized so that any state encoding may be used.

6.7   Write a description for the FSM shown in Figure 6.4 with inputs **Ain**, **Bin**, **Cin**, **clock**, and **reset**, and output **Y**.

A. A single always block

B. Two always blocks; one for the combinational logic and the other for the sequential.

C. Oops, this circuit is too slow. We can't have three gate delays between the flip flop outputs and inputs; rather only two. Change part B so that **Y** is a combinational output. i.e. Move the gate generating d2 to the other side of the flip flops.

D. Simulate all of the above to show that they are all functionally equivalent.

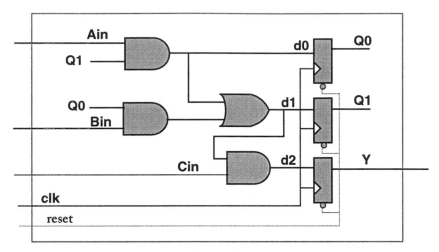

Figure 6.4 Control Over Synthesis

7 | Behavioral Synthesis

Behavioral synthesis is a just-emerging computer-aided design technology. Working at a higher level of abstraction, these tools have the capability of exploring design alternatives that are more far-reaching than found in logic synthesis. From a cycle-accurate specification they design and optimize a datapath and the finite state machine controlling it. This chapter overviews behavioral synthesis, presents the cycle accurate method of specification, and illustrates how to specify systems for design using behavioral synthesis.

7.1 Introduction to Behavioral Synthesis

Behavioral synthesis tools aid in the design of register transfer level systems — finite state machine with datapath systems. As illustrated in Figure 7.1, a cycle-accurate description is used to specify the functionality of the system. From the cycle accurate nature of the description, timing relationships involving the inputs and outputs of the system are derived. The behavioral synthesis tool designs a datapath and finite state machine implementing the functionality and meeting these timing relationships. The design is specified in terms of functional datapath modules such as ALUs, register files, and multiplexor/bus drivers that are provided in a technology library file. In addition, the finite state machine for the system is specified. Downstream design tools include logic synthesis to design the finite state machine and module generation to design the datapath.

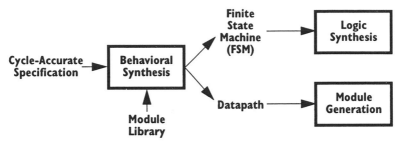

Figure 7.1 Behavioral Synthesis in a Tool Flow

Behavioral synthesis can be defined by its primary functions: scheduling, allocation, and mapping.

- *Scheduling* assigns operations to control states. Given that the input to a behavioral synthesis system is a cycle-accurate specification, one might wonder what role scheduling plays. To behavioral synthesis, cycle-accurate specifications only constrain when input ports are read and when results are made available on an output port. Internally, there is flexibility to schedule the operations that produce the results as long as the result is available at the appropriate time.

- *Allocation* specifies how many of an object are used to implement the datapath. The cycle-accurate specification only tells us how to calculate the outputs from the inputs. The behavioral synthesis tool selects the number of operators (i.e., should there be one multiplier or two?), the number of registers, and the number of buses in a design. In conjunction with scheduling, allocation provides a wide range of trade-offs in implementation. That is, if two multipliers are available, then two multiply operations could be done in one control state, making the implementation faster but larger.

- *Mapping* assigns operations (e.g. the "+" and "-" in Verilog procedural statements) to functional modules. Given that a behavioral synthesis tool has decided to have two adders in the datapath, select which of the + operators in the description are going to be mapped into which of the functional modules.

These functions of a behavioral synthesis tool are specified here in a general sense. Between available synthesis tools, there is considerable difference in how each of these is implemented. Additionally, the style of input description varies greatly among different tools. Indeed, although we show cycle-accurate specifications as input to behavioral synthesis tools, most will take a higher level specification.

The discussion in this section is based on experience using the behavioral synthesis tools available from DASYS, Inc. Read your synthesis tool manual for tool specifics.

7.2 **Cycle-Accurate Specification**

Cycle-accurate specification was introduced in section 1.6 and will be further detailed here. The basis for cycle-accurate specifications is the always statement, which is viewed as a specification of a thread of control: a process. The resulting register-transfer level implementation of the always statement will include a data path to perform the processing specified in the always statement, and a description of a finite-state machine to evoke the register-transfer operations in the data path. A module may have multiple always statements in it. Each will be synthesized to a separate, although communicating, data path-finite state machine pairs.

7.2.1 **Inputs and Outputs of an Always Block**

Although an always block is a behavioral construct that does not have a formal specification of ports, we can think of them as having ports. Consider a module with a single always block and no other continuous assign or module/gate instantiations as shown in Example 7.1. It is clear that the input and output ports of the module correspond to the inputs and outputs of the always block. That is, entities the always block needs as inputs come from outside the module, and entities the always block produces are made available outside the module. Of course, there may be some internal registers with values produced by the execution of the always block and also used as input to it. But, since such registers are not made available outside of the always block, they are not considered outputs. And, since they are generated internally, their use is not considered an input.

```
module inOutExample (r, s, qout);
    input    [7:0]   r, s;
    output   [7:0]   qout;
    reg      [7:0]   qout, q;

    always begin
        @ (posedge clock)
            q <= r + s;
        @ (posedge clock)
            qout <= q + qout;
    end
endmodule
```

Example 7.1 Illustration of always Block Input, Output, and Internal Sets

More formally, the *internal register set* of an always block is the set of all named entities on the left-hand side of the procedural assignment statements in the always block that are only used internal to the always block. These include registers and memories. In Example 7.1, register **q** is a member of the internal register set. Register **qout** is not a member of the internal set because it is also used outside of the module.

The *input set* of an always block includes all of the named entities on the right-hand side of the procedural assignments in the always block and all of the named entities in conditional expressions that are not members of the internal register set. That is, they are generated by a gate primitive, continuous assign, or another always block. In Example 7.1, **r** and **s** are members of the input set.

The *output set* of an always statement is the set of all named entities on the left-hand side of the procedural assignment statements that are not members of the internal set. That is, these entities are used on the right-hand side of a continuous assign, are input to a gate primitive, or are in the input set of another always block. In Example 7.1, **qout** is a member of the output set. Even though **qout** is also used on the right-hand side of this always block, it is the fact that it is used outside of the always block that puts it in the output set.

An always block used in cycle-accurate specification often has clock and reset inputs as well. Indeed, Example 7.1 shows the use of input **clock**. For the sake of the above definitions, we do not consider these to be inputs of the always block. Rather we will view them as special control inputs. This is similar to the practice in finite state machine design where clock and reset are not considered part of the systems inputs. (To make our point, we intentionally left clock out of the input port list.)

A module has many always blocks, gate instantiations, and continuous assign statements. Conceptually, we consider an always block as having ports made up of its input set and output set. Although these ports are not formally listed, we view each always block as reading its inputs and producing its outputs and interacting with the rest of a system through them.

7.2.2 Input/Output Relationships of an Always Block

A cycle-accurate description is an always block that specifies the timing relationships between reading elements from the input set and producing values in the output set. The input/output relationships define the interface of the system to the outside world. These relationships are specified by inserting clock edge specifications in the procedural statements. The clock edge specifications are called *clock events*. Thus, we might state:

```
always begin
   @ (posedge clock)
      q <= r + s;              State A
   @ (posedge clock)
      qout <= q + qout;        State B
end
```

Here, the clock events are the event control statements with the posedge specifier. Of course, they could have been specified as negedge clocks as well.

Consider how to read the above statements. The statement labelled **State A** above indicates the action that occurs in one state of the system. When the posedge of the **clock** is seen, q will be loaded with the sum of r and s. That is, even though q <= r + s is written on the text line after the event statement waiting for the edge, we know from the simulation semantics of the language that q will be calculated based on values of r and s existing just before the clock edge. q will be updated after all such right-hand sides have been calculated. Likewise, qout will be loaded at the second **clock** edge based on the value of q and qout just before this edge (this will be the q calculated in the previous state). From this specification, we infer that we have one clock period in which to calculate the sum of r, s, and qout. That is, in state A, the r and s inputs are sampled and summed to produce q. State B then accumulates that sum into **qout**.

The Verilog description is shown again in Figure 7.2, this time with a timing diagram and a state transition diagram. Note that the clock edge that transits the system from state A to state B is the same one that loads the new value generated for q in state A. Thus, the new value of q is generated by state A; it will not be available in register q until the system is in state **B**.

When modeling systems using the cycle-accurate approach, we are only sampling the always block inputs on the edge of the clock at the end of the state. Thus, as shown in the figure, even though r and s were generated earlier in time (possibly at the previous clock event), we only require that they be valid at the clock edge at the end of the state. After all, the specification is only accurate at the clock cycles (clock events); thus the name. Since all actions occur at the clock edge, assignments to members of the output set must be non-blocking.

An important notion in behavioral synthesis is that the timing relationships between the input and output sets specify the complete interface with the rest of the system. That is, it is possible to synthesize alternate implementations of the behavior that have the same input/output timing relationships which may vary in the size of

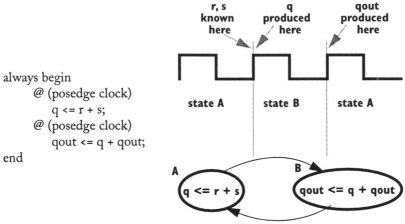

always begin
    @ (posedge clock)
        q <= r + s;
    @ (posedge clock)
        qout <= q + qout;
end

Figure 7.2 Cycle-Accurate Behavior

the implementation or its maximum clock frequency. Consider the Verilog fragment
in Example 7.2.

```
input    [7:0]    i, j, k;
output   [7:0]    f, h;
reg      [7:0]    f, g, h, q, r, s;

always begin
    ...
    @ (posedge clock)
        f <= i + j;              State A
        g = j * 23;
    @ (posedge clock)
        h <= f + k;              State B
    @ (posedge clock)
        f <= f * g;              State C
        q = r * s;
    ...
```

Example 7.2 Alternate Implementations of Cycle-Accurate Specifications

Assume the output set is f and h, the input set is i, j, and k, and registers g, q, r, and s
are part of the internal set. Note that either of the multiplies in state C could have
been executed in state B because the values being multiplied in each of the statements
were calculated before state B. Rescheduling one of these would be advantageous
because state C has two multiplies scheduled in it. That means that the data path to
implement this Verilog fragment would have to have two separate multiply cells to
execute both multiplies in the same state. If we moved one of the multiplies to state B,

then each of the states would only need one multiply in the data path — a savings in area. Behavioral synthesis tools are capable of recognizing the opportunities of rescheduling operators into other states to make such savings.

If q = r * s was moved into **state B**, there would be no change in input/output functionality. However, if f <= f * g is moved, then f would appear one state too early. The timing relationships of the input and output sets would be changed. A behavioral synthesis tool knows to insert a temporary register to load this value in **state B**, and then transfer the value to the output f in **state C**. It is possible that an extra register already exists in the design. For instance, if g is not accessed after **state C** before it is rewritten in the next iteration of the always statement, the result of the multiply could be loaded into register g and then transferred to register f in **state C**. The states B and C are rewritten below as **Bnew** and **Cnew** to illustrate this:

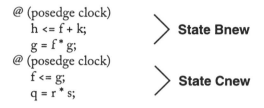

@ (posedge clock)
  h <= f + k;   **State Bnew**
  g = f * g;
@ (posedge clock)
  f <= g;   **State Cnew**
  q = r * s;

One might observe that a designer can recognize these opportunities for optimization and could perform them. In fact, a designer could rewrite the descriptions as we have to specify different schedulings of operations to control states. However, a behavioral synthesis tool, given one of these specifications, can *rapidly* suggest alternate implementations that exhibit different trade-offs. The designer can select from the most appropriate. Not all behavioral synthesis tools can make all of these transformations. Your mileage may vary.

References: always 2.1; thread of control 2.1; input set 6.3.1

7.2.3 **Specifying the Reset Function**

The example discussed above is expanded here in Example 7.3 to include a specification for the behavior of the circuit when it is reset. Module accumulate has ports for the output (**qout**), ports for the inputs (**r** and **s**), as well as the special inputs for the system (**clock** and **reset**).

The reset function for the always block is specified by an initial statement. Here we have specified an asynchronous reset that is asserted low. The initial block begins by waiting for a negative edge on **reset**. When that occurs, the **main** block in the always is disabled, **qout** is set to 0, and the next negative edge of **reset** is waited for. This action causes the named begin-end block (**main**) to exit. When it exits, the always restarts it again and waits for **reset** to be TRUE (unasserted). At some point, **reset** becomes unasserted and the system will be in state **A**; at the first clock event, the system will transit from state **A** to state **B**. Note, though, that **qout** has been initialized to 0 through the reset, and the system will begin accumulating values from 0. The functionality described is captured by the Verilog description and illustrated by the state transition diagram in Example 7.3.

```
module accumulate (qout, r, s, clock, reset);
        output  [11:0]  qout;
        input   [11:0]  r, s;
        input           clock, reset;
        reg     [11:0]  qout, q;

        initial
            forever @(negedge reset) begin
                disable main;
                qout <= 0;
            end

        always begin : main
            wait (reset);
            @ (posedge clock)
                q <= r + s;
            @ (posedge clock)
                qout <= q + qout;
        end
endmodule
```

Example 7.3 Specifying the Reset Functionality

There are a few points to note. If **reset** is unasserted, the behavior of the always block is that of the example in the previous section. Reset could have been specified as asserted-high by waiting for the positive edge of **reset** in the initial block, and then waiting for ~**reset** in the always block. Finally, no action can be specified between the "wait(reset);" and the "@(posedge clock)". Such an action can't be part of state B because it would have to be conditioned by the **reset** — an action not normally allowed in finite state machine design. Any such action there would have to be implemented as another state executing when reset becomes unasserted and a clock event would be needed so that it would clearly be part of a state. Thus a clock event always follows the wait for an unasserted reset.

Our full, cycle-accurate specification of a system now includes both the always and initial blocks. Together these specify a thread of control and how that thread is reset into a known state. When discussing the input and output sets of an always block at this level of design, it is more accurate to consider both the always and initial blocks together. Analyze only the always block to determine the sets. The initial block only specifies the reset behavior.

7.3 Mealy/Moore Machine Specifications

Examples in the previous sections described the basics of modeling systems using the cycle-accurate approach. This section illustrates how these descriptions can be used as input to behavioral synthesis tools.

The examples illustrate several features in specification for behavioral synthesis. First, the placement of the clock events is arbitrary. They may be placed in conditionals, and there may be different numbers of them in different conditional control paths. That is, each branch of an if-then-else need not have an equivalent number of states. Arbitrary placement of clock events in conditionals and loops allows the specification of very complicated state transitions. For instance, you may traverse into several nested loops before coming to a clock event. The only restriction on their placement is that a loop body must have at least one clock event specifier; it can be anywhere in the loop body.

7.3.1 A Complex Control Specification

Example 7.4 specifies an interpolating 3rd order FIR filter that samples its input (**in**) either every second or fourth clock period. Based on the sampled input, a new output value **y** is calculated. This value will appear on the output either two or four clock periods in the future. The interpolated values for either one or three intermediate clock periods are calculated as the difference between the new value (**out**) and the previous value of **y** (**yold**). This is stored in **delta** and divided by two. If **switch** is equal to zero, **delta** is added to **yold** (also named **out**) to produce the single interpolated output in the next state. If **switch** is equal to 1, **delta** is divided by two again and used to produce the interpolated outputs for the next three states.

In the example, the final value of **delta** in **state** A depends on whether the then path of the if statement is taken. That is, the control signals to the data path depend on state information (we're in state A) as well as the system input **switch**. This requires a Mealy machine implementation.

Note that when writing to elements in the output set (in this case, **out**), a non-blocking assignment is used. This removes any problems with race conditions with any other assignments. All of the other assignments are blocking, allowing the values assigned in one statement to be used in the next statements.

7.3.2 Data and Control Path Trade-offs

In this section we consider two descriptions of an 8-point FIR filter specified for behavioral synthesis using the cycle-accurate approach. In Example 7.5, arrays **coef_array** and **x_array** are used to store the coefficients and previous inputs respec-

```
module synSwitchFilter (Clock, reset, in, switch, out);
    input               Clock, reset, switch;
    input      [7:0]    in;
    output     [7:0]    out;
    reg        [7:0]    out, x1, x2, x3, y, yold, delta;

    initial forever @(negedge reset) begin
        disable main;
        out = 0;
        y = 1;
        x2 = 2;
        x3 = 3;
    end

    always begin :main
        wait (reset);
        @(posedge Clock)
        x1 = in;
        out <= y;
        yold = y;
        y = x1 + x2 + x3;                        State A
        delta = y - yold;
        delta = delta >> 1;
        if (switch == 1) begin
            delta = delta >> 1;
            @(posedge Clock) out <= out + delta;
            @(posedge Clock) out <= out + delta;
        end
        @(posedge Clock) out <= out + delta;
        x3 = x2;
        x2 = x1;
    end
endmodule
```

Example 7.4 Specification for Behavioral Synthesis

tively. The filter reads a sample x every eight clock cycles and produces a result y every
eight cycles. Examples 7.5 and 7.6 produce the same simulation results but represent
different implementations.

Module **firFilt** in Example 7.5 takes two states to specify the FIR algorithm. The
first state (**A**) determines initial values for the accumulator (**acc**), and the **x_array**
value. In addition, the **index** is initialized to the starting position (**start_pos**). The second state (**B**) executes the body and end-condition check for the loop. Thus it has two

next states. The loop body will always generate new values for **acc** and **index**. If the loop is exited, based on the updated value of **index**, a new value of the output **y** and the next starting position (**start_pos**) in the array are also generated. A disable statement is used to specify a test-at-the-end loop. When synthesized, the datapath and a two-state controller will be generated.

```
module firFilt (clock, reset, x, y);
      input              clock, reset;
      input    [7:0]     x;
      output   [7:0]     y;

      reg      [7:0]     coef_array [7:0];
      reg      [7:0]     x_array [7:0];
      reg      [7:0]     acc, y;

      reg      [2:0]     index, start_pos;
                         //important: these roll over from 7 to 0

      initial
         forever @ (negedge reset) begin
               disable firmain;
               start_pos = 0;
         end

      always begin: firmain
         wait (reset);
         @ (posedge clock);              // State A;
         x_array[start_pos] = x;
         acc = x * coef_array[start_pos];
         index = start_pos + 1;
         begin :loop1
               forever begin
                     @ (posedge clock);    // State B;
                     acc = acc + x_array[index] * coef_array[index];
                     index = index + 1;
                     if (index == start_pos) disable loop1;
               end
         end // loop1
         y <= acc;
         start_pos = start_pos + 1;
      end
endmodule
```

Example 7.5 Basic FIR

When using cycle-accurate specification, only one non-blocking assignment is made to any member of the output set in a state. If two such assignments were made to a register, its final value would be indeterminate.

The state transition diagram of Example 7.5 is shown on the left-hand side of Figure 7.3. Along with the conditionals, only the names of the registers that are written in the state are shown; the actual expression is not shown. The state transition diagram is quite straight-forward.

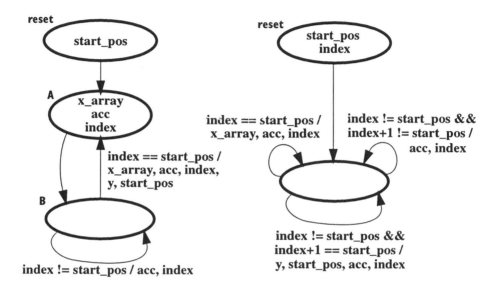

Figure 7.3 State Transition Diagrams for Examples 7.5 (left) and 7.6 (right)

Module **firFiltMealy** in Example 7.6 is a one-state specification of the FIR algorithm. As is typical with Mealy machine implementations, actions are encoded on the different next state arcs of the finite state machine. Here, the actions of **firFilt** above are so encoded. **firFiltMealy** shows three separate actions that can occur; all with the same next state (which is the current state). The first action is the then part of the first if statement. This corresponds to the initialization of the loop in **firFilt**. The second action is the else part, which actually has two possible actions. The first action, where **loop1** is not disabled, updates **acc** and **index** and corresponds to the loop body of **fir-filt**. The second action updates **acc** and **index**, but also updates **y** and **start_pos**. This corresponds to exiting the loop in module **firFilt**. Interesting, when **firFiltMealy** is synthesized, there is no identifiable finite state machine. All actions are conditioned by the comparison of registers **index** and **start_pos**; only datapath registers are clocked.

The state transition diagram for Example 7.6 is shown on the right-hand side of Figure 7.3. The same notation is used here; only the register name that are written are shown. In this case, the next state arc transited depends on the current value of index and also the updated value of index. This updated value is shown here as **index+1**.

These examples illustrate the control a designer has in specifying complex control structures.

7.4 **Summary**

This chapter has described the use Verilog as the input to behavioral synthesis tools. Input to these tools uses the cycle-accurate style of specification. Since synthesis technology is still young, the restrictions on the language styles will evolve. The user manual for the tools must be consulted.

```
module firFiltMealy (clock, reset, x, y);
    input           clock, reset;
    input   [7:0]   x;
    output  [7:0]   y;

    reg     [7:0]   coef_array [7:0];
    reg     [7:0]   x_array [7:0];
    reg     [7:0]   acc, y;
    reg     [2:0]   index, start_pos;

    initial
        forever @ (negedge reset) begin
            disable firmain;
            start_pos = 0;
            index = 0;
        end

    always begin: firmain
        wait (reset);
        begin: loop1
            forever begin
                @ (posedge clock);      // State 1 — the only state
                if (index == start_pos) begin
                    x_array[index] = x;
                    acc = x * coef_array[index];
                    index = index + 1;
                end
                else begin
                    acc = acc + x_array[index] * coef_array[index];
                    index = index + 1;
                    if (index == start_pos) disable loop1;
                end
            end
        end
        y <= acc;
        start_pos = start_pos + 1;
        index = start_pos;
    end
endmodule
```

Example 7.6 Mealy FIR

8 | User-Defined Primitives

Verilog provides a set of 26 gate level primitives for modeling the actual logic implementation of a digital system. From these primitives, presented in Chapter 4, larger structural models may be hierarchically described. This chapter presents an advanced method for extending the set of gate level primitives to include user-defined combinational, and level- and edge-sensitive sequential circuits.

There are several reasons for wanting to extend the set of gate level primitives. First, user-defined primitives are a very compact and efficient way of describing a possibly arbitrary block of logic. Secondly, it is possible to reduce the pessimism with respect to the unknown x value in the simulator's three valued logic, thus creating more realistic models for certain situations. Finally, simulation efficiency may be gained through their use. Note, however, that these may not be used to specify designs for logic synthesis.

8.1 **Combinational Primitives**

8.1.1 **Basic Features of User-Defined Primitives**

As shown in Example 8.1, user-defined primitives are defined in a manner similar to a truth table enumeration of a logic function. Primitives are defined at the same lexical

```
primitive carry(carryOut, carryIn, aIn, bIn);
output   carryOut;
input    carryIn,
         aIn,
         bIn;

   table
      0    00  :  0;
      0    01  :  0;
      0    10  :  0;
      0    11  :  1;
      1    00  :  0;
      1    01  :  1;
      1    10  :  1;
      1    11  :  1;
   endtable
endprimitive
```

Example 8.1 A User-Defined Combinational Primitive

level as modules. i.e. primitives are not defined within modules. This example describes a primitive for generating the carry out of a single-bit full adder. **carryOut** is the output, and **carryIn**, **aIn**, and **bIn** are the inputs. A table is then specified showing the value of the output for the various combinations of the inputs. A colon separates the output on its right from the inputs on its left. The order of inputs in the table description must correspond to the order of inputs in the port list of the primitive definition statement. Reading from the fourth line of the table, if **carryIn** was 0, **aIn** was 1, and **bIn** was 1, then **carryOut** would be 1.

There are a number of rules that must be considered:

- Primitives have multiple input ports, but exactly one output port. They may not have bidirectional inout ports.
- The output port must be the first port in the port list.
- All primitive ports are scalar. No vector ports are allowed.

- Only logic values of 1, 0, and x are allowed on input and output. The z value cannot be specified, although on input, it is treated as an x.

The user-defined primitives act the same as other gate primitives and continuous assign statements. When one of their inputs changes, then the new output is determined from the table and is propagated on the output. The input values in a row of the table must correspond exactly to the values of the input ports for the row's output value to be selected. If a set of inputs appears on the ports for which there is no exact match, then the output will default to x. Any time delay to be associated with the primitive is specified when instances of the primitive are defined. Because primitives cannot generate the value z, only two delays (rising and falling) can be specified per instance.

As can be seen, the definition of a user-defined primitive follows closely the definition of a module. However, the keyword primitive introduces the definition and the keyword endprimitive closes it. Declarations within a primitive can only be inputs, outputs, and registers (i.e. no inouts).

udp_declaration
      ::= **primitive** *udp*_identifier (udp_port_list);
            udp_port_declaration { udp_port_declaration }
            udp_body
            endprimitive

udp_port_list
      ::= *output_port*_identifier , *input_port*_identifier {, *input_port*_identifier }

udp_port_ declaration
      ::= output_declaration
      | input_declaration
      | reg_declaration

Beyond this point, the primitive definition departs greatly from that of a module definition. The primitive has no internal instantiations, assign statements, or always statements. (However, sequential primitives may have initial statements.) Rather, the primitive requires a table definition whose syntax is partially detailed below.

udp_body
      ::= combinational_body
      | sequential_body

combinational_body
      ::= **table**
            combinational_entry { combinational_entry }
            endtable

combinational_entry
    ::= level_input_list : output_symbol ;

sequential_body
    ::= [udp_initial_statement]
            table_sequential_entry {sequential_entry }
            endtable

udp_initial_statement
    ::= **initial** *udp_output_port*_identifier = init_val ;

References: sequential primitives 8.2

8.1.2 **Describing Combinational Logic Circuits**

The usefulness of Example 8.1 might be rather low as nothing is stated about what happens when there is an unknown (x) input on any of the inputs. Since the table made no mention of what happens when there is an x input, the output of the primitive will be x. This is rather pessimistic in that if the other two inputs were both 1, then the output should be 1 regardless of the third input.

The table enumeration allows for the specification of 1, 0, and x values in its input and output sections. Further, it allows for the specification of a don't care in the table meaning that any of the three logic values are to be substituted for it when evaluating the inputs. Consider the expanded definition of the carry primitive shown in Example 8.2. Here, the last six lines of the table specify the output in the presence of unknown inputs. For instance (third line from bottom of table), if **carryIn** and **aIn** were 1, and **bIn** was x, then **carryOut** will be 1 regardless of the value of **bIn**. Of course, if there were two unknowns on the inputs to this gate, then the output would be unknown since there is no table entry specifying what to do in that case.

The table may be abbreviated using the ? symbol to indicate iterative substitution of 0, 1, and x. Essentially, the ? allows for us to state that we don't care what a certain value is, the other inputs will specify the output. The carry primitive example can be rewritten more compactly as shown in Example 8.3.

We can read any line of the table in two ways. Taking the first line of the table as an example, we can state that if the first two inputs are both zero, then the third input can be considered a don't care and the output will be zero. Second, we can mentally triplicate the line substituting in values of 0, 1, and x for the ?. The shorthand provided by the don't care symbol improves the readability of the specification remarkably.

```
primitive carryX(carryOut, carryIn, aIn, bIn);
output   carryOut;
input    aIn,
         bIn,
         carryIn;

    table
        0    00  :   0;
        0    01  :   0;
        0    10  :   0;
        0    11  :   1;
        1    00  :   0;
        1    01  :   1;
        1    10  :   1;
        1    11  :   1;
        0    0x  :   0;
        0    x0  :   0;
        x    00  :   0;
        1    1x  :   1;
        1    x1  :   1;
        x    11  :   1;
    endtable
endprimitive
```

Example 8.2 A Carry Primitive

8.2 **Sequential Primitives**

In addition to describing combinational devices, user-defined primitives may be used to describe sequential devices which exhibit level- and edge-sensitive properties. Since they are sequential devices, they have internal state that must be modeled with a register variable and a state column must be added to the table specifying the behavior of the primitive. The output of the device is driven directly by the register. The output field in the table in the primitive definition specifies the next state.

The level- and edge-sensitive primitives are harder to describe correctly because they tend to have far more combinations than normal combinational logic. This should be evident from the number of edge combinations that must be defined. Should any of the edges go unspecified, the output will become unknown (x). Thus, care should be taken to describe all combinations of levels and edges, reducing the pessimism.

```
primitive carryAbbrev (carryOut, carryIn, aIn, bIn);
output  carryOut;
input   aIn,
        bIn,
        carryIn;

    table
        0   0?  :  0;
        0   ?0  :  0;
        ?   00  :  0;
        ?   11  :  1;
        1   ?1  :  1;
        1   1?  :  1;
    endtable
endprimitive
```

Example 8.3 A Carry Primitive With Shorthand Notation

8.2.1 Level-Sensitive Primitives

The level-sensitive behavior of a latch is shown in Example 8.4. The latch output holds its value when the **clock** is one, and tracks the input when the **clock** is zero.

```
primitive latch (q, clock, data);
output  q;
reg     q;
input   clock, data;
    table
//          clock  data state output
            0      1   :?:   1;
            0      0   :?:   0;
            1      ?   :?:   -;
    endtable
endprimitive
```

Example 8.4 A User-Defined Sequential Primitive

Notable differences between combinational and sequential device specification are the state specification (surrounded by colons), and a register specification for the output.

To understand the behavior specification, consider the first row. When the **clock** is zero and the **data** is a one, then when the state is zero, one or **x** (as indicated by the ?), the output is one. Thus, no matter what the state is, the output (next state) depends only on the input. Line two makes a similar statement for having zero on the **data** input.

If the **clock** input is one, then no matter what the **data** input is (zero, one, or **x**) there will be no change in the output (next state). This "no change" is signified by the minus sign in the output column.

8.2.2 **Edge-Sensitive Primitives**

The table entries for modeling edge-sensitive behavior are similar to those for level-sensitive behavior except that a rising or falling edge must be specified on one of the inputs. It is illegal to specify more than one edge per line of the table. Example 8.5 illustrates the basic notation with the description of an edge-triggered D-type flip flop.

```
primitive dEdgeFF (q, clock, data);
output   q;
reg      q;
input    clock, data;

      table
//       clock   data   state   output
         (01)     0     : ? :     0;
         (01)     1     : ? :     1;
         (0x)     1     : 1 :     1;
         (0x)     0     : 0 :     0;
         (?0)     ?     : ? :     -;
          ?      (??)   : ? :     -;
      endtable
   endprimitive
```

Example 8.5 Edge-Sensitive Behavior

The terms in parentheses represent the edge transitions of the clock variable. The first line indicates that on the rising edge of the **clock** (01) when the **data** input is zero, the next state (as indicated in the output column) will be a zero. This will occur regardless of the value of the current state. Line two of the table specifies the results of having a one at the **data** input when a rising edge occurs; the output will become one.

If the **clock** input goes from zero to don't care (zero, one, or **x**) and the **data** input and state are one, then the output will become one. Any unspecified combinations of transitions and inputs will cause the output to become **x**.

The second to the last line specifies that on the falling edge of the **clock**, there is no change to the output. The last line indicates that if the **clock** line is steady at either zero, one, or **x**, and the data changes, then there is no output change.

Similar to the combinational user-defined primitive, the primitive definition is very similar to that of a module. Following is the formal syntax for the sequential entries in a table within the primitive.

udp_body
        ::=   combinational_body
        | sequential_body

combinational_body
        ::= **table**
              combinational_entry { combinational_entry }
              endtable

combinational_entry
        ::= level_input_list : output_symbol ;   // see section 8.1

sequential_body
        ::= [udp_initial_statement]
              table_sequential_entry {sequential_entry }
              endtable

udp_initial_statement
        ::= **initial** *udp_output_port*_identifier = init_val ;

init_val
        ::= **1'b0 | 1'b1 | 1'bx | 1'bX | 1'B0 | 1'B1 | 1'Bx | 1'BX | 1 | 0**

sequential_entry
        ::= seq_input_list : current_state : next_state ;

seq_input_list
        ::= level_input_list
        | edge_input_list

level_input_list
        ::= level_symbol { level_symbol }

edge_input_list
        ::= { level_symbol } edge_indicator { level_symbol }

edge_indicator
        ::= (level_symbol level_symbol)
        | edge_symbol   //see section 8.3

current_state
     ::= level_symbol

next_state
     ::= output_symbol
     | -   // a literal hyphen, see text

References: combinational primitives 8.1; edge symbols 8.3

8.3 **Shorthand Notation**

Example 8.6 is another description of the edge-triggered flip flop in Example 8.5 except that this one is written using some of Verilog's shorthand notation for edge conditions.

```
primitive dEdgeFFShort (q, clock, data);
output   q;
reg      q;
input    clock, data;

        table
//      clock      data  state  output
          r          0   : ? :   0;
          r          1   : ? :   1;
         (0x)        0   : 1 :   1;
         (0x)        1   : 1 :   1;
         (?0)        ?   : ? :   -;
          ?          *   : ? :   -;
        endtable
endprimitive
```

Example 8.6 Edge -Sensitive Behavior With Shorthand Notation

The symbol "r" in the table stands for rising edge or (zero to one), and "*" indicates any change, effectively substituting for "(??)". Table 8.1 lists all of the shorthand specifications used in tables for user-defined primitives.

Table 8.1 Summary of Shorthand Notation

Symbol	Interpretation	Comments
0	Logic 0	
1	Logic 1	
x	Unknown	
?	Iteration of 0, 1, and x	Cannot be used in output field
b	Iteration of 0 and 1	Cannot be used in output field
-	No change	May only be given in the output field of a sequential primitive
(vw)	Change of value from v to w	v and w can be any one of 0, 1, x, or b
*	Same as (??)	Any value change on input
r	Same as (01)	Rising edge on input
f	Same as (10)	Falling edge on input
p	Iteration of (01), (0x), and (x1)	Positive edge including x
n	Iteration of (10), (1x), and (x0)	Negative edge including x

8.4 **Mixed Level- and Edge-Sensitive Primitives**

It is quite common to mix both level- and edge-sensitive behavior in a user-defined primitive. Consider the edge-sensitive JK flip flop with asynchronous clear and preset shown in Example 8.7

In this example, the **preset** and **clear** inputs are level-sensitive. The **preset** section of the table specifies that when **preset** is zero and **clear** is one, the output will be one. Further, if there are any transitions (as specified by the "*") on the **preset** input and **clear** and the internal state are all ones, then the output will be one. The **clear** section of the table makes a similar specification for the clear **input**.

The table then specifies the normal clocking situations. The first five lines specify the normal JK operations of holding a value, setting a zero, setting a one, and toggling. The last line states that no change will occur on a falling edge of the **clock**.

The **j** and **k** transition cases specify that if the **clock** is a one or zero, then a transition on either **j** or **k** will not change the output.

```
primitive jkEdgeFF (q, clock, j, k, preset, clear);
output   q;
reg      q;
input    clock, j, k, preset, clear;

    table
    //clock  jk   pc     state  output
    // preset logic
        ?     ??   01     : ? :    1;
        ?     ??   *1     : 1 :    1;

    // clear logic
        ?     ??   10     : ? :    0;
        ?     ??   1*     : 0 :    0;

    // normal clocking cases
        r     00   11     : ? :    -;
        r     01   11     : ? :    0;
        r     10   11     : ? :    1;
        r     11   11     : 0 :    1;
        r     11   11     : 1 :    0;
        f     ??   ??     : ? :    -;

    // j and k transition cases
        b     *?   ??     : ? :    -;
        b     ?*   ??     : ? :    -;

    //cases reducing pessimism
        p     00   11     : ? :    -;
        p     0?   1?     : 0 :    -;
        p     ?0   ?1     : 1 :    -;
        (x0)  ??   ??     : ? :    -;
        (1x)  00   11     : ? :    -;
        (1x)  0?   1?     : 0 :    -;
        (1x)  ?0   ?1     : 1 :    -;
        x     *0   ?1     : 1 :    -;
        x     0*   1?     : 0 :    -;
    endtable
endprimitive
```

Example 8.7 A JK Flip Flop

Finally, we have the cases that reduce the pessimism of the example by specifying outputs for more situations. The first three lines include the full set of rising-edge cases, i.e. those **clock** edges including **x**. Following these, the next four lines make further specifications on when a negative edge including **x** occurs on the **clock**. Finally, the specification for **clock** having the value **x** is given. In all of these "pessimism reducing" cases, we have specified no change to the output.

There are times when an edge-sensitive and level-sensitive table entry will conflict with each other. The general rule is that when the input and current state conditions of both a level-sensitive table row and an edge-sensitive table row specify conflicting next-states, the level-sensitive entry will dominate the edge-sensitive entry. Consider the table entry in Example 8.7:

```
//clock  jk   pc    state  output
   ?      ??   01    : ? :    1;        // Case A
```

which includes the case:

```
   1      00   01    : 0 :    1;        // Case B
```

Another entry:

```
   f      ??   ??    : ? :    -;        // Case C
```

includes the case:

```
   f      00   01    : 0 :    0;        // Case D
```

Case B is a level-sensitive situation and case D is an edge-sensitive situation, but they define conflicting next state values for the same input combinations. In these two cases, the **j, k, p,** and **c** inputs are the same. Case B states that when the **clock** is one and the state is zero, then the next state is one. However, case D states that when there is a one to zero transition on the **clock** and the state is zero, then the next state is zero. But for a falling edge to be on the **clock** with the other inputs as given, the **clock** must just previously have been one and thus the next state should have already changed to one, and not zero. In all cases, the level-sensitive specification dominates and the next state will be one.

8.5 Summary

The user-defined primitives represent an advanced capability in the language for specifying combinational and sequential logic primitives. The specifications are efficient and compact and allow for the reduction of pessimism with respect to the **x** value.

8.6 **Exercises**

8.1 Write combinational user defined primitives that are equivalent to:

A. the predefined 3-input XOR gate,

B. the equation ~((a & b) | (c & d)), and

C. the multiplexor illustrated as follows:

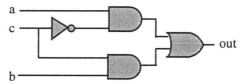

Try to reduce pessimism in the multiplexor description when the select line is unknown.

8.2 Try to reduce the pessimism in Example 8.4 for cases when the clock becomes unknown. Can more entries in Example 8.5 be given to further reduce pessimism?

8.3 Write a sequential user defined primitive of a simple two input positive edge triggered toggle flip flop with an asynchronous clear input.

8.4 Write a combinational user defined primitive of a strobed difference detector. The device is to have 3 inputs: **inA**, **inB** and strobe, such that when strobe is 1, **inA** is compared with **inB**. The output should be 0 when **inA** equals **inB**, and 1 when the comparison fails. When **inB** is unknown this indicates a don't-care situation such that regardless of the value of **inA** the output is a 0.

8.5 Develop a gate level description of an edge-sensitive JK flip flop with asynchronous clear and preset, and compare it against the user defined primitive in Example 8.7 with respect to pessimism from the unknown value.

9 Switch Level Modeling

Designs at the logic level of abstraction, describe a digital circuit in terms of primitive logic functions such as OR, and NOR, etc., and allow for the nets interconnecting the logic functions to carry 0, 1, **x** and **z** values. At the analog-transistor level of modeling, we use an electronic model of the circuit elements and allow for analog values of voltages or currents to represent logic values on the interconnections.

The switch level of modeling provides a level of abstraction between the logic and analog-transistor levels of abstraction, describing the interconnection of transmission gates which are abstractions of individual MOS and CMOS transistors. The switch level transistors are modeled as being either on or off, conducting or not conducting. Further, the values carried by the interconnections are abstracted from the whole range of analog voltages or currents to a small number of discrete values. These values are referred to as signal *strengths*.

9.1 A Dynamic MOS Shift Register Example

We began our discussion of logic level modeling in Chapter 4 by listing the primitive set of gates provided by the Verilog language (the list is reproduced as Table 9.1).

At the time, only the logic level primitives were discussed. We can see from the switch level primitives, shown in the right three columns of the table, that they all model individual MOS/CMOS transistors.

Table 9.1 Gate and Switch Level Primitives

n_input gates	n_output gates	tristate gates	pull gates	MOS switches	bidirec- tional switches
and	buf	bufif0	pullup	nmos	tran
nand	not	bufif1	pulldown	pmos	tranif0
nor		notif0		cmos	tranif1
or		notif1		rnmos	rtran
xor				rpmos	rtranif0
xnor				rcmos	rtranif1

Figure 9.1 illustrates the differences in modeling at the switch and logic levels. The circuit is a three stage, inverting shift register controlled by two phases of a clock. The relative timing of the clock phases is also shown in the figure. The Verilog description is shown in Example 9.1.

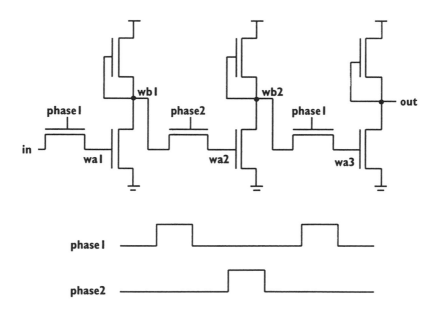

Figure 9.1 MOS Shift Register and Clock Phases

```
module shreg (out, in, phase1, phase2);
/* IO port declarations, where 'out' is the inverse
of 'in' controlled by the dual-phased clock */

        output   out;      //shift register output
        input    in,       //shift register input
                 phase1, //clocks
                 phase2;

        tri      wb1, wb2, out;      //tri nets pulled up to VDD
        pullup   (wb1), (wb2), (out);//depletion mode pullup devices

        trireg   (medium) wa1, wa2, wa3; //charge storage nodes

        supply0      gnd;          //ground supply

        nmos #3      //pass devices and their interconnections
                 a1(wa1, in, phase1), b1(wb1, gnd, wa1),
                 a2(wa2, wb1, phase2), b2(wb2, gnd, wa2),
                 a3(wa3, wb2, phase1), gout(out, gnd, wa3);
endmodule
```

Example 9.1 MOS Shift Register

The circuit consists only of **nmos** transistors and depletion mode pullup transistors interconnected by nets of type tri and trireg. *tri* nets model tristate nets. In this example, tri nets **wb1, wb2,** and **out** are pulled up to VDD through the declaration of three unnamed pullup gates.

Three trireg nets, **wa1, wa2,** and **wa3,** are declared. Trireg nets are different from other types of nets in that they store a value when all gates driving the net have turned off. That is, a driver can drive them (i.e. charge them) and then turn off. The value driven will remain on the trireg net even though it is no longer being driven. These nets are used in this example to model the dynamic storage of the shift register stages. The declaration of the nets shows them being given the *medium* capacitor strength (which also happens to be the default).

A net of type supply0 is defined and named **gnd,** modeling a connection to the ground terminal of the power supply. Finally, the nmos pass transistors are instantiated and connected, completing the shift register definition.

It is instructive to evoke the inputs to the shift register model and follow its simulation output. The module in Example 9.2 instantiates a copy of the **shreg** module

```
module waveShReg;
    wire    shiftout;        //net to receive circuit output value
    reg     shiftin;         //register to drive value into circuit
    reg     phase1, phase2;  //clock driving values

    parameter   d = 100;   //define the waveform time step

    shreg   cct (shiftout, shiftin, phase1, phase2);

    initial
        begin :main
            shiftin = 0;    //initialize waveform input stimulus
            phase1 = 0;
            phase2 = 0;
            setmon;         // setup the monitoring information
            repeat(2)       //shift data in
                clockcct;
        end

    task setmon;     //display header and setup monitoring
        begin
            $display("            time   clks   in out wa1-3 wb1-2");
            $monitor ($time,,,,phase1, phase2,,,,,,shiftin,,,, shiftout,,,,,
                cct.wa1, cct.wa2, cct.wa3,,,,,cct.wb1, cct.wb2);
        end
    endtask

    task clockcct;     //produce dual-phased clock pulse
        begin
            #d phase1 = 1; //time step defined by parameter d
            #d phase1 = 0;
            #d phase2 = 1;
            #d phase2 = 0;
        end
    endtask
endmodule
```

Example 9.2 Simulating the MOS Shift Register

described in Example 9.1, drives its inputs and monitors its outputs. Table 9.2 lists the output from the simulation of this example.

Module **waveShReg** initializes **shiftin, phase1,** and **phase2** to zero, prints a header line for the output table, and then sets up the monitoring of certain nets within instance **cct** of module **shreg**. Note that the nets within instance **cct** are referenced with the hierarchical naming convention (e.g. "cct.wb1"). The **clockcct** task is executed twice, evoking actions within the shift register. After two iterations of **clockcct**, the simulation is finished.

Table 9.2 lists the output from the simulation. Initially, the outputs are all unknown. After 100 time units the **phase1** clock is set to one. This enables the pass transistor to conduct and the zero value at the input to be driven onto trireg net **wa1** after one gate delay. After one more gate delay, tri net **wb1** becomes one because transistor **b1** is cutoff and **wb1** is connected to a pullup. No more gate action occurs until the **phase1** clock goes to zero at time 200. At this point, we see the value on trireg net **wa1** persisting even though there is no driver for that net. The **phase2** clock then becomes 1 and the value on **wb1** is transferred to **wa2**, driving transistor **b2** and net **wb2** to zero. **Phase2** is lowered and **phase1** is raised, shifting the bit to **wa3**, making the complement of the original input available at the output. (Note that charge will remain on a net indefinitely unless there is a three-delay specifier placed on the net — the first being the delay to one, the second is the delay to zero, and the last is the delay to x.)

References: Verilog gates D; strengths 9.2

Table 9.2 Results of Simulating the MOS Shift Register

time	clks	in	out	wa1-3	wb1-2
0	00	0	x	xxx	xx
100	10	0	x	xxx	xx
103	10	0	x	0xx	xx
106	10	0	x	0xx	1x
200	00	0	x	0xx	1x
300	01	0	x	0xx	1x
303	01	0	x	01x	1x
306	01	0	x	01x	10
400	00	0	x	01x	10
500	10	0	x	01x	10
503	10	0	x	010	10
506	10	0	1	010	10
600	00	0	1	010	10
700	01	0	1	010	10

9.2 **Switch Level Modeling**

Switch level modeling allows for the *strength* of a driving gate and the size of the capacitor storing charge on a trireg net to be modeled. This capability provides for more accurate simulation of the electrical properties of the transistors than would a logic simulation.

9.2.1 **Strength Modeling**

Consider the description of a static RAM cell shown in Example 9.3 and Figure 9.2. Among other declarations, two NOT gates are instantiated, each with a "pull" drive strength; *pull0* for the zero output strength, and *pull1* for the one output strength. The pull drive strength is one of the possible strengths available in Verilog. It is weaker than the default *strong* drive which models a typical active drive gate output.

   In the example, the two NOT gates form a feedback loop that latches a value driven on **w4** through the tranif1 gate. The *tranif1* gate is a transfer gate that conducts when its control input (**address** in this case) is one, and is nonconducting otherwise. The bufif1 gate is the read/write control for the circuit. In read mode, the bufif1 control line (**write**) is zero and its output is high impedance. When the cell is addressed, the value in the latch is connected to the output buffer **g5**. In write mode when the cell is addressed, the bufif1 gate drives **w4** through the tranif1 gate, possibly changing the latch's state.

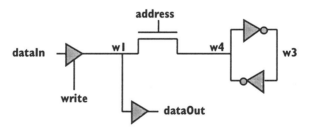

Figure 9.2 A Static RAM Cell

   Example 9.3 also shows a Verilog module that will evoke the **sram** module and print out the state of the nets in the circuit. The output is shown in Table 9.3 in a tabular form. The method of modeling in this example shows us a static view of the circuit; values are printed out after the "minor" gate changes have occurred. (Note: The actual printout from simulating Example 9.3 has been edited for display in Table 9.3. Only the values printed are shown; the textual information such as "addr=" has been omitted. This is also true of Tables 9.6 and 9.8. In addition, the three values for **w134** are not shown in Table 9.3.)

```
module sram (dataOut, address, dataIn, write);
    output   dataOut;
    input    address, dataIn, write;
    tri      w1, w3, w4, w43;

    bufif1              g1(w1, dataIn, write);
    tranif1             g2(w4, w1, address);
    not (pull0, pull1)  g3(w3, w4), g4(w4, w3);
    buf                 g5(dataOut, w1);
endmodule

module wave_sram;        //waveform for testing the static RAM cell
    wire     dataOut;
    reg      address, dataIn, write;

    sram cell (dataOut, address, dataIn, write);

    parameter d = 100;
    initial begin
        #d dis;
        #d address = 1;      #d dis;
        #d dataIn = 1;       #d dis;
        #d write = 1;        #d dis;
        #d write = 0;        #d dis;
        #d write = 'bx;      #d dis;
        #d address = 'bx;    #d dis;
        #d address = 1;      #d dis;
        #d write = 0;        #d dis;
    end

    task dis;     //display the circuit state
        $display($time,, "addr=%v d_In=%v write=%v d_out=%v",
            address, dataIn, write, dataOut,
            " (134)=%b%b%b", cell.w1, cell.w3, cell.w4,
            " w134=%v %v %v", cell.w1, cell.w3, cell.w4);
    endtask
endmodule
```

Example 9.3 A Static RAM Cell

Table 9.3 Results of Simulating Static RAM

time	addr	d_in	wr	d_out	134	Comments
100	x	x	x	x	xxx	
300	1	x	x	x	xxx	
500	1	1	x	x	xxx	
700	1	1	1	1	101	write function
900	1	1	0	1	101	read function
1100	1	1	x	1	101	
1300	x	1	x	x	x01	ram holds value
1500	1	1	x	1	101	
1700	1	1	0	1	101	read function

Note first that all values in the circuit start at **x**. By time 500, the **dataIn** and **address** value are both 1. The tranif1 gate will transfer values in both directions. The bufif1 gate, having an **x** on its control input, is driving its output to level H (meaning 1 or **z**). Since this table only shows the Boolean values (as specified with the %b in the $display statement) we see an **x** on the bufif1 output **w1**.

At time 700, the **write** line has been one for 100 time units, driving **w1** and **dataOut** to a one. Since the tranif1 gate is conducting, **w1** and **w4** are connected. At this point, we have gate **g4** (the NOT gate) and **g1** (the bufif1 gate) both driving these connected lines. However, since **g4** has been defined to have driving strength *pull0* and *pull1* in the zero and one states respectively, its drive strength is not as strong as the bufif gate which has the default *strong* drive strengths. In this case, the strong drive overwhelms the pull drive and **w4** follows **w1**, and **w3** becomes the complement. **w3** on the input to **g4** then completes the changing of the ram cell value.

At time 900, the **write** line is at zero, but the **address** line still selects the cell. This is the read function of the **sram** module; the **dataOut** indicates the saved state.

At time 1300, both **address** and **write** are **x**, and thus so is **w1** and **dataOut**. However, the **sram** still holds its value. By time 1700, **address** and **write** indicate the read function and the value stored earlier is again conducted through the tranif1 gate to the **dataOut**.

References: $display F.1; resistive gates 9.2.4

9.2.2 **Strength Definitions**

The above example showed two of the levels of strength available in modeling switch level circuits; Table 9.4 is a complete list. Again we can see that the strong drive of the bufif1 gate is stronger than the pull drive of the NOT gate.

Table 9.4 Strength Specifications

Strength Name	Strength Level	Element Modeled	Declaration Abbreviation	Printed Abbreviation
Supply Drive	7	Power supply connection	supply	Su
Strong Drive	6	Default gate and assign output strength	strong	St
Pull Drive	5	Gate and assign output strength	pull	Pu
Large Capacitor	4	Size of trireg net capacitor	large	La
Weak Drive	3	Gate and assign output strength	weak	We
Medium Capacitor	2	Size of trireg net capacitor	medium	Me
Small Capacitor	1	Size of trireg net capacitor	small	Sm
High Impedance	0	Not applicable	highz	Hi

There are four driving strengths and three charge storage strengths. The driving strengths are associated with gate and continuous assignment outputs, and the charge storage strengths are associated with the trireg net type. The strengths may be associated with either a 1, 0, or x value. That is, a gate may drive a weak zero, a weak one, or a weak x. The declaration abbreviation should be used with a zero or one (e.g. pull0) when gate instances and strengths are declared. The printed abbreviation column indicates how the strength is printed when the %v format is used (see later examples).

Strengths associated with gate instances and assign statements are specified within parentheses as shown in the examples and in the following formal syntax:

gate instantiation
::= n_input_gatetype [drive_strength] [delay2] n_input_gate_instance {,
      n_input_ gate_instance } ;
| ...

continuous_assign
::= **assign** [drive_strength] [delay3] list_of_net_assignments ;

drive_strength
      ::= (strength0, strength1)
      | (strength1, strength0)
      | (strength0, highly)
      | (strength1, **highz0**)
      | (**highz1**, strength0)
      | (**highz0**, strength1)

strength0
      ::= **supply0 | strong0 | pull0 | weak0**

strength1
      ::= **supply1 | strong1 | pull1 | weak1**

If the strengths are not given, then strong drives are assumed. Only the gate types shown in Table 9.5 support drive strength specifications:

Table 9.5 Gate Types Supporting Drive Strength Specifications

and	or	xor	buf	bufif0	bufif1	pullup
nand	nor	xnor	not	notif0	notif1	pulldown

When a trireg net is declared, a charge storage strength is specified to model the size of the capacitance exhibited by the net. However, charge stored in the net does not decay with time unless a three-delay specification is given. The third delay parameter specifies the time until the stored charge decays to an **x** value. Trireg declarations are a form of net specifications as shown in the formal syntax:

net_declaration
      ::= net_type [**vectored** | **scalared**] [range] [delay3] list_of_net_identifiers;
      | trireg [**vectored** | **scalared**] [charge_strength] [range] [delay3]
          list_of_net_identifiers;
      | net type [**vectored** | **scalared**] [drive strength] [range] [delay3]
          list_of_net_decl_assignrnents;

charge strength
      ::= (**small**) | (**medium**) | (**large**)

References: net declarations 4.2.3

9.2.3 **An Example Using Strengths**

We now look more closely at Example 9.3 and observe the gate strengths as they are calculated and printed. The $display statement:

```
$display ($time,,
        "address=%b dataIn=%b write=%b dataOut=%b",
         address, dataIn, write, dataOut,
        "(134)=%b%b%b", cell.w1, cell.w3, cell.w4,
        " w134=%v %v %v", cell.w1, cell.w3, cell.w4);
```

prints the w134 signals as binary numbers, using the %b control, and then as strengths, using the %v control. Table 9.6 shows the strengths printed out when using this statement. (Note that the simulation trace has been edited for display purposes.)

Table 9.6 Simulation Results Showing Strengths

time	addr	d_in	write	d_out	(134)	w134	Comments
100	StX	StX	StX	StX	xxx	StX PuX StX	
300	St1	StX	StX	StX	xxx	StX PuX StX	
500	St1	St1	StX	StX	xxx	56X PuX 56X	
700	St1	St1	St1	St1	101	St1 Pu0 St1	Write function
900	St1	St1	St0	St1	101	Pu1 Pu0 Pu1	Read function
1100	St1	St1	StX	St1	101	651 Pu0 651	
1300	StX	St1	StX	StX	x01	StH Pu0 651	
1500	St1	St1	StX	St1	101	651 Pu0 651	
1700	St1	St1	St0	St1	101	Pu1 Pu0 Pu1	Read function

The strength outputs in Table 9.6 have one of two formats. If a strength is listed with a value, then the net is being driven by that value with the specified strength. The printing abbreviations for the strengths are listed in Table 9.4. Thus **St1** indicates a strong 1, **StH** indicates a strong 1 or z, **Pu0** indicates a pull 0, and **PuX** indicates a driver of strength pull driving an **x**. If two numbers are given with the value, then the net is being driven by multiple sources and the numbers indicate the minimum and maximum strength levels (see level numbers in Table 9.4) driving the net. For instance, at time 1100, net **w1** is being driven by a strong (6) and pull (5) value one.

At time 100, all of the nets have unknown values on them, but notice that there is a strength associated with each of them corresponding to their driver's declaration. Thus, **address**, **dataIn**, **write**, **w1**, and **dataOut** are all strong-strength signals, whereas **w3** is a pull strength. **w4** is connected to **g4** which is a pull-strength gate and to the tranif1 gate. Since it is connected to more than one gate output, we would have expected to see a range of strengths driven on it. Indeed this could be the case. However, it is not the tranif1 gate driving **w4**. Rather it is the bufif1 gate driving **w4** through the tranif1. The mos gates do not have their own drive strength. They merely propagate the values and strengths at their input (with a possible reduction in strength depending on gate type and strength input).

At time 500, we see net **w1** listed as 56X, indicating that it is being driven by both a pull x and strong 1 driver. This indication arises because the bufif1 gate (strong) is driving an H (its control line is x) and the tranif1 gate is passing a pull-strength x from gate **g4**. The two combine to drive an x on **w1**. Since **w1** and **w4** are connected together through the tranif1 gate, they both have the same indication.

Following the operation of the sram at time 700, we see again that the strong strength of the bufif1 gate transmitted through the tranif1 gate overrides the value driven by **g4** onto **w4**, thus allowing for a new value to be saved. At 1300, we see that even when **address** and **write** become unknown, the **sram** still holds its value.

9.2.4 **Resistive MOS Gates**

The MOS gates can be modeled as either resistive or nonresistive devices. Nonresistive gates (nmos, pmos, cmos, tran, tranif0, and tranif1) do not effect the signal strength from input to output (i.e. between bidirectional terminals) except that a supply strength will be reduced to a strong strength. In addition, pullup and pulldown gates drive their output with a pull strength. However, when the resistive model is used (rnmos, rpmos, rcmos, rtran, rtranif0, rtranif1), then a value passing through the gate undergoes a reduction in drive strength as enumerated in Table 9.7

Table 9.7 Strength Reduction Through Resistive Transfer Gates

Input Strength	Reduced Strength
Supply Drive	Pull Drive
Strong Drive	Pull Drive
Pull Drive	Weak Drive
Weak Drive	Medium Capacitor
Large Capacitor	Medium Capacitor
Medium Capacitor	Small Capacitor
Small Capacitor	Small Capacitor
High Impedance	High Impedance

Consider another change in the **sram** specification where the tranif1 gate is declared to be a resistive transfer gate, *rtranif1*, with the following statement:

```
rtranif1
    g2(w4, w1, address);
```

Then with the detailed display statement shown in Example 9.3, we obtain the simulation results shown in Table 9.8. (Note that the simulation trace has been edited for display purposes.)

Table 9.8 Simulation Showing Strength Reduction

time	addr	d_in	write	d_out	(134)	w134	Comments
100	StX	StX	StX	StX	xxx	StX PuX StX	
300	St1	StX	StX	StX	xxx	StX PuX StX	
500	St1	St1	StX	StX	xxx	36X PuX PuX	
700	St1	St1	St1	St1	1xx	St1 PuX PuX	Write
900	St1	St1	St0	StX	xxx	WeX PuX PuX	Read
1100	St1	St1	StX	StX	xxx	36X PuX PuX	
1300	StX	St1	StX	StX	xxx	36X PuX PuX	
1500	St1	St1	StX	StX	xxx	36X PuX PuX	
1700	St1	St1	St0	StX	xxx	WeX PuX PuX	Read

Considering the values and strengths at time 500, we now see that w1 and w4 are different because they are separated by a resistive device. On w1 there is a 36x, the 6 arises from the bufif1 output driving a strong logic one and the 3 arises from g4 driving a logic zero as reduced from a pull drive (5) to a weak drive (3) by the rtranif1 gate.

It is important to note that this version of the **sram** does not work! The previous versions of the **sram** changed the stored value because the strong output of the bufif1 gate overpowered the pull output of **g4**. But in this case, the rtranif1 gate reduces the strong output to a pull output which does not overpower the output of **g4**. Thus, **g3** does not change its output and the latching mechanism comprised of **g3** and **g4** does not capture the new value.

9.3 **Ambiguous Strengths**

A possible way of representing a scalar net value is with two bytes of information; the first byte indicates the strength of the 0 portion of the net value, and the second byte indicates the strength of the 1 portion. The bit positions within each byte are numbered from most significant down to least significant. The bit position corresponds to the strength level values as given in Table 9.4. The higher place value positions correspond to higher strengths. These are illustrated in Figure 9.3   When a logic gate is simulated, the value on its input in terms of zero, one, x, and z is determined from the strength bytes. If the zero[th] bit in either of the bytes is set when the rest of the bits are zero, or both bytes are zero, then the input is **z**. If the zero[th] bits of both bytes are zero, then for known values only one of these bytes will be non-zero. For unknown (**x**) values, both bytes will be non-zero.

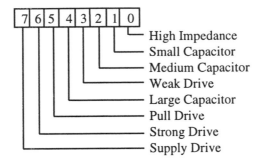

Figure 9.3 Bit Ordering For Strength Modeling

Ambiguous situations arise when multiple gates drive a common net, and in situations where there is an unknown value driving a tristate control input. These situations are modeled by the net taking on a range of values, i.e. contiguous bits in the two strength bytes are set.

9.3.1 Illustrations of Ambiguous Strengths

We will list a few examples to illustrate the reasoning process. Imagine the two bytes joined together as shown in Figure 9.4

```
        0-Strength              1-Strength
      ┌─┬─┬─┬─┬─┬─┬─┬─┬─┬─┬─┬─┬─┬─┬─┬─┐
      │7│6│5│4│3│2│1│0│7│6│5│4│3│2│1│0│
      └─┴─┴─┴─┴─┴─┴─┴─┴─┴─┴─┴─┴─┴─┴─┴─┘
```

Figure 9.4 Two Strength Bytes End-to-End

Consider the following examples where two outputs drive the same net. The representation used for the 0-strength and 1-strength bytes in the examples is that shown in Figure 9.4.

<0-strength:1-strength>=logic value.

Both the 0- and 1-strength bytes are given in binary notation. The logic value corresponding to each of the two strength bytes is given as one of 0, 1, x, or z.

0100_0000:0000_0000 =0	output 1
<u>0000_0000:0010_0000 =1</u>	output2
0100_0000:0000_0000 =0	result on net

In the above case, output 1 is a strong zero and output 2 is a pull 1. The result on the net is a zero due to the strong driver.

```
0000_0000:0110_0000 =1    output 1
0110_0000:0000_0000 =0    output 2
0111_1111:0111_1111 =x    result on net
```

In this case, each output has an ambiguous strength, listed here as being both strong and pull. When these two outputs, one driving a one and the other driving a zero, are combined on the net, the result is an x. All the bits between the values are set as shown in the result.

```
0000_0000:0010_0000 =1    output 1
0000_0111:0111_1111 =x    output 2
0000_0000:0110_0000 =1    result on net
```

In the above case, a pull 1 and an unknown with ambiguous strengths both drive the net. The drives range from a zero of medium capacitor (2) strength through a strong one. The result is a one with ambiguous strengths ranging between strong and pull.

9.3.2 **The Underlying Calculations**

The above illustrations were meant to give an intuitive feel for the operation of the simulator in the presence of ambiguous strengths. In this section we present portions of the **miniSim** example shown in full detail in Section 9.4. The **miniSim** is a Verilog description of a very simple simulator that handles strengths. We will present only the portions of the Verilog description that do the strength calculations.

Example 9.4 illustrates the **log3** function which is called when a gate input is evaluated. The function converts the value **inVal** specified with two strength bytes into a three-valued logic. In the description, the first strength byte is the zero byte and the second is the one byte. The first **casez** expression says that if none of the strength bits are set, then the value is a x. The second expression states that if only some of the zero strength bits are one, the value is a zero. Next, if only some of the one strength bits are one, the value is a one. If none of the above conditions hold, the value is unknown.

The above function would be used when gates are evaluated. Example 9.5 illustrates a task used to simulate a NAND gate.

Although we will not describe all of the details of the task, we will describe enough to give the basic understanding of the simulation. First we call the **storeInVal** task to store the input values to this element in the global memories **in0Val** and **in1Val**. We then convert these strength values into three-valued logic and store them in **in0** and **in1**. Next, **out** is set as per the three-valued NAND of the two values. Finally, if there was a change in **out**, then we **schedule** the output to change.

```
`define Val0 3'd0
`define Val1 3'd1
`define ValX 3'd2
// Convert a full strength value to a three-valued logic (0, 1 or X)
function [1:0] log3;
input [15:0] inVal;
    begin
        casez (inVal)
            16'b00000000_00000000: log3 = `ValX;
            16'b???????0_00000000: log3 = `Val0;
            16'b00000000_???????0: log3 = `Val1;
            default: log3 = `ValX;
        endcase
    end
endfunction
```

Example 9.4 The log3 Function

```
// Evaluate a 'Nand' gate primitive.
task evalNand;
input fanout; //first or second fanout indicator
    begin
        storeInVal(fanout);
        // calculate new output value
        in0 = log3(in0Val[evalElement]);
        in1 = log3(in1Val[evalElement]);
        out = ((in0 == `Val0) || (in1 == `Val0)) ?
            strengthVal(`Val1) :
            ((in0 == `ValX) || (in1 == `ValX)) ?
                strengthVal(`ValX):
                strengthVal(`Val0);
        // schedule if output value is different
        if (out != outVal[evalElement])
            schedule(out);
    end
endtask
```

Example 9.5 The evalNand Task

Consider evaluating a wire which is driven by two inputs as shown in Example 9.6. This example parallels the above **evalNand** task, except that within the task, we deal with the strengths. Specifically, function **getMast**, shown in Example 9.7, is called to

```
// Evaluate a wire with full strength values
task evalWire;
input          fanout;
reg   [7:0]    mask;
     begin
        storeInVal(fanout);
        in0 = in0Val[evalElement];
        in1 = in1Val[evalElement];
        mask = getMask(in0[15:8]) & getMask(in0[7:0]) &
             getMask(in1[15:8]) & getMask(in1[7:0]);
        out = fillBits((in0 | in1) & {mask, mask});

        if (out != outVal[evalElement])
             schedule(out);
        if (DebugFlags[2])
             $display(
    "in0 = %b_%b\nin1 = %b_%b\nmask= %b %b\nout = %b_%b",
                in0[15:8],in0[7:0], in1[15:8],in1[7:0],
                mask,mask, out[15:8],out[7:0]);
     end
endtask
```

Example 9.6 The evalWire Task

develop a mask for the final result and function **fillBits**, shown in Example 9.8, actually constructs the strength bytes for the result.

Let's consider the following example presented in the previous section. In this case, we have ambiguous strengths on both outputs driving the wire.

0000_0000:0110_0000 =1	output 1 — in0
0110_0000:0000_0000 =0	output 2 — in1
0111_1110:0111_1110 =x	result on net

Following along in task **evalWire**, we see that **in0** and **in1** are each loaded with the two strength bytes for the inputs to the wires. A mask is generated by calling **getMask** four times, each with a different strength byte. The results are AND-ed together and put in **mask**. The results, in order, are:

```
// Given either a 0-strength or 1-strength half of a strength value
// return a masking pattern for use in a wire evaluation.
function [7:0] getMask;
input [7:0] halfVal; //half a full strength value

    casez (halfVal)
        8'b???????1: getMask = 8'b11111111;
        8'b??????10: getMask = 8'b11111110;
        8'b?????100: getMask = 8'b11111100;
        8'b????1000: getMask = 8'b11111000;
        8'b???10000: getMask = 8'b11110000;
        8'b??100000: getMask = 8'b11100000;
        8'b?1000000: getMask = 8'b11000000;
        8'b10000000: getMask = 8'b10000000;
        8'b00000000: getMask = 8'b11111111;
    endcase
endfunction
```

Example 9.7 The getMask Function

```
1111_1111
1110_0000
1110_0000
1111_1111
1110_0000    mask
```

Two copies of mask concatenated together are then ANDed with the result of OR-ing the inputs in0 and in1 together.

```
0110_0000:0110_0000    OR of in0 and in1
1110_0000:1110_0000    mask, mask
0110_0000:0110_0000    result passed to fillBits
```

This result is passed to **fillBits** which will determine that this value is x and will then execute the two casez statements. In the first casez, **fillBits** will be set to 0111_1111:0110_0000, and the second casez will OR in the value 0000_0000:0111_1111. **fillBits** will have the final value:

0111_1111:0111_1111.

This result, if different from the previous value on the wire, is scheduled.

References: casez 2.4.4

```
//Given an incomplete strength value, fill the missing strength bits.
// The filling is only necessary when the value is unknown.
function [15:0] fillBits;
input [15:0] val;
 begin
   fillBits = val;
   if (log3(val) == `ValX)
     begin
       casez (val)
16'b1??????_????????: fillBits = fillBits | 16'b11111111_00000001;
16'b01?????_????????: fillBits = fillBits | 16'b01111111_00000001;
16'b001????_????????: fillBits = fillBits | 16'b00111111_00000001;
16'b0001???_????????: fillBits = fillBits | 16'b00011111_00000001;
16'b00001??_????????: fillBits = fillBits | 16'b00001111_00000001;
16'b000001?_????????: fillBits = fillBits | 16'b00000111_00000001;
16'b0000001?_????????: fillBits = fillBits | 16'b00000011_00000001;
       endcase
       casez (val)
16'b????????_1???????: fillBits = fillBits | 16'b00000001_11111111;
16'b????????_01??????: fillBits = fillBits | 16'b00000001_01111111;
16'b????????_001?????: fillBits = fillBits | 16'b00000001_00111111;
16'b????????_0001????: fillBits = fillBits | 16'b00000001_00011111;
16'b????????_00001???: fillBits = fillBits | 16'b00000001_00001111;
16'b????????_000001??: fillBits = fillBits | 16'b00000001_00000111;
16'b????????_0000001?: fillBits = fillBits | 16'b00000001_00000011;
       endcase
     end
 end
endfunction
```

Example 9.8 The fillBits Function

9.4 The miniSim Example

9.4.1 Overview

MiniSim is a description of a very simplified gate level simulator. Only three primitives have been included: a NAND gate, a D positive edge-triggered flip flop, and a wire that handles the full strength algebra that is used in Verilog. All primitive timing is unit delay, and a record is kept of the stimulus pattern number and simulation time within each pattern. Each primitive is limited to two inputs and one output that has a maximum fanout of two.

Two circuits are illustrated. The first to be loaded and simulated is a flip flop toggle circuit. The second circuit has two open-collector gates wired together with a pullup, and illustrates some cases when combining signal strengths.

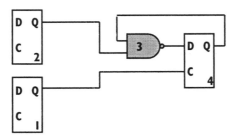

Figure 9.5 The Flip Flop Toggle Circuit

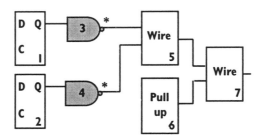

Figure 9.6 Two Open Collector Gates Driving a Wire

9.4.2 **The miniSim Source**

```
module miniSim;

// element types being modeled
`define Nand 0
`define DEdgeFF 1
`define Wire 2

// literal values with strength:
//   format is 8 0-strength bits in decreasing strength order
//   followed by 8 1-strength bits in decreasing strength order
`define Strong0 16'b01000000_00000000
`define Strong1 16'b00000000_01000000
`define StrongX 16'b01111111_01111111
`define Pull0   16'b00100000_00000000
`define Pull1   16'b00000000_00100000
`define Highz0  16'b00000001_00000000
`define Highz1  16'b00000000_00000001

// three-valued logic set
`define Val0 3'd0
`define Val1 3'd1
`define ValX 3'd2

parameter//set  DebugFlags to 1 for message
    DebugFlags =              'b11000,
//                            | | | | |
// loading             <------+ | | | |
//  event changes      <--------+ | | |
//  wire calc          <----------+ | |
//  evaluation         <------------+ |
//  scheduling         <--------------+

    IndexSize = 16,    //maximum size for index pointers
    MaxElements = 50,  //maximum number of elements
    TypeSize = 12;     //maximum number of types

reg [IndexSize-1:0]
    eventElement,           //output value change element
    evalElement,            //element on fanout
    fo0Index[1:MaxElements], //first fanout index of eventElement
    fo1Index[1:MaxElements], //second fanout index of eventElement
    currentList,            //current time scheduled event list
```

```
      nextList,            //unit delay scheduled event list
      schedList[1:MaxElements]; //scheduled event list index
   reg [TypeSize-1:0]
      eleType[1:MaxElements]; //element type
   reg
      fo0TermNum[1:MaxElements],  //first fanout input terminal number
      fo1TermNum[1:MaxElements],  //second fanout input terminal number
      schedPresent[1:MaxElements]; //element is in scheduled event list flags
   reg [15:0]
      eleStrength[1:MaxElements], //element strength indication
      outVal[1:MaxElements],    //element output value
      in0Val[1:MaxElements],    //element first input value
      in1Val[1:MaxElements],    //element second input value
      in0, in1, out, oldIn0;    //temporary value storage

   integer pattern, simTime; //time keepers

   initial
     begin
       // initialize variables
       pattern = 0;
       currentList = 0;
       nextList = 0;

       $display("Loading toggle circuit");
       loadElement(1, `DEdgeFF, 0, `Strong1,0,0, 4,0,0,0);
       loadElement(2, `DEdgeFF, 0, `Strong1,0,0, 3,0,0,0);
       loadElement(3, `Nand, (`Strong0|`Strong1),
           `Strong0,`Strong1,`Strong1, 4,0,1,0);
       loadElement(4, `DEdgeFF, (`Strong0|`Strong1),
           `Strong1,`Strong1,`Strong0, 3,0,1,0);

       // apply stimulus and simulate
       $display("Applying 2 clocks to input element 1");
       applyClock(2, 1);
       $display("Changing element 2 to value 0 and applying 1 clock");
       setupStim(2, `Strong0);
       applyClock(1, 1);

       $display("\nLoading open-collector and pullup circuit");
       loadElement(1, `DEdgeFF, 0, `Strong1,0,0, 3,0,0,0);
       loadElement(2, `DEdgeFF, 0, `Strong0,0,0, 4,0,0,0);
       loadElement(3, `Nand, (`Strong0|`Highz1),
           `Strong0,`Strong1,`Strong1, 5,0,0,0);
       loadElement(4, `Nand, (`Strong0|`Highz1),
```

```
      `Highz1,`Strong0,`Strong1, 5,0,1,0);
    loadElement(5, `Wire, 0,
      `Strong0,`Strong0,`Highz1, 7,0,1,0);
    loadElement(6, `DEdgeFF, 0, `Pull1,0,0, 7,0,0,0);
    loadElement(7, `Wire, 0,
      `Strong0,`Pull1,`Strong0, 0,0,0,0);

    // apply stimulus and simulate
    $display("Changing element 1 to value 0");
    pattern = pattern + 1;
    setupStim(1, `Strong0);
    executeEvents;
    $display("Changing element 2 to value 1");
    pattern = pattern + 1;
    setupStim(2, `Strong1);
    executeEvents;
    $display("Changing element 2 to value X");
    pattern = pattern + 1;
    setupStim(2, `StrongX);
    executeEvents;
  end

// Initialize data structure for a given element.
task loadElement;
input [IndexSize-1:0] loadAtIndex; //element index being loaded
input [TypeSize-1:0] type;       //type of element
input [15:0] strengthCoercion;    //strength specification of element
input [15:0] oVal, i0Val, i1Val;  //output and input values
input [IndexSize-1:0] fo0, fo1;   //fanout element indexes
input fo0Term, fo1Term;          //fanout element input terminal indicators
  begin
    if (DebugFlags[4])
      $display(
        "Loading element %0d, type %0s, with initial value %s(%b_%b)",
        loadAtIndex, typeString(type),
        valString(oVal), oVal[15:8], oVal[7:0]);
    eleType[loadAtIndex] = type;
    eleStrength[loadAtIndex] = strengthCoercion;
    outVal[loadAtIndex] = oVal;
    in0Val[loadAtIndex] = i0Val;
    in1Val[loadAtIndex] = i1Val;
    fo0Index[loadAtIndex] = fo0;
    fo1Index[loadAtIndex] = fo1;
    fo0TermNum[loadAtIndex] = fo0Term;
    fo1TermNum[loadAtIndex] = fo1Term;
```

```
      schedPresent[loadAtIndex] = 0;
   end
endtask

// Given a type number, return a type string
function [32*8:1] typeString;
input [TypeSize-1:0] type;
   case (type)
     `Nand: typeString = "Nand";
     `DEdgeFF: typeString = "DEdgeFF";
     `Wire: typeString = "Wire";
     default: typeString = "*** Unknown element type";
   endcase
endfunction

// Setup a value change on an element.
task setupStim;
input [IndexSize-1:0] vcElement; //element index
input [15:0] newVal;          //new element value
   begin
     if (! schedPresent[vcElement])
       begin
         schedList[vcElement] = currentList;
         currentList = vcElement;
         schedPresent[vcElement] = 1;
       end
     outVal[vcElement] = newVal;
   end
endtask

// Setup and simulate a given number of clock pulses to a given element.
task applyClock;
input [7:0] nClocks;
input [IndexSize-1:0] vcElement;
   repeat(nClocks)
     begin
       pattern = pattern + 1;
       setupStim(vcElement, `Strong0);
       executeEvents;
       pattern = pattern + 1;
       setupStim(vcElement, `Strong1);
       executeEvents;
     end
endtask
```

```
// Execute all events in the current event list.
// Then move the events in the next event list to the current event
// list and loop back to execute these events. Continue this loop
// until no more events to execute.
// For each event executed, evaluate the two fanout elements if present.
task executeEvents;
reg [15:0] newVal;
  begin
    simTime = 0;
    while (currentList)
      begin
        eventElement = currentList;
        currentList = schedList[eventElement];
        schedPresent[eventElement] = 0;
        newVal = outVal[eventElement];
        if (DebugFlags[3])
          $display(
            "At %0d,%0d Element %0d, type %0s, changes to %s(%b_%b)",
            pattern, simTime,
            eventElement, typeString(eleType[eventElement]),
            valString(newVal), newVal[15:8], newVal[7:0]);
        if (fo0Index[eventElement]) evalFo(0);
        if (fo1Index[eventElement]) evalFo(1);
        if (! currentList) // if empty move to next time unit
          begin
            currentList = nextList;
            nextList = 0;
            simTime = simTime + 1;
          end
      end
  end
endtask

// Evaluate a fanout element by testing its type and calling the
// appropriate evaluation routine.
task evalFo;
input fanout; //first or second fanout indicator
  begin
    evalElement = fanout ? fo1Index[eventElement] :
                  fo0Index[eventElement];
    if (DebugFlags[1])
      $display("Evaluating Element %0d type is %0s",
        evalElement, typeString(eleType[evalElement]));
    case (eleType[evalElement])
    `Nand: evalNand(fanout);
```

```
    `DEdgeFF: evalDEdgeFF(fanout);
    `Wire: evalWire(fanout);
  endcase
 end
endtask

// Store output value of event element into
// input value of evaluation element.
task storeInVal;
input fanout; //first or second fanout indicator
 begin
  // store new input value
  if (fanout ? fo1TermNum[eventElement] : fo0TermNum[eventElement])
    in1Val[evalElement] = outVal[eventElement];
  else
    in0Val[evalElement] = outVal[eventElement];
 end
endtask

// Convert a given full strength value to three-valued logic (0, 1 or X)
function [1:0] log3;
input [15:0] inVal;
  casez (inVal)
   16'b00000000_00000000: log3 = `ValX;
   16'b???????0_00000000: log3 = `Val0;
   16'b00000000_???????0: log3 = `Val1;
   default:        log3 = `ValX;
  endcase
endfunction

// Convert a given full strength value to four-valued logic (0, 1, X or Z),
// returning a 1 character string
function [8:1] valString;
input [15:0] inVal;
  case (log3(inVal))
   `Val0: valString = "0";
   `Val1: valString = "1";
   `ValX: valString = (inVal & 16'b11111110_11111110) ? "X" : "Z";
  endcase
endfunction

// Coerce a three-valued logic output value to a full output strength value
// for the scheduling of the evaluation element
function [15:0] strengthVal;
input [1:0] logVal;
```

```
    case (logVal)
     `Val0: strengthVal = eleStrength[evalElement] & 16'b11111111_00000000;
     `Val1: strengthVal = eleStrength[evalElement] & 16'b00000000_11111111;
     `ValX: strengthVal = fillBits(eleStrength[evalElement]);
    endcase
  endfunction

  // Given an incomplete strength value, fill the missing strength bits.
  // The filling is only necessary when the value is unknown.
  function [15:0] fillBits;
  input [15:0] val;
    begin
     fillBits = val;
     if (log3(val) == `ValX)
       begin
         casez (val)
  16'b1??????_????????: fillBits = fillBits | 16'b11111111_00000001;
  16'b01?????_????????: fillBits = fillBits | 16'b01111111_00000001;
  16'b001????_????????: fillBits = fillBits | 16'b00111111_00000001;
  16'b0001???_????????: fillBits = fillBits | 16'b00011111_00000001;
  16'b00001??_????????: fillBits = fillBits | 16'b00001111_00000001;
  16'b000001?_????????: fillBits = fillBits | 16'b00000111_00000001;
  16'b0000001_????????: fillBits = fillBits | 16'b00000011_00000001;
         endcase
         casez (val)
  16'b????????_1???????: fillBits = fillBits | 16'b00000001_11111111;
  16'b????????_01??????: fillBits = fillBits | 16'b00000001_01111111;
  16'b????????_001?????: fillBits = fillBits | 16'b00000001_00111111;
  16'b????????_0001????: fillBits = fillBits | 16'b00000001_00011111;
  16'b????????_00001???: fillBits = fillBits | 16'b00000001_00001111;
  16'b????????_000001??: fillBits = fillBits | 16'b00000001_00000111;
  16'b????????_0000001?: fillBits = fillBits | 16'b00000001_00000011;
         endcase
       end
    end
  endfunction

  // Evaluate a 'Nand' gate primitive.
  task evalNand;
  input fanout; //first or second fanout indicator
    begin
     storeInVal(fanout);
     // calculate new output value
     in0 = log3(in0Val[evalElement]);
     in1 = log3(in1Val[evalElement]);
```

```
      out = ((in0 == `Val0) || (in1 == `Val0)) ?
         strengthVal(`Val1) :
         ((in0 == `ValX) || (in1 == `ValX)) ?
            strengthVal(`ValX):
            strengthVal(`Val0);
      // schedule if output value is different
      if (out != outVal[evalElement])
         schedule(out);
   end
endtask

// Evaluate a D positive edge-triggered flip flop
task evalDEdgeFF;
input fanout; //first or second fanout indicator
   // check value change is on clock input
   if (fanout ? (fo1TermNum[eventElement] == 0) :
            (fo0TermNum[eventElement] == 0))
      begin
      // get old clock value
      oldIn0 = log3(in0Val[evalElement]);
      storeInVal(fanout);
      in0 = log3(in0Val[evalElement]);
      // test for positive edge on clock input
      if ((oldIn0 == `Val0) && (in0 == `Val1))
         begin
         out = strengthVal(log3(in1Val[evalElement]));
         if (out != outVal[evalElement])
            schedule(out);
         end
      end
   else
      storeInVal(fanout); // store data input value
endtask

// Evaluate a wire with full strength values
task evalWire;
input fanout;
reg [7:0] mask;
 begin
   storeInVal(fanout);

   in0 = in0Val[evalElement];
   in1 = in1Val[evalElement];
   mask = getMask(in0[15:8]) & getMask(in0[7:0]) &
      getMask(in1[15:8]) & getMask(in1[7:0]);
```

```
    out = fillBits((in0 | in1) & {mask, mask});

    if (out != outVal[evalElement])
        schedule(out);

    if (DebugFlags[2])
        $display("in0 = %b_%b\nin1 = %b_%b\nmask= %b %b\nout = %b_%b",
            in0[15:8],in0[7:0], in1[15:8],in1[7:0],
            mask,mask, out[15:8],out[7:0]);
    end
endtask

// Given either a 0-strength or 1-strength half of a strength value
// return a masking pattern for use in a wire evaluation.
function [7:0] getMask;
input [7:0] halfVal; //half a full strength value
    casez (halfVal)
    8'b???????1: getMask = 8'b11111111;
    8'b??????10: getMask = 8'b11111110;
    8'b?????100: getMask = 8'b11111100;
    8'b????1000: getMask = 8'b11111000;
    8'b???10000: getMask = 8'b11110000;
    8'b??100000: getMask = 8'b11100000;
    8'b?1000000: getMask = 8'b11000000;
    8'b10000000: getMask = 8'b10000000;
    8'b00000000: getMask = 8'b11111111;
    endcase
endfunction

// Schedule the evaluation element to change to a new value.
// If the element is already scheduled then just insert the new value.
task schedule;
input [15:0] newVal; // new value to change to
  begin
    if (DebugFlags[0])
        $display(
            "Element %0d, type %0s, scheduled to change to %s(%b_%b)",
            evalElement, typeString(eleType[evalElement]),
            valString(newVal), newVal[15:8], newVal[7:0]);
    if (! schedPresent[evalElement])
      begin
        schedList[evalElement] = nextList;
        schedPresent[evalElement] = 1;
        nextList = evalElement;
      end
```

```
      outVal[evalElement] = newVal;
   end
endtask
endmodule
```

9.4.3 Simulation Results

Loading toggle circuit
Loading element 1, type DEdgeFF, with initial value 1(00000000_01000000)
Loading element 2, type DEdgeFF, with initial value 1(00000000_01000000)
Loading element 3, type Nand, with initial value 0(01000000_00000000)
Loading element 4, type DEdgeFF, with initial value 1(00000000_01000000)
Applying 2 clocks to input element 1
At 1,0 Element 1, type DEdgeFF, changes to 0(01000000_00000000)
At 2,0 Element 1, type DEdgeFF, changes to 1(00000000_01000000)
At 2,1 Element 4, type DEdgeFF, changes to 0(01000000_00000000)
At 2,2 Element 3, type Nand, changes to 1(00000000_01000000)
At 3,0 Element 1, type DEdgeFF, changes to 0(01000000_00000000)
At 4,0 Element 1, type DEdgeFF, changes to 1(00000000_01000000)
At 4,1 Element 4, type DEdgeFF, changes to 1(00000000_01000000)
At 4,2 Element 3, type Nand, changes to 0(01000000_00000000)
Changing element 2 to value 0 and applying 1 clock
At 5,0 Element 1, type DEdgeFF, changes to 0(01000000_00000000)
At 5,0 Element 2, type DEdgeFF, changes to 0(01000000_00000000)
At 5,1 Element 3, type Nand, changes to 1(00000000_01000000)
At 6,0 Element 1, type DEdgeFF, changes to 1(00000000_01000000)

Loading open-collector and pullup circuit
Loading element 1, type DEdgeFF, with initial value 1(00000000_01000000)
Loading element 2, type DEdgeFF, with initial value 0(01000000_00000000)
Loading element 3, type Nand, with initial value 0(01000000_00000000)
Loading element 4, type Nand, with initial value Z(00000000_00000001)
Loading element 5, type Wire, with initial value 0(01000000_00000000)
Loading element 6, type DEdgeFF, with initial value 1(00000000_00100000)
Loading element 7, type Wire, with initial value 0(01000000_00000000)
Changing element 1 to value 0
At 7,0 Element 1, type DEdgeFF, changes to 0(01000000_00000000)
At 7,1 Element 3, type Nand, changes to Z(00000000_00000001)
At 7,2 Element 5, type Wire, changes to Z(00000000_00000001)
At 7,3 Element 7, type Wire, changes to 1(00000000_00100000)
Changing element 2 to value 1
At 8,0 Element 2, type DEdgeFF, changes to 1(00000000_01000000)
At 8,1 Element 4, type Nand, changes to 0(01000000_00000000)
At 8,2 Element 5, type Wire, changes to 0(01000000_00000000)
At 8,3 Element 7, type Wire, changes to 0(01000000_00000000)
```
```

Changing element 2 to value X
At 9,0 Element 2, type DEdgeFF, changes to X(01111111_01111111)
At 9,1 Element 4, type Nand, changes to X(01111111_00000001)
At 9,2 Element 5, type Wire, changes to X(01111111_00000001)
At 9,3 Element 7, type Wire, changes to X(01111111_00111111)

9.5 **Summary**

We have seen in this chapter how strengths may be assigned to gate outputs and assign statements, and how logic values driven at these strengths may be propagated through gates, driven on nets, and stored on trireg nets. The chapter closed with a brief discussion of the **miniSim**, a simulator written in the Verilog language that demonstrates how the logic strengths are combined together. Following this, the whole **miniSim** example was presented.

9.6 **Exercises**

9.1   Change the method of monitoring in Example 9.2 to that of strobing the signals 1 time unit before the positive edge of the **phase1** clock. Do this in such a way as to be independent of the absolute value of **d**, i.e. keep the timing parameterizable.

9.2   Without using a **wand** net, model a wired-AND configuration by employing open-collector NAND gates and a pullup primitive.

9.3   Model the following charge sharing circuit using appropriate trireg declarations:

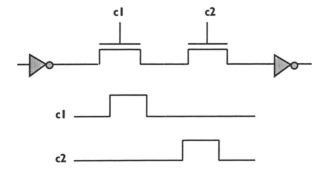

9.4 What results from passing the following strength values through a resistive MOS gate:

        A)   0(00110000_00000000)

        B)   X(00000011_00000001)

        C)   1(00000000_11111110)

9.5 In the following two examples of combining strength values, one of them has an incorrect result, which one, and what should the result be?

      x(00000001_01111111)   output 1

      0(00100000_00000000)   output 2

      x(00111111_01111111)   result on net

      0(01100000_00000000)   output 1

      x(01111111_00111111)   output 2

      0(01100000_00000000)   result on net

9.6 Given the following about combining strength values for a wired-AND net type:

      0(01000000_00000000)   output 1

      1(00000000_01000000)   output 2

      0(01000000_00000000)   result on wired-AND net

What is the correct result for the following wired-AND combination?

      0(01100000_00000000)   output 1

      1(00000000_01100000)   output 2

9.7 Extend the miniSim description to include a cross-coupled NAND latch element.

9.8 Extend the miniSim description to include a bufif1 gate element. What output values are generated when the control input is unknown and the data input is 0 or 1?

9.9 Add another net type that models a two input wired-AND element to the **miniSim** description. This element must allow the 0-strength component to win in situations of equal 0 and 1 strength (hint: the solution involves an alteration of the masking operation only).

10 | Projects

The exercises at the end of the previous chapters have been short questions to help you think about the material in the chapter. This chapter contains two projects that each encompass many aspects of the Verilog language. Each of these projects has been used in Junior level university classes for electrical and computer engineering students.

The projects are all open-ended; there is no one correct answer. Instructors should realize that the projects were aimed at a set of students with a certain course background that may not match the background of their current students. Further, the projects were tailored to the specific material being presented in class at the time. Alter the projects by adding or deleting portions as needed.

Some of these projects have supporting Verilog descriptions. These may be obtained from the e-mail reflector as described in the book's Preface.

10.1 Modeling Power Dissipation

Hardware description languages are used to model various aspects of a system; performance and functionality being the two main ones. With all the interest in building low-power devices for handheld electronics, it is also important to model the power dissipation of a circuit during its operation. This problem asks you to write a Verilog description of several versions of a small system, and use these descriptions to compare and contrast the power dissipation of each.

10.1.1 **Modeling Power Dissipation**

In this assignment, we choose to model circuits at the gate level. In CMOS circuits, power is only dissipated when a gate switches state. More specifically, when the gate output changes from a zero to a one, charge is drawn from the power supply to charge up the output connection and drive the gates in the fanout list. In this model, we will assume that it takes no energy to hold a gate's output value. Also, changing from an output 1 to 0 takes no energy. As a further tweak of the model, the energy needed to switch from 0 to 1 is proportional to the gate's fanout.

We'll build our circuit completely out of NAND gates. But, Verilog's built-in gate primitives don't count zero-to-one transitions — they only keep track of time and logic value. Thus we need to build our own model of a NAND gate that keeps track of the number of zero-to-one transitions. This number will then be proportional to power dissipated in the circuit.

10.1.2 **What to do**

We'll build several versions of a circuit to implement the equation:

a = b + c + d + e

Several versions? Well, let's see. Assume that these are all 16-bit adds, and that each add has a combinational logic delay of time τ. Here's three versions to consider:

- The adds are organized like a balanced tree and the operations occur in a single clock period of 2τ (essentially implementing a = ((b + c) + (d + e)). i.e., b and c are added together at the same time d and e are added together. Then the sums are added producing a.

- There is an unbalanced tree of adds and a single clock period of 3τ (essentially implementing a = (b + (c + (d + e)))).

- And yet another version that takes two clock periods, each of time τ, to implement the balanced tree. That is, during the first clock period, b and c are added and stored in a register. Also during that first clock period, d and e are added and put into a separate register. During the second clock period, these two registers are added.

What you will do in this assignment is build these three circuits, run thousands of input vectors through them (hey, what's a little computer time), and measure the power dissipated by each.

10.1.3 **Steps**

A. Build a full adder module by instantiating 2-input NAND gates. At first, use gate primitives and give them all a unit gate delay (#1). Then build a 16-bit adder by instantiating full adder modules. Use any form of carry logic you wish — ripple carry might be the easiest.

B. Build the different circuits suggested above. Instantiate and connect the 16-bit adder modules built in part A to do this. Ignore the carryout from the most significant bit. For each circuit, build a testbench module that will present input vectors to your circuit. Use a random number generator (see $random) to generate 2000 different input sets. (An input set includes different numbers for b, c, d, and e.) Check a few to see if your circuits really do add the numbers correctly!

C. Now that you have things working correctly, change the full adder module to use a new type of NAND gate called "myNAND" (or similar). Write a behavioral model for myNAND that can be directly substituted for the original NANDs. That is, anytime any of the inputs change, the behavioral model should execute, determine if a zero-to-one output transition will occur, and then update a global counter indicating that the transition occurred. Of course, it should schedule its output to change after a gate delay of time. The global counter is a register in the top module of the simulation which you will initialize to zero when simulation starts. Anytime a zero-to-one transition occurs in any instantiated gate in the system, this counter will be updated. Use hierarchical naming to get access to it. You may want to consider what to do if the gate output changes from zero-to-one and one-to-zero in zero time — there should be no expenditure of power nor change in logic output value.

D. Change the delays of the myNAND module to be proportional to the number of fanouts. Let's say delay will just equal fanout. Define a parameter in myNAND that initializes the delay to 1. When you instantiate myNAND, override the parameter with a count of the gate's fanout. (Be as accurate as you can.) Also change the model so that the global counter is incremented by the delay number. Thus a gate with large fanout will take more power every time it changes from zero to one, and it will also take more time to propagate the change.

E. Compare the different circuits. Can you explain the differences in dissipation based on the model we're using?

F. Extra, for fun. Can you come up with a version that dissipates even less energy?

10.2 **A Floppy Disk Controller**

10.2.1 **Introduction**

In this project, each two-person team will use Verilog to create a model of part of a floppy disk controller. A floppy disk controller takes a stream of data bits mingled with a clock signal, decodes the stream to separate the clock and data, and computes the Cyclic Redundancy Checksum (CRC) of the data to ensure that no errors have occurred. Once the data is found to be correct, it is placed in a FIFO, and from there it is placed into main memory via direct memory access (DMA). Your Verilog model will take the stream of data bits from the disk as input, and will negotiate with the memory bus as output.

The parts of the controller are shown in Figure 10.1. For this project, you will build Verilog models of the functions in the shaded area of Figure 10.1. Verilog models for everything else are provided on the e-mail reflector. Each box in the figure represents a concurrent process. The box labeled 'CRC' should be implemented at the gate level, but all other boxes can be implemented at the behavioral level. The next section describes the format of the disk media, which will be followed by a description of the function of each of the boxes.

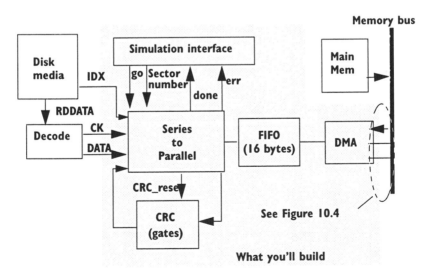

Figure 10.1 Block diagram of floppy disk controller

10.2.2 **Disk Format**

The format of the disk is shown in Figure 10.2. Figure 10.2a depicts the relationship between the sectors and index holes used to generate the IDX signal, while Figure 10.2b shows the format of each sector. IDX is used to find the proper sector for a transfer. IDX pulses high at the beginning of every sector. You may assume for this project that when the simulation starts that the disk is just before the beginning of sector 0. So the first IDX pulse signals the beginning of sector 0, the second the beginning of sector 1, etc. There are only 10 sectors on our disk.

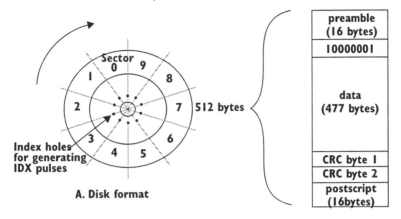

A. Disk format

B. Sector format

Figure 10.2 Formats

The other output from the disk media is RDDATA. RDDATA is the stream of data bits mingled with the clock signal. Module DECODE extracts the data from the clock signal and presents both to module Series-to-parallel (SerPar). Module SerPar then collects the bits into bytes and interprets them as per the sector format.

At the beginning of each sector is a preamble. The preamble consists of 16 bytes of 0's. Immediately following the preamble is the sync byte (10000001). The sync byte signals the end of the preamble and the beginning of the data to the controller. This is necessary because the head of the disk may have landed in the middle of the preamble and you may not have seen all 16 bytes of 0's. When the sync byte is seen, the controller can start counting the bits and bytes of the rest of the sector.

After the sync byte comes the actual data stored in the sector. There are 477 bytes of data stored in each sector. The least significant bit (LSB) of the each byte of data is written to (and read from) the disk first. Using Figure 10.3 as an example, if the byte 5B hex (01011011) were stored on the disk, the bits would be read from the disk 11011010.

At the end of each sector is a postscript which, like the preamble, consists of 16 bytes of 0's. The 2 bytes immediately preceding the postscript contain the checksum for the data in the sector (See section 10.2.5.). In our disk format, each sector contains 512 bytes. So the amount of data in a sector is 512 - 16 - 1 - 16 - 2 = 477 bytes.

Figure 10.3 RDDATA signal from the disk media

10.2.3 Function Descriptions

Decode: Decode takes as its input RDDATA, which is a stream of data bits mingled with a clock signal, from the disk media. Decode separates the clock from the data, and outputs each of them to SerPar. The RDDATA signal at the beginning of the sector (in the preamble) only contains clock pulses as shown in Figure 10.3. The data embedded in RDDATA is placed between the clock pulses. (No pulse between the clocks means a zero bit of data, a one pulse between the clocks means a one bit of data.) Since there are 16 bytes of zeros at the beginning, the controller has a chance to lock on to the clock signal embedded in RDDATA. The sync byte is the first byte that has any 1 bits in it.

The rightmost end of the RDDATA signal of Figure 10.3 shows what RDDATA would look like if the byte 01011011 were being read from the disk. The nominal period of the RDDATA clock pulses is 4 μs, with a duty cycle of 1/8. For the sake of readability, the duty cycle is not accurately represented in Figure 10.3.

SerPar: SerPar takes as its input IDX, the sector index signal from the disk media; the clock and data signals from Decode; and the sector number and go signals from the simulation interface. On the positive edge of go, SerPar resets the CRC, and begins counting IDX pulses until the proper sector is found. Once the proper sector is found, SerPar begins monitoring the data line from Decode for the sync byte. SerPar then transfers the data a bit at a time to CRC, and a byte at a time to FIFO. When it has received all the data from the sector it compares the 16-bit checksum stored after the data in the sector to the one that has just been computed by CRC for the data. If the two checksums are the same, then SerPar raises the done signal for the simulation interface. If the two checksums are different, then SerPar raises the err signal for the simulation interface.

CRC: CRC takes the data one bit at a time from SerPar, and computes its checksum on the data bytes. The CRC should be reset by SerPar before the data from the sector is read in. You must implement CRC at the gate/flip-flop level.

FIFO: FIFO is a 16-byte First In, First Out queue. It serves as a buffer for the data between SerPar, and DMA and memory. Once it receives a byte from SerPar, FIFO should signal to DMA that a transaction is necessary. When DMA has gained access to main memory, FIFO will transfer its contents to memory via DMA.

DMA: DMA transfers bytes from FIFO to main memory. When FIFO signals that a transaction is necessary, DMA arbitrates with main memory for control of the memory bus. The DMA asserts hrq to request the bus. The memory asserts hack (how appropriate are these names?) to tell the DMA it can use the bus. Once DMA has gained control of the bus, it transfers the bytes of data from FIFO to main memory. The data is transferred by asserting the address and data lines and then memw. When FIFO has no more data, DMA relinquishes control of the memory bus by deasserting hrq and waits until FIFO again signals that a transaction is necessary. Figure 10.4 shows the protocol for gaining control of the bus, and then strobing the data into memory. Assume that the data will be placed in the first N bytes of memory, so you won't have to worry about getting a starting address or block size. In the real world, controllers need to know where to place data and how much data is going to be placed.

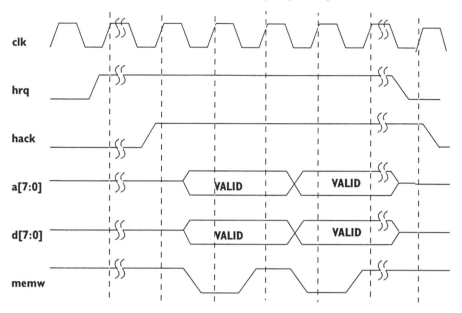

Figure 10.4 Memory bus timing diagram

Table 10.1 Memory Bus Signal Descriptions

Signal	Type wrt DMA	Description
clk	Input	Clock, 8 MHz
hrq	Output	Memory bus Hold Request. Active high.
hack	Input	Memory bus Hold Acknowledge. Indicates that the bus is available for DMA transfer. Active high.
a[7:0]	Output	Address lines. Should be tristated when not in use.
d[7:0]	Output	Data. Should be tristated when not in use.
memw	Output	Memory Write strobe. Active low.

10.2.4 **Reality Sets In…**

We told you in the Disk Format section that the clock embedded in the RDDATA signal has a nominal period of 4 µs, and that the data is put halfway between clock pulses. "No big deal," you say, "when I get a clock pulse, I'll wait 2 µs and see if RDDATA is high. If it is, I have a 1. If not, I have a 0." If you write a simulation where the clock comes along every 4 µs and the data is exactly between the clock pulses, the simulation works, and you're happy. But real disk drives depend on motors and magnetic media, so sometimes the clock comes along at 4 µs, and sometimes it comes along at 4.2 µs, with the data at 2.2 µs.

Disk drive controllers use something called a phase-locked loop (PLL) to latch onto the frequency of the clock and to adjust to its variations as the motor changes speed and the bits jitter around. You need to come up with a way to find the data in between the clock pulses without depending on the clock pulses being exactly 4 µs apart. The RDDATA from our input modules is going to vary like RDDATA does in the real world. In order to make the problem a little easier though, we'll guarantee that the clock period will be 4 µs +/- 5%, and that the center of the data will be within +/- 5% of the center of the pulses. Make sure your Decode module can lock onto the embedded clock during the preamble and hold onto it even as the frequency changes slightly. In real life, that's why the preamble is there. A Verilog description that produces these waveforms is provided on the e-mail reflector.

10.2.5 **Everything You Always Wanted to Know about CRC's**

The disk will use a 16 bit cyclic redundancy check (CRC) word calculated from the data bytes by the binary polynomial:

$$x^{16} + x^{12} + x^5 + 1$$

The CRC computation uses a shift register and XOR gates. Unlike a normal shift register, some of the stages shift in the previous bit XOR'd with the bit being shifted out of the shift register. The bits from the data stream are shifted in from the left. Numbering the bits from 1 on the left to 16 on the right, the input to the first, sixth, and thirteenth bits of the register are XOR'd with the output of the sixteenth bit.

The shift register is initialized to zero. After the entire data stream has been read in, the content of the shift register is the checksum for the sector. It is compared bit-by-bit with the checksum stored with the sector on the disk. If the two checksums match, then it is unlikely that a bit error has occurred, and the controller can transfer the data to memory. If the checksums do not match, then some bit(s) of data must have been corrupted. The controller should then signal that an error has occurred.

The CRC should be build out of XOR gates and flip-flop modules (the FF's may be described behaviorally).

10.2.6 **Supporting Verilog Modules**

There are several Verilog modules providing the stream of data and clock coming from the disk. Some modules will have correct data and some erroneous data; the file names are "correct*x*.v" and "error*x*.v." The memory and bus controller modules are provided in "memory.v." The module declarations for these files are shown in Figure 10.5. The Verilog descriptions mentioned here can be found on the e-mail reflector.

```
module memory(clock, hrq, hack, memw, d, a);
     output          clock, hack;
     input           hrq, memw;
     inout    [0:7]  d, a;

module disk(idx, rddata);
     output          idx, rddata;

module simint(go, count, done, err);
     output          go;
     output   [0:2]  count;
     input           done, err;
```

Figure 10.5 Module Declarations

A | Tutorial Questions and Discussion

This appendix contains questions, answers, and discussion to accompany Chapter 1, the tutorial introduction. The goal of this appendix is to provide far more help and guidance than we could in Chapter 1. This appendix contains tutorial help for the beginning student and questions appropriate for use with an introductory course in digital systems design or computer architecture. The sections here are referenced from the sections of Chapter 1.

Some of the questions assume that the reader has access to a Verilog simulator — the one included on the book's CD will suffice. A few of the questions assume access to a synthesis tool; limited access to one is available through the CD. Finally, the book's CD includes copies of the books examples; retrieve them from there to avoid retyping.

A.1 Structural Descriptions

The questions in this section accompany Section 1.1.2. The first two include a detailed presentation of how to develop a simple Verilog description, including a discussion of common mistakes. The questions following assume more familiarity with a hardware description language and simulator.

A.1 Write a Verilog description of the logic diagram shown in Figure A.1. This logic circuit implements the Boolean function $F=(A\overline{B})+C$ which you can probably see by inspection of the K-map. Since this is the first from-scratch description, the discussion section has far more help.

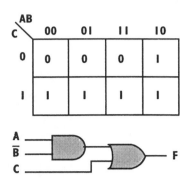

C\\AB	00	01	11	10
0	0	0	0	1
1	1	1	1	1

Figure A.1 $F=(A\overline{B})+C$

Do This — Write a module specification for this logic circuit. The module will not have inputs or outputs. Use primitives gates (AND, OR, and NOT), connect them with wires, and include an initial statement to fully test your circuit. To produce $\overline{B}$ from B, add a NOT gate (inverter) to the above diagram. Specify that NOT gates have a delay of 1 time unit and the others have delays of 2 time units. Oh, and try not to look at the answer below! If you're not sure what to do, read on.

Discussion: The first thing to write is the module header and name — give it any name you wish. Next, break the description down into the individual gates, assigning distinct names to the wires connecting the gates. Now write the gate instantiations and specify the ports for interconnecting them. A gate is instantiated as shown here:

    and   #5 myFirstAnd (q, r, s);

Here an AND gate with delay five, instance name **myFirstAnd**, and ports q, r, and s is defined. Which connection is first in the list? The output; q it the output and the others are inputs. Finish instantiating the gates.

In answering the question, you might have written the following module description. Clearly, you probably used a different name for the module (it's **top** here) and also for the gate instance names (e.g., **g1**). The delay specification, which is optional when specifying gate instantiations, is required in the description because the problem statement asked for it. There are other ways to start writing this problem.

```
module top;
    not     #1  g1 (d, b);
    and     #2  g2 (e, d, a);
    or      #2  g3 (f, c, d);
endmodule
```

This description will not parse; *some* of the identifiers have not been declared. Some?

Do This — Explain which ones? Why not the others? There are no declarations in this description, so why don't all of the identifiers produce an error?

The reason is that an output of a primitive gate is declared as a wire by default. Thus, identifiers **d**, **e**, and **f** are all defaulted to be of type wire. **a**, **b**, and **c** are not declared and will thus cause errors. Why is the output of a primitive gate defaulted to be a wire? Real combinational logic gates are connected to wires. In the Verilog language, new values are either driven on nets (wires are the default type of net) or loaded into registers. Primitive gates always drive wires.

Now continue the example by declaring the gate inputs (**a**, **b**, and **c**) to be registers. This will allow us to assign values to them in an initial statement and to test the output of our logic function. We could add the following declarations.

```
wire   d, e, f;
reg    a, b, c;
```

But remember that the wire declaration is not needed because gate outputs default to wire declarations. The following description would parse without errors.

```
module top;
     reg    a, b, c;

     not    #1  g1 (d, b);
     and    #2  g2 (e, d, a);
     or     #2  g3 (f, c, d);
endmodule
```

But, this description wouldn't do much except parse correctly. The goal is to simulate the design and convince yourself that the specification performs the logic function that you expect. Now we need to specify a set of inputs (called test vectors) so that we can simulate the circuit and observe its output.

Do This — write an initial block that will provide several different inputs to these gates and display all values in the circuit. The block should be part of the **top** module. The ordered series of inputs that we will put into our design will be (**a**, **b**, **c**): 100, 110, 010, 011. This is a fairly extensive test set, even though it does not test every input combination.

Discussion: To use the registers that we put in the description for the gate inputs, we need to write an initial block — registers can only be loaded by assignment statements in initial and always blocks. We'll use an initial block since these are often used to provide test vector inputs.

Here's our first try. Following the statements, the first three put 100 on the inputs (**a**, **b**, **c**). The next assignment changes **b** to make the input 110. The fifth assignment changes **a** to make the input 010, and the last assignment makes the input 011. That is the sequence of inputs we want, but alas this specification will not work.

```
initial begin
    a = 1;
    b = 0;
    c = 0;
    b = 1;
    a = 0;
    c = 1;
end
```

Do This — Explain why this initial block will not work.

Discussion: There are two errors here. One error is there is no means of displaying the output when the inputs change. Let's add a $monitor statement to display the data to the screen whenever any value changes. Additionally, we will have the simulation time reported. In our case we will use the statement:

```
$monitor($time,,"a=%b, b=%b, c=%b, d=%b, e=%b, f=%b", a, b, c, d, e, f);
```

The monitor statement is not just a print statement. It will cause a printing of the quoted string when executed but then it will continue to monitor for changes on any of the input identifiers (**a, b, c, d, e,** and **f** here), printing the quoted string when any one changes. Only one of these $monitor statements can be active at the same time. If one is reached while another is active, the new one cancels the old.

The second error is more fundamental. The error is that the only input value the gates will see is the last one: 011. The simulation didn't stop to let the intermediate values flow through the gates. Here's how to think about how the simulator works. At the start of the simulation, all values in the system (both nets and registers) have the value x (i.e., unknown). The initial and always blocks start executing in an arbitrary order. In this system, we only have one initial block; it runs, making all of the assignments, and then it stops with **a** = 0, **b** = 1, and **c** = 1. When the initial block stops, the gates notice that their inputs have changed and they calculate their output values. The other input combinations are never seen by the gates.

Indeed, if we simulated our current version of the module shown below we would get the simulation trace showing only the final inputs and output. Not cool.

```
module top;
      wire      d, e, f;
      reg       a, b, c;

      not       #1   g1(d, b);
      and       #2   g2(e, a, d);
      or        #2   g3(f, e, c);    // (AB̄)+C

      initial begin
            $monitor($time,, "a=%b, b=%b, c=%b, d=%b, e=%b, f=%b\n",
                                              a,b,c,d,e,f);
            a = 1;             // initialization
            b = 0;
            c = 0;
            b = 1;             // first change of input
            a = 0;             // second change of input
            c = 1;             // third change of input

            #20 $finish;       // this tells the simulator to stop
      end
endmodule
```

Here is the simulated output showing the values in the circuit. The first value on the line is the time at which the values occur. The first line shows the inputs valid at time 0, the output of the **not** gate (d) changes one time unit later, and the output of g2 (e) and g3 (f) change at time 2. Note that the value of 1 on c causes f to change at time 2. We don't have to wait for the output of the **not** gate to propagate through gate g2 and g3.

```
0 a=0, b=1, c=1, d=x, e=x, f=x
1 a=0, b=1, c=1, d=0, e=x, f=x
2 a=0, b=1, c=1, d=0, e=0, f=1
```

Back to our problem: no delay was used in the assignment of the registers, and they were all assigned (in order, from top to bottom) during the same time. We need to add delay statements that will stop the execution of the initial block long enough so that the gates can produce their outputs. The new initial block could be:

```
initial begin
    $monitor($time,, "a=%b, b=%b, c=%b, d=%b, e=%b, f=%b\n",
                        a, b, c, d, e, f);
    a = 1;              // initialization
    b = 0;
    c = 0;
    #2 b = 1;           //first change of input
    #2 a = 0;           // second change of input
    #2 c = 1;           // third change of input

    #20 $finish;
end
```

Although this does add delay to the circuit and allows the values to propagate into the circuit, it doesn't allow enough time, as these results show:

```
0 a=1, b=0, c=0, d=x, e=x, f=x
1 a=1, b=0, c=0, d=1, e=x, f=x
2 a=1, b=1, c=0, d=1, e=x, f=x
3 a=1, b=1, c=0, d=0, e=0, f=x
4 a=0, b=1, c=0, d=0, e=0, f=x
5 a=0, b=1, c=0, d=0, e=0, f=0
6 a=0, b=1, c=1, d=0, e=0, f=0
8 a=0, b=1, c=1, d=0, e=0, f=1
```

The problem is that the inputs change again before the logic values have time to propagate to the output. The delay we include in the description needs to be longer than the longest delay through the gates. In this case, setting it to six would work since the longest path from inputs to outputs is five. You could also set it to #3072 with no change in the results.

The following description is correct.

```
module top;
    wire    d, e, f;
    reg     a, b, c;

    not     #1  g1(d, b);
    and     #2  g2(e, a, d);
    or      #2  g3(f, e, c);        // (A̅B̅)+C

    initial begin
        $monitor($time,, "a=%b, b=%b, c=%b, d=%b, e=%b, f=%b\n",
                          a, b, c , d, e, f);

        a = 1;                  // initialization
        b = 0;
        c = 0;
        #20 b = 1;              // first change of input
        #20 a = 0;              // second change of input
        #20 c = 1;              // third change of input

        #20 $finish;
    end
endmodule
```

The simulation results should look like this:

```
1 a=1, b=0, c=0, d=1, e=x, f=x
3 a=1, b=0, c=0, d=1, e=1, f=x
5 a=1, b=0, c=0, d=1, e=1, f=1
20 a=1, b=1, c=0, d=1, e=1, f=1
21 a=1, b=1, c=0, d=0, e=1, f=1
23 a=1, b=1, c=0, d=0, e=0, f=1
25 a=1, b=1, c=0, d=0, e=0, f=0
40 a=0, b=1, c=0, d=0, e=0, f=0
60 a=0, b=1, c=1, d=0, e=0, f=0
62 a=0, b=1, c=1, d=0, e=0, f=1
```

A.2 Type in the following example and name the file adder.v. It implements the add function for two bits, producing a sum and a carry out. Create a module to test this **halfadder** module and instantiate them both in a test-bench module.

```
module halfadder (cOut, sum, a, b);
    output      cOut, sum;
    input       a, b;

    xor     #1  (sum, a, b);
    and     #2  (cOut, a, b);
endmodule
```

The first line gives the name of the module, and lists the inputs and outputs. The next two lines define which are inputs and which are outputs. Essentially it defines two outputs and two inputs, each to be single bit quantities.

Then we instantiate an XOR gate, with **a** and **b** as inputs, and **sum** as the output. The XOR gate is specified to have a delay of one time unit. That is, one time unit after an input changes, the output might change. The **and** gate is similar, but with a delay of two time units. Finally, we have the **endmodule** statement which indicates the end of the module description.

Do This — Create the **testadder** module. The idea is that we're going to connect this module to the **halfadder** module and have this module test it. Both modules will be instantiated within another module called **system**.

Discussion: A **testadder** module is shown below. The initial statement introduces a behavioral block; these blocks can be read much like you would read C (yes, there are many differences). The initial statement indicates that the block should only be executed once.

When the initial statement starts, it executes the $monitor statement (as described in the previous question), and assigns x and y to be 0. "#10" tells the simulator to wait for 10 time units and then continue execution. In 10 more time units, x is set to 1. After another 10, y is set to 1. Finally, after another 10, x is set to 0. Essentially, over the course of execution, x and y will have all four combinations of inputs for the half adder, and there is enough time for these values to propagate through the gates in the adder module.

$finish causes the simulator to exit after another 10 time units.

Finally, we need to connect the two modules together as shown in module system. The wire declaration defines four wires with the given names.

```
module system;
     wire     CarryOut, SumOut, in1, in2;

     halfadder    AddUnit (CarryOut, SumOut, in1, in2);
     testadder    TestUnit (in1, in2, CarryOut, SumOut);
endmodule
```

The module **system** is the top level of our design — it has no inputs or outputs and the other modules are instantiated within it. When the modules are instantiated, instance names are given to each: **halfadder** is named **AddUnit**, and **testadder** is named **TestUnit**. In effect, we have wired up a half adder module to a module that

```
module testadder ( x, y, c, s );
    output      x, y;
    reg         x, y;
    input       c, s;

    initial begin
        $monitor($time,,
        "x = %b, y = %b, Sum = %b, Carry = %b", x, y, s, c);
                x = 0;
                y = 0;
        #10     x = 1;
        #10     y = 1;
        #10     x = 0;
        #10     $finish;
    end
endmodule
```

creates inputs for the half adder. Outputs from the half adder are monitored by the test module.

Consider the two statements from module system:

```
halfadder   AddUnit (CarryOut, SumOut, in1, in2);
testadder   TestUnit (in1, in2, CarryOut, SumOut);
```

Do not think of this as executing the **halfadder**, then executing the **testadder** — these are not function calls. Rather, these define that an instance of each of these modules is to be connected together using wires as shown. Reversing the order of the two statements has no effect.

Do This — Run the simulator on this file. The simulator should display all the inputs and outputs, with the simulation time. Reason your way through the execution of these modules. Note that the **testadder** module will set x and y to certain values and then wait 10 time units. During that time, the XOR and AND gates in the halfadder module will execute and change their outputs. And then the **testadder** module will continue to execute.

A. What effect do the time delays in module **halfadder** have? Play around with them (they're integers). Make them 1.

B. Remove the $finish command; what changes?

C. Then also change the initial to always; what changes?

A.3 Example 1.2 is duplicated here as Example A.1. Expand the initial statement to cover all input patterns. Simulate the circuit, and create a truth table or K-map for this circuit. Draw out the seven-segment display patterns. Is the function correct?

Discussion: the example has four inputs and thus 2^4 distinct input patterns. Make sure all patterns are assigned to registers **A**, **B**, **C**, and **D** with enough time for the values to propagate to the output.

A.4 In the same example, change the gate types to AND and OR. Resimulate.

Discussion: Use DeMorgan's theorem to convert from NAND-NAND logic to AND-OR.

A.5 In the same example, change the gate types to NOR-NOR.

Discussion: Use DeMorgan's theorem.

A.6 Simulate Example A.1 using #6 instead of #1 for the gate delays. The results will not be the same. Explain.

A.7 Design a circuit using only NAND gates implementing the driver for segment a. Test it using the simulator.

```
module binaryToESegSim;
    wire    eSeg, p1, p2, p3, p4;
    reg     A, B, C, D;

    nand #1
        g1 (p1, C, ~D),
        g2 (p2, A, B),
        g3 (p3, ~B, ~D),
        g4 (p4, A, C),
        g5 (eSeg, p1, p2, p3, p4);

    initial       // two slashes introduce a single line comment
        begin
            $monitor ($time,,,
                "A = %b B = %b C = %b D = %b, eSeg = %b",
                A, B, C, D, eSeg);
            //waveform for simulating the binaryToESeg driver
            #10 A = 0; B = 0; C = 0; D = 0;
            #10 D = 1;
            #10 C = 1; D = 0;
            #10 $finish;
        end
endmodule
```

Example A.1 A Copy of Example 1.2

A.2 **Testbench Modules**

The questions in this section are to be used with Section 1.1.4.

A.8 In problem A.4 you developed an AND-OR version of Example A.1. Change it to use the testbench approach. Simulate using a complete set of test vectors.

A.9 In problem A.5 you developed an NOR-NOR version of Example A.1. Change it to use the testbench approach. Simulate using a complete set of test vectors.

A.3 **Combinational Circuits Using always**

These problems are to be used with Section 1.2. Problem A.11 includes a detailed discussion of problems encountered when writing such descriptions.

A.10 Substitute module **binaryToESeg_Behavioral** into the **testBench** module of Example 1.4. Compare the simulation results with those of the original example. What is different?

A.11 At this point, we have only covered the basic issues in describing combinational circuits using the always block. For a more detailed discussion, refer back to Chapter 6.

Do this — write a module using behavioral modeling techniques to describe the circuit in Figure A.2. Compile the module for simulation and synthesis. Is it functionally correct? If your circuit will not synthesize, read on to see if you hit upon any of these common mistakes!

Figure A.2 Logic diagram for F=(A$\overline{\text{B}}$)+C

Lack of Assignment — You might run into this particular problem if you assume that register values start at or default to 0. This is how our code would look if this assumption of f=0 by default was made.

```
module andOr(f, a, b, c);
    input    a, b, c;
    output   f;
    reg      f;

    always @(a or b or c)
        if (c + (a & ~b))
            f = 1;
endmodule
```

The simulator will initially assign f to have the value x. It will keep that value until it is assigned to 1, and will never assign it to zero. Obviously, we simply put in an else that will assign f to be 0. When describing modules for synthesis, it's a good general rule that for every if there should be an else to tell the logic what to do should that statement not be TRUE. Like this:

```
module andOr(f, a, b, c);
    input    a, b, c;
    output   f;
    reg      f;

    always @(a or b or c)
        if (c + (a & ~b))
            f = 1;
        else  f = 0;
endmodule
```

But we can break that rule. Here is a correct always block for the above problem with out an else. The trick is that the statement assigning f to zero creates a default value for f; the rest of the description can then concentrate on when to set it to 1.

```
    always @(a or b or c) begin
        f = 0;
        if (c + (a & ~b))
            f = 1;
    end
```

Missing Input Sensitivity — This is generally a simple matter that something was left out. A fundamental characteristic of combinational circuits is that they are always sensitive to all of their inputs. That is, a change on any input could cause a change on the output. Thus, the event statement ("@") in the always block has to include all of the combinational inputs. The expression in the parentheses of the event statement is called the sensitivity list. The following is how *not* to write the sensitivity list.

```
module andOr(f, a, b, c);
    input    a, b, c;
    output   f;
    reg      f;

    always @(a or c)          // OOPS! Forgot b!   This should be (a or b or c)
        if (c)
            f = 1;
        else
            f = a & ~b;
endmodule
```

This will have the effect of not updating the output when **b** changes, leaving it wherever it was until either **a** or **c** change. The simulation will give bad results. A synthesis tool will not think of this as a combinational circuit. It will think: anytime b changes, the circuit has to remember the previous before b changed. This requires memory in the circuit. Combinational circuits do not have memory; their outputs are a function only of the current inputs.

A.12 Rewrite Example 1.5 starting with "eSeg = 0". Then specify the conditions when it is to be set to one. The module should use only a single always block. Then insert into a **testBench** module and simulate to show correct function.

A.13 A case statement is often used in synthesizable Verilog descriptions. Example A.2 is a Verilog description for a BCD to seven segment display module using a case statement. Read ahead in section 2.4.2 to see how the case statement works.

Do this — Since this module only decodes the digits 0 through 9, change it to also decode and display the digits A through F.

Hints: Ignore the top-most bit. It is always one. The others are asserted low; a zero turns on a display segment. The segment bits are shown in order (either segments a-f or f-a). Figure out which is which from what you know about displays.

A.4 **Sequential Circuits**

These questions are to be used with Section 1.3. The first question includes a fairly lengthy discussion of writing a description of a sequential circuit. The others assume more background.

A.14 Design a two-bit counter. The circuit will count either up or down through the 2-bit binary number range. Your circuit has two external inputs:

```
module BCDtoSevenSeg ( led, bcd);
    output   [7:0]   led;
    input    [3:0]   bcd;
    reg      [7:0]   led;

    always @(bcd)
        case (bcd)
            0 :  led = 'h81;
            1 :  led = 'hcf;
            2 :  led = 'h92;
            3 :  led = 'h86;
            4 :  led = 'hcc;
            5 :  led = 'ha4;
            6 :  led = 'ha0;
            7 :  led = 'h8f;
            8 :  led = 'h80;
            9 :  led = 'h8c;
            default:led = 'bxxxxxxxx;
        endcase
endmodule
```

Example A.2 Verilog Description of BCD to Seven Segment Display

up   determines the count direction. It is asserted high.
reset   asynchronously sends the circuit to state 0. It is asserted low.

The counter will sequence between the four states: 0, 1, 2, 3 as follows:

if **up** = "1": 0 -> 1 -> 2 -> 3 -> 0 -> 1 -> 2 -> 3 -> ...
if **up** = "0": 0 -> 3 -> 2 -> 1 -> 0 -> 3 -> 2 -> 1 -> ...

Thus the circuit implements a counter that counts from 0 to 3, or 3 to 0, over and over. It can be asynchronously reset to 0, by asserting **reset**.

What states and state transitions exist? A state transition diagram is shown in Figure A.3.

How to represent the states? Let's use two bits to represent the states. An obvious state assignment is to have 00 represent state 0, 01 represent 1, 10 represent 2, and 11 represent 3.

Do this — Write the Verilog description for this counter. Here is the module header:

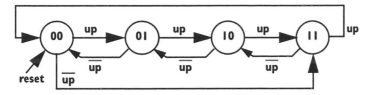

Figure A.3 State Transition Diagram

```
module counter_2_bit(up, clk, rst, count);
    input           up, clk, rst;
    output  [1:0]   count;
    reg     [1:0]   count;
```

An answer follows on the next page.

A.15 Why is the **default:** needed in the answer to the counter description in the above problem? Consider both simulation and synthesis when answering.

A.16 Create a testbench module for Example 1.6. You will need to include a clock for the circuit; use the one in Example 1.9. Your testbench module should reset the circuit and then provide the following inputs to the circuit

0, 0, 1, 0, 1, 1, 1, 1, 0, 0.

Simulate the fsm to show that it correctly transits through its states.

A.17 If you changed the non-blocking assignments (<=) to blocking assignments (=) in Example 1.6, would there be any difference in the outcome of a simulation. Explain.

A.18 Some simulators have a single step mode where individual events are simulated. figure out which of the two concurrent assignments is done first in the else in Example 1.7. Why can't we give you an answer as to which one is done first?

A.19 Here's one way to swap values in registers.

```
reg     [7:0] a, b, temp;

always begin
    ...
    temp = a;
    a = b;
    b = temp;
```

Rewrite this using only registers **a** and **b** (i.e., get rid of **temp**).

```
module counter_2_bit (up, clk, rst, count);        //Answer to problem A.14
    input              up, clk, rst;// Declarations
    output   [1:0]     count;
    reg      [1:0]     count, nextCount;

    always @(up or count)
        case (count)
            0: begin
                if (up) nextCount = 1;
                else nextCount = 3;
            end
            1: begin
                if (up) nextCount = 2;
                else nextCount = 0;
            end
            2: begin
                if (up) nextCount = 3;
                else nextCount = 1;
            end
            3: begin
                if (up) nextCount = 0;
                else nextCount = 2;
            end
            default:
                nextCount = 0;
        endcase

    always @(posedge clk or negedge rst)
        if(~rst)
            count <= 0;
        else
            count <= nextCount;
endmodule
```

A.5 **Hierarchical Descriptions**

These questions are to be used with Section 1.4.

A.20 What differences will be found when simulating Examples 1.13, 1.3, and 1.5?

A.21 Write the whole **board** example (Examples 1.3, 1.8, 1.9, and 1.10) as one module. Use behavioral models (always and initial) as much as possible. Explain the order of execution at the start of a simulation.

A.6 **Finite State Machine and Datapath**

These questions are to be used with Section 1.5.

A.22 For each register transfer on page 29, list which control inputs to the datapath must be asserted.

A.23 Assuming two's complement arithmetic, write a new module description for a LT0 function. The one 8-bit input is compared with zero. If it is less than zero, the single bit output is TRUE; else it is FALSE.

A.24 Draw timing diagrams, like Figure 1.11, showing the transitions between states C and D, and C and E.

A.25 Build a testbench for the **sillyComputation** module (Examples 1.17 and 1.18). You will need to initialize the value of y. Monitor values of x, y, cState, and i. Use 16-bit words.

A.26 Change the datapath and control unit of **sillyComputation**. Change i's register description so that the it can be cleared or incremented (i.e., a separate adder is not needed to increment i). Change the controller to accommodate this change. Simulate.

A.7 **Cycle-Accurate Descriptions**

These questions are to be used with Section 1.6.

A.27 Rewrite the cycle-accurate specification of Example 1.19 to match the state transition diagram of Figure 1.10.

A.28 Write a cycle-accurate specification of a Fibonacci number generator. The sequence should be 1, 1, 2, 3, 5, 8, ... Generate one new value each clock cycle. Parameterize the register and output widths to be 32 bits. Have a reset input to the system.

B | Lexical Conventions

Verilog source text files consist of a stream of lexical tokens separated by white space. The spacing of tokens is free format — the specific choice of tabs, spaces, or newlines to separate lexical tokens is not important to the compiler. However, the choice is important for giving a readable structure to the description. It is important that you develop a consistent style of writing your Verilog descriptions. We offer the examples in the book as a starting point to develop your own personal style.

The types of lexical tokens in the language are: white space, comments, operators, numbers, strings, identifiers, and keywords. This Appendix will discuss each of these.

B.1 White Space and Comments

White space is defined as any of the following characters: blanks, tabs, newlines, and formfeeds. These are ignored except for when they are found in strings.

There are two forms of comments. The single line comment begins with the two characters // and ends with a newline. A block comment begins with the two characters /* and ends with the two characters */. Block comments may span several lines. However, they may not be nested.

B.2 **Operators**

Operators are single, double or triple character sequences that are used in expressions. Appendix C lists and defines all the operators.

B.3 **Numbers**

Constant numbers can be specified in decimal, hexadecimal, octal, or binary. They may optionally start with a + or -, and can be given in one of two forms.

The first form is an unsized decimal number specified using the digits from the sequence 0 to 9. Although the designer may not specify the size, Verilog calculates a size for use in an expression. In an expression, the size is typically equivalent to the size of the operator's other (sized) operand. The appropriate number of bits, starting from the least significant bit, are selected for use. Appendix C.4 lists a set of rules for calculating the size.

The second form specifies the size of the constant and takes the form:

ss...s 'f nn...n

where:

Table 2.1 Parts of a number

ss...s	is the size in bits of the constant. The size is specified as a decimal number.
'f	is the base format. The **f** is replaced by one of the single letters: d, h, o, or b, for decimal, hexadecimal, octal, or binary. The letters may also be capitalized.
nn...n	is the value of the constant specified in the given base with allowable digits. For the hexadecimal base, the letters **a** through **f** may also be capitalized.

Unknown and high impedance values may be given in all but the decimal base. In each case, the **x** or **z** character represents the given number of bits of **x** or **z**. i.e. in hexadecimal, an **x** would represent four unknown bits, in octal, three.

Normally, zeros are padded on the left if the number of bits specified in **nn...n** is less than specified by **ss...s**. However, if the first digit of **nn...n** is **x** or **z**, then **x** or **z** is padded on the left.

An underline character may be inserted into a number (of any base) to improve readability. It must not be the first character of a number. For instance, the binary number:

    12 'b 0x0x_1101_0zx1

is more readable than:

    12 'b 0x0x11010zx1.

Examples of unsized constants are:

    792   // a decimal number

    7d9   // illegal, hexadecimal must be specified with 'h

    'h 7d9   // an unsized hexadecimal number

    'o 7746   // an unsized octal number

Examples of sized constants are:

    12 'h x   // a 12 bit unknown number

    8 'h fz   // equivalent to the binary: 8 'b 1111_zzzz

    10 'd 17   // a ten bit constant with the value 17.

B.4 **Strings**

A string is a sequence of characters enclosed by double quotes. It must be contained on a single line. Special characters may be specified in a string using the "\" escape character as follows:

    \n   new line character. Typically the **return** key.

    \t   tab character. Equivalent to typing the tab key.

    \\   is the \ character.

    \"   is the " character

    \ddd   is an ASCII character specified in one to three octal digits.

B.5 **Identifiers, System Names, and Keywords**

Identifiers are names that are given to elements such as modules, registers, ports, wires, instances, and begin-end blocks. An identifier is any sequence of letters, digits, and the underscore (_) symbol except that:

- the first character must not be a digit, and
- the identifier must be 1024 characters or less.

Upper and lower case letters are considered to be different.

System tasks and system functions are identifiers that always start with the dollar ($) symbol. A partial list of system tasks and functions is provided in Appendix F.

Escaped identifiers allow for any printable ASCII character to be included in the name. Escaped identifiers begin with white space. The backslash ("\") character leads off the identifier, which is then terminated with white space. The leading backslash character is not considered part of the identifier.

Examples of escaped identifiers include:

\bus-index

\a+b

Escaped identifiers are used for translators from other CAD systems. These systems may allow special characters in identifiers. Escaped identifiers should not be used under normal circumstances

Table 2.2 Verilog Keywords (See the Index for information on most of these)

always	and	assign	begin	buf
bufif0	bufif1	case	casex	casez
cmos	deassign	default	defparam	disable
edge	else	end	endcase	endfunction
endmodule	endprimitive	endspecify	endtable	endtask
event	for	force	forever	fork
function	highz0	highz1	if	initial
inout	input	integer	join	large
macromodule	medium	module	nand	negedge
nmos	nor	not	notif0	notif1
or	output	pmos	posedge	primitive
pull0	pull1	pulldown	pullup	rcmos
reg	release	repeat	rnmos	rpmos
rtran	rtranif0	rtranif1	scalared	small
specify	specparam	strong0	strong1	supply0
supply1	table	task	time	tran
tranif0	tranif1	tri	tri0	tri1
triand	trior	vectored	wait	wand
weak0	weak1	while	wire	wor
xnor	xor			

C | Verilog Operators

C.1 Table of Operators

Table 3.1 Verilog Operators

Operator Symbol	Name	Definition	Comments
{ , }	Concatenation	Joins together bits from two or more comma-separated expressions	Constants must be sized. Alternate form uses a repetition multiplier. {b, {3 {a, b}}} is equivalent to {b, a, b, a, b, a, b}.
+	Addition	Sums two operands.	Register and net operands are treated as unsigned. Real and integer operands may be signed. If any bit is unknown, the result will be unknown.
-	Subtraction	Finds difference between two operands.	Register and net operands are treated as unsigned. Real and integer operands may be signed. If any bit is unknown, the result will be unknown.
-	Unary minus	Changes the sign of its operand	Register and net operands are treated as unsigned. Real and integer operands may be signed. If any bit is unknown, the result will be unknown.

Table 3.1 Verilog Operators

*	Multiplication	Multiply two operands.	Register and net operands are treated as unsigned. Real and integer operands may be signed. If any bit is unknown, the result will be unknown.
/	Division	Divide two operands	Register and net operands are treated as unsigned. Real and integer operands may be signed. If any bit is unknown, the result will be unknown. Divide by zero produces an **x**.
%	Modulus	Find remainder	Register and net operands are treated as unsigned. Real and integer operands may be signed. If any bit is unknown, the result will be unknown.
>	Greater than	Determines relative value	Register and net operands are treated as unsigned. Real and integer operands may be signed. If any bit is unknown, the relation is ambiguous and the result will be unknown.
>=	Greater than or equal	Determines relative value	Register and net operands are treated as unsigned. Real and integer operands may be signed. If any bit is unknown, the relation is ambiguous and the result will be unknown.
<	Less than	Determines relative value	Register and net operands are treated as unsigned. Real and integer operands may be signed. If any bit is unknown, the relation is ambiguous and the result will be unknown.
<=	Less than or equal	Determines relative value	Register and net operands are treated as unsigned. Real and integer operands may be signed. If any bit is unknown, the relation is ambiguous and the result will be unknown.
!	Logical negation	Unary Complement	Converts a non-zero value (TRUE) into zero; a zero value (FALSE) into one; and an ambiguous truth value into **x**.
&&	Logical AND	ANDs two logical values.	Used as a logical connective in, for instance, **if** statements. e.g. if ((a > b) && (c < d)).
||	Logical OR	ORs two logical values.	Used as a logical connective in, for instance, **if** statements. c.g. if ((a > b) || (c < d)).

Table 3.1 Verilog Operators

= =	Logical equality	Compares two values for equality	Register and net operands are treated as unsigned. Real and integer operands may be signed. If any bit is unknown, the relation is ambiguous and the result will be unknown.
! =	Logical inequality	Compares two values for inequality	Register and net operands are treated as unsigned. Real and integer operands may be signed. If any bit is unknown, the relation is ambiguous and the result will be unknown.
= = =	Case equality	Compares two values for equality	The bitwise comparison includes comparison of **x** and **z** values. All bits must match for equality. The result is either TRUE or FALSE.
! = =	Case inequality	Compares two values for inequality	The bitwise comparison includes comparison of **x** and **z** values. Any bit difference produces inequality. The result is either TRUE or FALSE.
~	Bitwise negation	Complements each bit in the operand	Each bit of the operand is complemented. The complement of **x** is **x**.
&	Bitwise AND	Produces the bitwise AND of two operands.	See truth table below
|	Bitwise OR	Produces the bitwise inclusive OR of two operands.	See truth table below
^	Bitwise XOR	Produces the bitwise exclusive OR of two operands.	See truth table below
^~ or ~^	Equivalence	Produces the bitwise exclusive NOR of two operands	See truth table below
&	Unary reduction AND	Produces the single bit AND of all of the bits of the operand.	Unary reduction and binary bitwise operators are distinguished by syntax.
~ &	Unary reduction NAND	Produces the single bit NAND of all of the bits of the operand.	Unary reduction and binary bitwise operators are distinguished by syntax.

Table 3.1 Verilog Operators

		Unary reduction and binary bitwise operators are distinguished by syntax.	
|	Unary reduction OR	Produces the single bit inclusive OR of all of the bits of the operand.	Unary reduction and binary bitwise operators are distinguished by syntax.
~|	Unary reduction NOR	Produces the single bit NOR of all of the bits of the operand.	Unary reduction and binary bitwise operators are distinguished by syntax.
^	Unary reduction XOR	Produces the single bit XOR of all of the bits of the operand.	Unary reduction and binary bitwise operators are distinguished by syntax.
~^ or ^~	Unary reduction XNOR	Produces the single bit XNOR of all of the bits of the operand.	Unary reduction and binary bitwise operators are distinguished by syntax.
<<	Left shift	Shift the left operand left by the number of bit positions specified by the right operand	Vacated bit positions are filled with zeros
>>	Right shift	Shift the left operand right by the number of bit positions specified by the right operand	Vacated bit positions are filled with zeros
?:	Conditional	Assign one of two values based on expression	condExpr ? trueExpr : falseExpr. If condExpr is TRUE, the trueExpr is the result of the operator. If condExpr is FALSE, the falseExpr is the result. If the condExpr is ambiguous, then both trueExpr and falseExpr expressions are calculated and the result is produced in a bitwise fashion. For each bit, if both expression bits are one, the result is one. If both are zero, the result is zero. Otherwise, the resulting bit is x. The operator is right associative.

C.2 **Operator Precedence**

The operator precedences are shown below. The top of the table is the highest precedence, and the bottom is the lowest. Operators listed on the same line have the same precedence. All operators associate left to right in an expression (except ?:). Parentheses can be used to change the precedence or clarify the situation. When in doubt, use parentheses. They are easier to read, and reread!

unary operators:	! ~ + -	(highest precedence)
	* / %	
	+ -	(binary)
	<< >>	
	< <= > >=	
	== != === !==	
	& ~&	
	^ ~^	
	| ~|	
	&&	
	||	
	?:	(lowest precedence)

C.3 **Operator Truth Tables**

Table 3.2 Bitwise AND

&	0	1	x
0	0	0	0
1	0	1	x
x	0	x	x

Table 3.3 Bitwise OR

|	0	1	x
0	0	1	x
1	1	1	1
x	x	1	x

Table 3.4 Bitwise XOR

^	0	1	x
0	0	1	x
1	1	0	x
x	x	x	x

Table 3.5 Bitwise XNOR

~^	0	1	x
0	1	0	x
1	0	1	x
x	x	x	x

C.4 **Expression Bit Lengths**

In the following table, L(i) refers to the length in bits of operand i.

Table 3.6 Expression Bit Lengths

Expression	Bit Length	Comments
unsized constant number	same as integer (usually 32)	
sized constant number	as given	
i OP j	max (L(i), (L(j))	OP is +, -, /, *, %, &, |, ^, ~^
+i, -i	L(i)	
~i	L(i)	
i OP j	1 bit	OP is ===, !==, ==, !=, &&, ||, <, <=, >, >= and the reduction operators &, ~&, |, ~|, ^, ~^
i >> j, i << j	L(i)	
i ? j : k	max (L(j), L(k))	
{i, ..., j}	L(i) + ... + L(j)	
{i {j, ..., k}}	i * (L(j) + ... + L(k))	

D | Verilog Gate Types

D.1 Logic Gates

These gates all have one scalar output and any number of scalar inputs. When instantiating one of these modules, the first parameter is the output and the rest are inputs. Zero, one or two delays may be specified for the propagation times. Strengths may be specified on the outputs.

AND	0	1	x	z
0	0	0	0	0
1	0	1	x	x
x	0	x	x	x
z	0	x	x	x

NAND	0	1	x	z
0	1	1	1	1
1	1	0	x	x
x	1	x	x	x
z	1	x	x	x

OR	0	1	x	z
0	0	1	x	x
1	1	1	1	1
x	x	1	x	x
z	x	1	x	x

NOR	0	1	x	z
0	1	0	x	x
1	0	0	0	0
x	x	0	x	x
z	x	0	x	x

XOR	0	1	x	z
0	0	1	x	x
1	1	0	x	x
x	x	x	x	x
z	x	x	x	x

XNOR	0	1	x	z
0	1	0	x	x
1	0	1	x	x
x	x	x	x	x
z	x	x	x	x

D.2 **BUF and NOT Gates**

These gates have one or more scalar outputs and one scalar input. The input is listed last on instantiation. Zero, one, or two delays may be specified. Strengths may be specified on the outputs.

BUF	output
0	0
1	1
x	x
z	x

NOT	output
0	1
1	0
x	x
z	x

D.3 **BUFIF and NOTIF Gates**

These gates model three-state drivers. Zero, one, two, or three delays may be specified. Each of the gates has one output, one data input, and one control input. On instantiation, the ports are listed in that order. (L indicates 0 or z; H indicates 1 or z)

		Control Input			
	Bufif0	0	1	x	z
D	0	0	z	L	L
A	1	1	z	H	H
T	x	x	z	x	x
A	z	x	z	x	x

		Control Input			
	Bufif1	0	1	x	z
D	0	z	0	L	L
A	1	z	1	H	H
T	x	z	x	x	x
A	z	z	x	x	x

		Control Input			
	Notif0	0	1	x	z
D	0	1	z	H	H
A	1	0	z	L	L
T	x	x	z	x	x
A	z	x	z	x	x

	Notif1	Control Input			
		0	**1**	**x**	**z**
D	**0**	z	1	H	H
A	**1**	z	0	L	L
T	**x**	z	x	x	x
A	**z**	z	x	x	x

D.4 **MOS Gates**

These gates model NMOS and PMOS transistors. The "r" versions model NMOS and PMOS transistors with significantly higher resistivity when conducting. The resistive forms reduce the driving strength from input to output. The nonresistive forms only reduce the supply strength to a strong strength. See Table 9.7. Drive strengths may not be specified for these gates.

Each gate has one scalar output, one scalar data input, and one scalar control input, and on instantiation, are listed in that order. (L indicates 0 or z; H indicates 1 or z)

	(r)pmos	Control Input			
		0	**1**	**x**	**z**
D	**0**	0	z	L	L
A	**1**	1	z	H	H
T	**x**	x	z	x	x
A	**z**	z	z	z	z

	(r)nmos	Control Input			
		0	**1**	**x**	**z**
D	**0**	z	0	L	L
A	**1**	z	1	H	H
T	**x**	z	x	x	x
A	**z**	z	z	z	z

D.5 **Bidirectional Gates**

The following gates are true bidirectional transmission gates: tran, tranif1, tranif0, rtran, rtranif1, and rtranif0. Each of these has two scalar inout terminals. The tranif and rtranif gates have a control input which is listed last on instantiation.

The rise delay indicates the turn-on delay for the pass device and the fall delay indicates the turn-off delay.

D.6 **CMOS Gates**

CMOS gates represent the typical situation where nmos and pmos transistors are paired together to form a transmission gate. The first terminal is the data output, the second is the data input, the third is the n-channel control, and the last is the p-channel control. The cmos gate is a relatively low impedance device. The rcmos version has a higher impedance when conducting.

D.7 **Pullup and Pulldown Gates**

These are single output gates that drive pull strength values (the default) onto the output net. Pullup drives a logic one and pulldown drives a logic zero. The strength may be specified.

E | Registers, Memories, Integers, and Time

E.1 **Registers**

Registers are abstractions of storage devices found in digital systems. They are defined with the **reg** keyword and are optionally given a size (or bit width). The default size is one. Thus:

 reg tempBit;

 defines a single bit register named **tempBit**, while

 reg [15:0] tempNum;

defines a 16-bit register named tempNum. Single bit registers are termed *scalar*, and multiple bit registers are termed *vector*. The bit width specification gives the name of the most significant bit first (in this case, 15) and the least significant bit last.

 The register could have been declared as

 reg [0:15] tempNum;

with the only difference being that the most significant bit is named (numbered) 0. Of course, all the other bits are differently numbered.

The general form of a register specification is:

reg_declaration ::= **reg** [range] list_of_register_identifiers ;

list_of_register_identifiers ::= register_name { , register_name }

register_name ::=
      ::= *register*_identifier
      | *memory*_identifier [*upper_limit*_constant_expression :
        *lower_limit*_constant_expression]

range ::= [*msb*_constant_expression : *lsb*_constant_expression]

Either a single bit, or several contiguous bits of a vector register (or net) can be
addressed and used in an expression. Selecting a single bit is called a *bit-select*, and
selecting several contiguous bits is known as a *part-select*. Examples of these include:

```
reg   [10:0]   counter;
reg            a;
reg   [2:0]    b;
reg   [-5:7]   c
      ...
a = counter [7];      // bit seven of counter is loaded into a
b = counter [4:2];    // bits 4, 3, 2 of counter are loaded into b
```

In a bit-select, the bit to be selected may be specified with an expression or by a literal. The bits selected in a part-select must be specified with constant expressions or
literals; the values may be positive or negative. The general form for bit- and part-
select is given below:

primary ::=
      ::=   identifier [expression]
      | identifier [*msb*_constant_expression : *lsb*_constant_expression]

E.2 Memories

Memories are defined using the register declaration:

```
reg   [10:0]   lookUpTable [0:31];
```

This declares a 32 word array named **lookUpTable** where each word consists of 11
bits. The memory is used in an expression, for example, as follows:

```
lookUpTable [5] = 75;
```

This loads the fifth word of **lookUpTable** with the value 75.

The formal syntax specification in the previous section covers both register and memory declarations.

Bit-selects and part-selects are not allowed with memories. To specify this, the memory must be first transferred to a register and then a bit- or part-select may be performed on the register.

E.3 **Integers and Times**

Registers are used to model hardware. Sometimes though, it is useful to perform calculations for simulation purposes. For example, we may want to turn off monitoring after a certain time has passed. If we use registers for this purpose, the operations on them may be confused with actions of the actual hardware. *Integer* and *time* variables provide a means of describing calculations pertinent to the simulation. They are provided for convenience and make the description more self documenting.

An integer declaration uses the *integer* keyword and specifies a list of variables. The time declaration is the same except for the *time* keyword:

```
integer  a, b;        //two integers
integer  c [1:100];   // an array of integers
time     q, r;        // two time variables
time     s [1:100];   // an array of times
```

An integer is a general purpose 32-bit variable. Operations on it are assumed to be two's complement and the most significant bit indicates the sign.

A time variable is a 64-bit variable typically used with the $time system function.

F | System Tasks and Functions

In this section we present some of the built in Verilog System Tasks and Functions. Our philosophy for this book is not to become a substitute for the simulator manual. Rather, we want to illustrate a few of the basic methods of displaying the results of simulation, and stopping the simulation.

F.1 Display and Write Tasks

There are two main tasks for printing information during a simulation: $display and $write. These two are the same except that $display always prints a newline character at the end of its execution. Examples of the $display task were given throughout the main portion of the book. A few details will be given here.

The typical form of the parameters to these tasks is

$display ("Some text %d and maybe some more: %h.", a, b);

This statement would print the quoted string with the value of **a** substituted in for the format control "%d", and **b** is substituted in for the format control "%h". The "%d" indicates that the value should be printed in a decimal base. %h specifies hexadecimal.

Allowable letters in the format control specification are:

h or H	display in hexadecimal
d or D	display in decimal
o or O	display in octal
b or B	display in binary
c or C	display ASCII character
v or V	display net signal strength (see "printed abbreviation" in Table 9.4).
m or M	display hierarchical name
s or S	display string

Using the construct "%0d" will print a decimal number without leading zeros or spaces. This may be used with **h**, **d**, and **o** also.

Two adjacent commas (,,) will print a single space. Other special characters may be printed with escape sequences:

\n	is the new line character
\t	is the tab character
\\	is the \ character
\"	is the " character
\ddd	is the character specified in up to 3 octal digits

For instance:

$display ("Hello world\n");

will print the quoted string with two newline characters (remember, $display automatically adds one at the end of its execution).

F.2 **Continuous Monitoring**

The $monitor command is used to print information whenever there is a *change* in one or more specified values. The monitor prints at the end of the current time so that all changes at the current time will be reflected by the printout. The parameters for the $monitor task are the same as for the $display task.

   The command is:

   $monitor (parameters as used in the $display task);

   Whenever the $monitor task is called, it will print the values and set up the simulator to print them anytime one of the parameters changes. Only one $monitor display list may be active at a time. If time is being printed as in the following $monitor statement, a change in simulation time will not trigger the $monitor to print.

   $monitor ($time,, "regA = ", regA);

F.3 **Strobed Monitoring**

The $strobe task also uses the same parameter list format as the $display task. Unlike $display, it will print just before simulation time is about to advance. In this way, $strobe insures that all of the changes that were made at the current simulation time have been made, and thus will be printed.

F.4 **File Output**

The $display, $write, $monitor, and $strobe tasks have a version for writing to a file. They each require an extra parameter, called the file descriptor, as shown below:

   $fdisplay (descriptor, parameters as in the display command);
   $fwrite (descriptor, parameters as in the write command);
   $fmonitor (descriptor, parameters as in the monitor command);
   $fstrobe (descriptor, parameters as in the strobe command);

   The descriptor is a 32-bit value returned from the $fopen function. The descriptor may be stored in a 32-bit reg. The $fopen function takes the form:

   $fopen ("name of file");

   $fopen will return 0 if it was unable to open the file for writing. When finished writing to a file, it is closed with the function call:

$fclose (descriptor);

The descriptors are set up so that each bit of the descriptor indicates a different channel. Thus, multiple calls to $fopen will return a different bit set. The least signifi cant bit indicates the "standard output" (typically a terminal) and need not be opened. By passing the OR of two or more descriptors to one of the printing commands, the same message will be printed into all of the files (and standard output) indicated by the ORed descriptors.

F.5 **Simulation Time**

$time is a function that returns the current time as a 64-bit value. $stime will return a 32-bit value. The time may be printed, for instance, with the $monitor command as shown below:

$monitor ($time,,, "regA = ", regA);

Note that the change of simulation time will not trigger the $monitor to print.

F.6 **Stop and Finish**

The $stop and $finish tasks stop simulation. They differ in that $stop returns control back to the simulator's command interpreter, while $finish returns back to the host operating system.

$stop;
$stop(n);
$finish;
$finish(n);

A parameter may be passed to these tasks with the following effects.

Parameter Value	Diagnostics
0	prints nothing
1	gives simulation time and location
2	same as 1, plus a few lines of run statistics

If the forms with no parameter are used, then the default is the same as passing a 1 to it.

F.7 **Random**

The $random system function provides a random number mechanism, returning a new random number each time the function is called. The size of the returned value is the same as an integer variable. The function may be called with or without a parameter:

```
$random;
$random(<seed>);
```

The <seed> parameter is an inout which is used to control the numbers that $random returns. An argument for <seed> must be a register, integer, or time variable, and should be assigned to the variable before calling $random.

F.8 **Reading Data From Disk Files**

The $readmemb and $readmemh system tasks are used to load information stored in disk files into Verilog memories. The "b" version reads binary numbers and the "h" version reads hexadecimal numbers.

The general syntax for the task call is:

```
$readmemx ("filename", <memname>, <<start_addr> <,<finish_addr>>?>?);
```

where:

- x is "b" or "h"
- <memname> specifies the Verilog IDENTIFIER of the memory to be loaded.
- <start_addr> optionally specifies the starting address of the data. If none is specified, the left-hand address given in the memory declaration is used. If the <finish_addr> is specified, loading begins at the <start_addr> and continues to the <finish_addr>. Also see below for an alternate specification of the starting address.
- <finish_addr> is the last address to be written into.

Addresses can be specified within the file as well. The construct "@hhh...h" within the file specifies the hexadecimal address to use as the starting address. Subsequent data is loaded starting at that memory address. Note that the "h" specifies hexadecimal digits only. There is no length or base format specified. There may be several address specifications allowing several sub-blocks of memory to be loaded while the rest remains untouched.

The format for data in the file is either binary or hexadecimal numbers only. The length and base is not specified. The numbers are separated by white space. Verilog comments are allowed.

G | Formal Syntax Definition

This formal syntax specfication is provided in BNF. This information, starting in section G.2 and continuing through the end of this sppendix, is reprinted from IEEE Standard 1364-1995 "IEEE Standard Verilog Hardware Description Language Reference Manual (LRM)", Copyright © 1995 by the Institute of Electrical and Electronics Engineers, Inc (IEEE). The IEEE disclaims any responsibility or liability resulting from the placement and use in this publication. This information is reprinted with the permission of the IEEE.

G.1 Tutorial Guide to Formal Syntax Specification

The formal syntax notation will be introduced through an example — in this case Example G.1, an edge triggered D flip flop, **dEdgeFF**. Using this example we will describe the formal syntax of a module definition.

To this point, we have, by example, demonstrated that a module definition uses certain keywords ("module", "endmodule") and has other entities associated with it ("ports", "instantiations", etc.). The formal syntax for a module is:

```
module dEdgeFF (q, clock, data);
    input    clock, data;
    output   q;
    reg      reset;
    wire     q, qBar, r, s, r1, s1;

    initial begin
        reset = 1;
        #20 reset = 0;
    end

    nor #10
        a (q, qBar, r, reset);
    nor
        b (qBar, q, s),
        c (s, r, clock, s1),
        d (s1, s, data),
        e (r, r1, clock),
        f (r1, s1, r);

endmodule
```

Example G.1 An Edge-Triggered Flip Flop

```
module_declaration
    ::=  module_keyword module_identifier [ list_of_ports ];
         { module_item }
         endmodule

module_keyword
    ::=  module
    |    ...
```

In plain words, the module construct ("module_declaration") is defined by a "module_keyword," followed by the "module_identifier." The name is optionally followed by a list of ports (the "[ ]" indicates an optional item), and then by a ";". Next come zero or more module items (the "{ }" indicates zero or more) followed by the "endmodule" keyword. The module_keyword is the keyword "module" and the "module_identifier" is the name of the module. A definition of this can be found under "identifier." Examples of all of these items can be seen in Example G.1.

As a key, the construct before the "::=" is the item to be defined. The line with the "::=" starts the definition of the construct (later we will see that "|" indicates an alternate definition). Any other items in regular text are constructs that are defined elsewhere. Finally, bold text indicates literal text — text like "module" or ";" that will appear directly in the description. Typically, these are keywords and language punctuation. Some items are listed with the first part being italic and the rest being regular text. The italic part adds extra semantic information to the regular text item. The item to be used is found under the definition of the regular text item.

Table G.1 Definition of Items in Formal Syntax Specifications

Item	Meaning
White space	May be used to separate lexical tokens
name ::=	Starts off the definition of a syntax construct item. Sometimes name contains embedded underscores "_". Also, the "::=" may be found on the next line.
|	Introduces an alternative syntax definition, unless it appears in bold. (see next item)
name	Bold text is used to denote reserved keywords, operators, and punctuation marks required in the syntax
[item]	Is an optional item that may appear zero or one time.
{item}	Is an optional item that may appear zero, one or more times. If the braces appear in bold, they are part of the syntax.
*name1*_name2	This is equivalent to the syntax construct item name2. The name1 (in italics) imparts some extra semantic information to name2. However, the item is defined by the definition of name2.
| ...	Used in the non-appendix text to indicate that there are other alternatives, but that due to space or expediency they are not listed here. This is not used in the full syntax specification in the Appendix.

We still need to define the syntax construct items. Below are the rest of the definitions for a module. In some cases, the text "..." is used to indicate that there are more alternatives but that due to space or expediency, they won't be list and discussed here. All syntax construct items used in the normal text of the book are keyed to the identically named items in the Appendix.

More of the formal syntax for a module:

*module*_identifier
  ::= IDENTIFIER

A module is named using a *module*_identifier. The full definition of IDENTIFIER is not included here. However, the later appendix has the full definition. We will see that other items will be named using the same definition of an identifier. The italic *module* is added to the definition here to make it more readable. For instance, later we'll see *port*_identifier used; this has the same definition as *module*_identifier.

Now let's consider the ports. Above we see that a module has an optional list_of_ports. Below we see that a list_of_ports is one or more comma-separated ports listed within parentheses. Thus if there are no ports to the module (after all, they're optional), then nothing is specified — not even a null "()". However, if there is at least one port, then parentheses are used to contain the list of comma-separated ports.

list_of_ports
    ::= (port {, port })

A port is an optional port_expression which in turn is either a port_reference or a concatenation of port_references. A port_reference is either a *port*_identifier (which is actually an IDENTIFIER), a bit-select of a *port*_identifier (the second alternative in the list), or a part-select of a *port*_identifier (the third alternative). The items in the bit- and part-selects are constants indicating which bits are to be used. The selects are enclosed in literal square brackets and the constants of a part-select are separated by a literal colon.

port
    ::= [port_expression]
    | ...

port_expression
    ::= port_reference
    | { port_reference {, port reference} }

port_reference
    ::= *port*_identifier
    | *port*_identifier [constant_expression]
    | *port*_identifier [*msb*_constant_expression : *lsb*_constant_expression]

Going further with the module definition, we see that it also includes zero, one, or more module_items. There is a long list of alternatives in this list — some of which we see in Example G.1. For instance, the Example contains gate instantiations, initial constructs, and always constructs. Also, there are module_item_declarations such as register and net declarations. We also see other familiar items — gate and module instantiations, and continuous assignments. These will be detailed in later chapters.

module_item
    ::= module_item_declaration
    | continuous_assign
    | gate_instantiation
    | module_instantiation

```
        |    initial_construct
        |    always_construct
        |    ...
```

module_item_declaration
```
        ::=  input_declaration
        |    output_declaration
        |    inout_declaration
        |    net_declaration
        |    reg_declaration
        |    ...
```

Let's follow the input_declaration item.

input_declaration
```
        ::=  input [range] list_of_port_identifiers ;
```

range
```
        ::=  [ msb_constant_expression: lsb _constant_expression ]
```

constant_expression
```
        ::=  constant_primary
        |    ...
```

constant_primary
```
        ::=  number
        |    ...
```

list_of_port_identifiers
```
        ::=  port_identifier {, port_identifier }
```

We can see the basic form of an input declaration within a module is to have the keyword input followed by an optional range (bitwidth) specification, and then followed by a comma-separated list of at least one identifier with a semicolon at the end. The range, if present, consists of one or two constant expressions separated by a colon and enclosed in square brackets. The constant expression is a general expression which may contain operators but must evaluate to a constant at compile time.

References: register specifications E.1; IDENTIFIERS B.5, G.10

G.2 Source Text

source_text ::= {description}
description ::=
                module_declaration

    | udp_declaration
module_declaration ::=
    module_keyword *module*_identifier [list_of_ports] ; { module_item
    } **endmodule**
module_keyword ::= **module** | **macromodule**
list_of_ports ::= (port { , port })
port ::=
    [port_expression]
    | . *port*_identifier ([port_expression])
port_expression ::=
    port_reference
    | { port_reference { , port_reference} }
port_reference ::=
    *port*_identifier
    | *port*_identifier [constant_expression]
    | *port*_identifier [*msb*_constant_expression : *lsb*_constant_expression
    ]
module_item ::=
    module_item_declaration
    | parameter_override
    | continuous_assign
    | gate_instantiation
    | udp_instantiation
    | module_instantiation
    | specify_block
    | initial_construct
    | always_construct
module_item_declaration ::=
    parameter_declaration
    | input_declaration
    | output_declaration
    | inout_declaration
    | net_declaration
    | reg_declaration
    | integer_declaration
    | real_declaration
    | time_declaration
    | realtime_declaration
    | event_declaration
    | task_declaration
    | function_declaration
parameter_override ::= **defparam** list_of_param_assignments ;

G.3 **Declarations**

parameter_declaration ::= **parameter** list_of_param_assignments ;

list_of_param_assignments ::= param_assignment { , param_assignment }

param_assignment ::= *parameter*_identifier = constant_expression

input_declaration ::= **input** [range] list_of_port_identifiers ;

output_declaration ::= **output** [range] list_of_port_identifiers ;

inout_declaration ::= **inout** [range] list_of_port_identifiers ;

list_of_port_identifiers ::= *port*_identifier { , *port*_identifier }

reg_declaration ::= **reg** [range] list_of_register_identifiers ;

time_declaration ::= **time** list_of_register_identifiers ;

integer_declaration ::= **integer** list_of_register_identifiers ;

real_declaration ::= **real** list_of_real_identifiers ;

realtime_declaration ::= **realtime** list_of_real_identifiers ;

event_declaration ::= **event** *event*_identifier { , *event*_identifier } ;

list_of_real_identifiers ::= *real*_identifier { , *real*_identifier }

list_of_register_identifiers ::= register_name { , register_name }

register_name ::=

        *register*_identifier

        | *memory*_identifier **[** *upper_limit*_constant_expression **:**

        *lower_limit*_constant_expression **]**

range ::= **[** *msb*_constant_expression : *lsb*_constant_expression **]**

net_declaration ::=

        net_type [**vectored** | **scalared**] [range] [delay3] list_of_net_identifiers ;

        | **trireg** [**vectored** | **scalared**] [charge_strength] [range] [delay3]

        list_of_net_identifiers ;

        | net_type [**vectored** | **scalared**] [drive_strength] [range] [delay3]

        list_of_net_decl_assignments ;

net_type ::= **wire** | **tri** | **tri1** | **supply0** | **wand** | **triand** | **tri0** | **supply1** | **wor** | **trior**

list_of_net_identifiers ::= *net*_identifier { , *net*_identifier }

drive_strength ::=

        (strength0 , strength1)

        | (strength1 , strength0)

        | (strength0 , **highz1**)

        | (strength1 , **highz0**)

        | (**highz1** , strength0)

        | (**highz0** , strength1)

strength0 ::= **supply0** | **strong0** | **pull0** | **weak0**

strength1 ::= **supply1** | **strong1** | **pull1** | **weak1**

charge_strength ::= (**small**) | (**medium**) | (**large**)

delay3 ::= # delay_value | # (delay_value [, delay_value [, delay_value]])

delay2 ::= # delay_value | # (delay_value [, delay_value])

delay_value ::= unsigned_number | parameter_identifier |

constant_mintypmax_expression
list_of_net_decl_assignments ::= net_decl_assignment { , net_decl_assignment }
net_decl_assignment ::= *net*_identifier = expression
function_declaration ::=
        function [range_or_type] *function*_identifier ;
        function_item_declaration {function_item_declaration}
        statement
        endfunction
range_or_type ::= range | **integer** | **real** | **realtime** | **time**
function_item_declaration ::=
        block_item_declaration
        | input_declaration
task_declaration ::=
        task *task*_identifier ;
        {task_item_declaration}
        statement_or_null
        endtask
task_argument_declaration ::=
        block_item_declaration
        | output_declaration
        | inout_declaration
block_item_declaration ::=
        parameter_declaration
        | reg_declaration
        | integer_declaration
        | real_declaration
        | time_declaration
        | realtime_declaration
        | event_declaration

G.4 **Primitive Instances**

gate_instantiation ::=
        n_input_gatetype [drive_strength] [delay2] n_input_gate_instance { ,
        n_input_gate_instance } ;
        | n_output_gatetype [drive_strength] [delay2] n_output_gate_instance
        { , n_output_gate_instance } ;
        | enable_gatetype [drive_strength] [delay3] enable_gate_instance { ,
        enable_gate_instance} ;
        | mos_switchtype [delay3] mos_switch_instance { ,
        mos_switch_instance } ;
        | pass_switchtype pass_switch_instance { , pass_switch_instance } ;
        | pass_en_switchtype [delay3] pass_en_switch_instance { ,
        pass_en_switch_instance } ;

          | cmos_switchtype [delay3] cmos_switch_instance { ,
cmos_switch_instance } ;
          | **pullup** [pullup_strength] pull_gate_instance { , pull_gate_instance } ;
          | **pulldown** [pulldown_strength] pull_gate_instance { ,
pull_gate_instance } ;

n_input_gate_instance ::= [name_of_gate_instance] (output_terminal , input_terminal
        { , input_terminal })

n_output_gate_instance ::= [name_of_gate_instance] (output_terminal { ,
        output_terminal } , input_terminal)

enable_gate_instance ::= [name_of_gate_instance] (output_terminal , input_terminal
        , enable_terminal)

mos_switch_instance ::= [name_of_gate_instance] (output_terminal , input_terminal
        , enable_terminal)

pass_switch_instance ::= [name_of_gate_instance] (inout_terminal , inout_terminal)

pass_enable_switch_instance ::= [name_of_gate_instance] (inout_terminal ,
        inout_terminal , enable_terminal)

cmos_switch_instance ::= [name_of_gate_instance] (output_terminal , input_terminal
        ,
                        ncontrol_terminal , pcontrol_terminal)

pull_gate_instance ::= [name_of_gate_instance] (output_terminal)

name_of_gate_instance ::= *gate_instance*_identifier [range]

pullup_strength ::=
        (strength0 , strength1)
        | (strength1 , strength0)
        | (strength1)

pulldown_strength ::=
        (strength0 , strength1)
        | (strength1 , strength0)
        | (strength0)

input_terminal ::= *scalar*_expression

enable_terminal ::= *scalar*_expression

ncontrol_terminal ::= *scalar*_expression

pcontrol_terminal ::= *scalar*_expression

output_terminal ::= *terminal*_identifier | *terminal*_identifier [constant_expression]

inout_terminal ::= *terminal*_identifier | *terminal*_identifier [constant_expression]

n_input_gatetype ::= **and** | **nand** | **or** | **nor** | **xor** | **xnor**

n_output_gatetype ::= **buf** | **not**

enable_gatetype ::= **bufif0** | **bufif1** | **notif0** | **notif1**

mos_switchtype ::= **nmos** | **pmos** | **rnmos** | **rpmos**

pass_switchtype ::= **tran** | **rtran**

pass_en_switchtype ::= **tranif0** | **tranif1** | **rtranif1** | **rtranif0**

cmos_switchtype ::= **cmos** | **rcmos**

G.5 **Module Instantiation**

module_instantiation ::=
>   *module*_identifier [parameter_value_assignment] module_instance {
>   , module_instance } ;

parameter_value_assignment ::= # (expression { , expression })

module_instance ::= name_of_instance ([list_of_module_connections])

name_of_instance ::= *module_instance*_identifier [range]

list_of_module_connections ::=
>   ordered_port_connection { , ordered_port_connection }
> | named_port_connection { , named_port_connection }

ordered_port_connection ::= [expression]

named_port_connection ::= . *port*_identifier ([expression])

G.6 **UDP Declaration and Instantiation**

udp_declaration ::=
>   **primitive** *udp*_identifier (udp_port_list) ;
>   udp_port_declaration { udp_port_declaration }
>   udp_body
>   **endprimitive**

udp_port_list ::= *output_port*_identifier , *input_port*_identifier { ,
>   *input_port*_identifier }

udp_port_declaration ::=
>   output_declaration
> | input_declaration
> | reg_declaration

udp_body ::= combinational_body | sequential_body

combinational_body ::= **table** combinational_entry { combinational_entry } **endtable**

combinational_entry ::= level_input_list : output_symbol ;

sequential_body ::= [udp_initial_statement] **table** sequential_entry {
>   sequential_entry } **endtable**

udp_initial_statement ::= **initial** *udp_output_port*_identifier = init_val ;

init_val ::= **1'b0** | **1'b1** | **1'bx** | **1'bX** | **1'B0** | **1'B1** | **1'Bx** | **1'BX** | **1** | **0**

sequential_entry ::= seq_input_list : current_state : next_state ;

seq_input_list ::= level_input_list | edge_input_list

level_input_list ::= level_symbol { level_symbol }

edge_input_list ::= { level_symbol } edge_indicator { level_symbol }

edge_indicator ::= (level_symbol level_symbol) | edge_symbol

current_state ::= level_symbol

next_state ::= output_symbol | -

339

```
output_symbol ::= 0 | 1 | x | X
level_symbol ::= 0 | 1 | x | X | ? | b | B
edge_symbol ::= r | R | f | F | p | P | n | N | *


udp_instantiation ::= udp_identifier [ drive_strength ] [ delay2 ] udp_instance { , udp_instance
                } ;
udp_instance ::= [ name_of_udp_instance ] ( output_port_connection , input_port_connection
                                            { , input_port_connection } )
name_of_udp_instance ::= udp_instance_identifier [ range ]
```

G.7 Behavioral Statements

```
continuous_assign ::= assign [drive_strength] [delay3] list_of_net_assignments ;
list_of_net_assignments ::= net_assignment { , net_assignment }
net_assignment ::= net_lvalue = expression

initial_construct ::= initial statement
always_construct ::= always statement

statement ::=
                blocking_assignment ;
              | non_blocking assignment ;
              | procedural_continuous_assignments ;
              | procedural_timing_control_statement
              | conditional_statement
              | case_statement
              | loop_statement
              | wait_statement
              | disable_statement
              | event_trigger
              | seq_block
              | par_block
              | task_enable
              | system_task_enable

statement_or_null ::= statement | ;
blocking assignment ::= reg_lvalue = [ delay_or_event_control ] expression
non-blocking assignment ::= reg_lvalue <= [ delay_or_event_control ] expression
procedural_continuous_assignment ::=
                | assign reg_assignment ;
                | deassign reg_lvalue ;
                | force reg_assignment ;
                | force net_assignment ;
```

IEEE Std 1364-1995, Copyright © 1995, IEEE. All rights reserved

```
                | release reg_lvalue ;
                | release net_lvalue ;
procedural_timing_control_statement ::=
                delay_or_event_control statement_or_null
delay_or_event_control ::=
                delay_control
                | event_control
                | repeat ( expression ) event_control
delay_control ::=
                # delay_value
                | # ( mintypmax_expression )
event_control ::=
                @ event_identifier
                | @ ( event_expression )
event_expression ::=
                expression
                | event_identifier
                | posedge expression
                | negedge expression
                | event_expression or event_expression
conditional_statement ::=
                | if ( expression ) statement_or_null [ else statement_or_null ]
case_statement ::=
                | case ( expression ) case_item {case_item} endcase
                | casez ( expression ) case_item {case_item} endcase
                | casex ( expression ) case_item {case_item} endcase
case_item ::=
                expression { , expression } : statement_or_null
                | default [ : ] statement_or_null
loop_statement ::=
                | forever statement
                | repeat ( expression ) statement
                | while ( expression ) statement
                | for ( reg_assignment ; expression ; reg_assignment ) statement
reg_assignment ::= reg_lvalue = expression
wait_statement ::=
                | wait ( expression ) statement_or_null
event_trigger ::=
                | -> event_identifier ;
disable_statement ::=
                | disable task_identifier ;
                | disable block_identifier ;
seq_block ::= begin [ : block_identifier { block_item_declaration } ] { statement } end
par_block ::= fork [ : block_identifier { block_item_declaration } ] { statement } join
task_enable ::= task_identifier [ ( expression { , expression } ) ] ;
```

system_task_enable ::= system_task_name [(expression { , expression })] ;
system_task_name ::= $identifier   Note: The $ may not be followed by a space.

G.8 **Specify Section**

specify_block ::= **specify** [specify_item] **endspecify**
specify_item ::=
        specparam_declaration
        | path_declaration
        | system_timing_check
specparam_declaration ::= **specparam** list_of_specparam_assignments ;
list_of_specparam_assignments ::= specparam_assignment { , specparam_assignment
        }
specparam_assignment ::=
        *specparam*_identifier = constant_expression
        | pulse_control_specparam
pulse_control_specparam ::=
        PATHPULSE$ = (*reject*_limit_value [, *error*_limit_value]) ;
        |
        **PATHPULSE$**specify_input_terminal_descriptor$specify_output_te
        rminal_descriptor
                = (*reject*_limit_value [, *error*_limit_value
        ]) ;
limit_value ::= constant_mintypmax_expression
path_declaration ::=
        simple_path_declaration ;
        | edge_sensitive_path_declaration ;
        | state-dependent_path_declaration ;
simple_path_declaration ::=
        parallel_path_description = path_delay_value
        | full_path_description = path_delay_value
parallel_path_description ::=
        (specify_input_terminal_descriptor [polarity_operator] =>
        specify_output_terminal_descriptor)
full_path_description ::=
        (list_of_path_inputs [polarity_operator] *> list_of_path_outputs)
list_of_path_inputs ::=
        specify_input_terminal_descriptor { ,
        specify_input_terminal_descriptor }
list_of_path_outputs ::=
        specify_output_terminal_descriptor { ,
        specify_output_terminal_descriptor }
specify_input_terminal_descriptor ::=

```
                    input_identifier
                  | input_identifier [ constant_expression ]
                  | input_identifier [ msb_constant_expression :
                  lsb_constant_expression ]
specify_output_terminal_descriptor ::=
                    output_identifier
                  | output_identifier [ constant_expression ]
                  | output_identifier [ msb_constant_expression :
                  lsb_constant_expression ]
input_identifier ::= input_port_identifier | inout_port_identifier
output_identifier ::= output_port_identifier | inout_port_identifier
polarity_operator ::= + | -
path_delay_value ::=
                    list_of_path_delay_expressions
                  | ( list_of_path_delay_expressions )
list_of_path_delay_expressions ::=
                    t_path_delay_expression
                  | trise_path_delay_expression , tfall_path_delay_expression
                  | trise_path_delay_expression , tfall_path_delay_expression ,
                  tz_path_delay_expression
                  | t01_path_delay_expression , t10_path_delay_expression ,
                  t0z_path_delay_expression ,
                   tz1_path_delay_expression , t1z_path_delay_expression ,
                  tz0_path_delay_expression
                  | t01_path_delay_expression , t10_path_delay_expression ,
                  t0z_path_delay_expression ,
                   tz1_path_delay_expression , t1z_path_delay_expression ,
                  tz0_path_delay_expression ,
                   t0x_path_delay_expression , tx1_path_delay_expression ,
                  t1x_path_delay_expression ,
                   tx0_path_delay_expression , txz_path_delay_expression ,
                  tzx_path_delay_expression
path_delay_expression ::= constant_mintypmax_expression
edge_sensitive_path_declaration ::=
                    parallel_edge_sensitive_path_description = path_delay_value
                  | full_edge_sensitive_path_description = path_delay_value
parallel_edge_sensitive_path_description ::=
                    ( [ edge_identifier ] specify_input_terminal_descriptor =>
                               specify_output_terminal_descriptor [ polarity_operator
                  ] : data_source_expression ) )
full_edge_sensitive_path_description ::=
                    ( [ edge_identifier ] list_of_path_inputs *>
                               list_of_path_outputs [ polarity_operator ] :
                  data_source_expression ) )
data_source_expression ::= expression
edge_identifier ::= posedge | negedge
```

state_dependent_path_declaration ::=
        if (conditional_expression) simple_path_declaration
        | **if** (conditional_expression) edge_sensitive_path_declaration
        | **ifnone** simple_path_declaration

system_timing_check ::=
        $setup (timing_check_event , timing_check_event ,
        timing_check_limit [, notify_register]) ;
        | **$hold** (timing_check_event , timing_check_event ,
        timing_check_limit [, notify_register]) ;
        | **$period** (controlled_timing_check_event , timing_check_limit [,
        notify_register]) ;
        | **$width** (controlled_timing_check_event , timing_check_limit ,
        constant_expression [, notify_register]) ;
        | **$skew** (timing_check_event , timing_check_event ,
        timing_check_limit [, notify_register]) ;
        | **$recovery** (controlled_timing_check_event , timing_check_event ,
        timing_check_limit [, notify_register]) ;
        | **$setuphold** (timing_check_event , timing_check_event ,
        timing_check_limit ,
        timing_check_limit [, notify_register]) ;
timing_check_event ::=
        [timing_check_event_control] specify_terminal_descriptor [**&&&**
        timing_check_condition]
specify_terminal_descriptor ::=
        specify_input_terminal_descriptor
        | specify_output_terminal_descriptor
controlled_timing_check_event ::=
        timing_check_event_control specify_terminal_descriptor [**&&&**
        timing_check_condition]
timing_check_event_control ::=
        posedge
        | **negedge**
        | edge_control_specifier
edge_control_specifier ::= **edge** [edge_descriptor [, edge_descriptor]]
edge_descriptor ::=
        01
        | **10**
        | **0x**
        | **x1**
        | **1x**
        | **x0**
timing_check_condition ::=
        scalar_timing_check_condition
        | (scalar_timing_check_condition)
scalar_timing_check_condition ::=
        expression

```
              | ~ expression
              | expression == scalar_constant
              | expression === scalar_constant
              | expression != scalar_constant
              | expression !== scalar_constant
timing_check_limit ::= expression
scalar_constant ::=
              1'b0 | 1'b1 | 1'B0 | 1'B1 | 'b0 | 'b1 | 'B0 | 'B1 | 1 | 0
notify_register ::= register_identifier
```

G.9 **Expressions**

```
net_lvalue ::=
              net_identifier
              | net_identifier [ expression ]
              | net_identifier [ msb_constant_expression : lsb_constant_expression ]
              | net_concatenation
reg_lvalue ::=
              reg_identifier
              | reg_identifier [ expression ]
              | reg_identifier [ msb_constant_expression : lsb_constant_expression ]
              | reg_concatenation
constant_expression ::=
              constant_primary
              | unary_operator constant_primary
              | constant_expression binary_operator constant_expression
              | constant_expression ? constant_expression : constant_expression
              | string
constant_primary ::=
              number
              | parameter_identifier
              | constant_concatenation
              | constant_multiple_concatenation
constant_mintypmax_expression ::=
              constant_expression
              | constant_expression : constant_expression : constant_expression
mintypmax_expression ::=
              expression
              | expression : expression : expression
expression ::=
              primary
              | unary_operator primary
              | expression binary_operator expression
              | expression ? expression : expression
```

```
                | string
unary_operator ::=
                + | - | ! | ~ | & |  ~& |  | | ~| | ^ | ~^ | ^~
binary_operator ::=
                + | - | * | / | % | == | != | === | !== | && | ||
                | < | <= | > | >= | & | | | ^ | ^~ | ~^ | >> | <<
primary ::=
                number
                | identifier
                | identifier [ expression ]
                | identifier [ msb_constant_expression : lsb_constant_expression ]
                | concatenation
                | multiple_concatenation
                | function_call
                | ( mintypmax_expression )
number ::=
                decimal_number
                | octal_number
                | binary_number
                | hex_number
                | real_number
real_number ::=
                [ sign ] unsigned_number . unsigned_number
                | [ sign ] unsigned_number [ . unsigned_number] e [ sign ]
                unsigned_number
                | [ sign ] unsigned_number [ . unsigned_number] e [ sign ]
                unsigned_number
decimal_number ::=
                [ sign ] unsigned_number
                | [size] decimal_base unsigned_number
binary_number ::= [size] binary_base binary_digit { _ | binary_digit}
octal_number ::= [size] octal_base octal_digit { _ | octal_digit}
hex_number ::= [size] hex_base hex_digit { _ | hex_digit}
sign ::= + | -
size ::= unsigned_number
unsigned_number ::= decimal_digit { _ | decimal_digit }
decimal_base ::= 'd | 'D
binary_base ::= 'b | 'B
octal_base ::= 'o | 'O
hex_base ::= 'h | 'H
decimal_digit ::= 0 | 1 | 2 | 3 | 4 | 5 | 6 | 7 | 8 | 9 | 0
binary_digit ::= x | X | z | Z | 0 | 1
octal_digit ::= x | X | z | Z | 0 | 1 | 2 | 3 | 4 | 5 | 6 | 7
hex_digit ::= x | X | z | Z | 0 | 1 | 2 | 3 | 4 | 5 | 6 | 7 | 8 | 9 | a | b | c | d | e | f | A | B | C |
                D | E | F
```

concatenation ::= { expression { , expression} }
multiple_concatenation ::= { expression { expression { , expression } } }
function_call ::=
                *function*_identifier (expression { , expression})
                | name_of_system_function [(expression { , expression})]
name_of_system_function ::= $identifier
string ::= " { Any_ASCII_Characters_except_new_line } "

NOTES

    1)   —Embedded spaces are illegal.

    2)   —The $ in name_of_system_function may not be followed by a space.

G.10 **General**

comment ::=
                short_comment
                | long_comment
short_comment ::= // comment_text \n
long_comment ::= /* comment_text */
comment_text ::= { Any_ASCII_character }
identifier ::= IDENTIFIER [{ . IDENTIFIER }]
IDENTIFIER ::=
                simple_identifier
                | escaped_identifier
simple_identifier ::= [a-zA-Z][a-zA-Z-_$]
escaped_identifier ::= \ {Any_ASCII_character_except_white_space} white_space
white_space ::= space | tab | newline

NOTE—The period in identifier may not be preceded or followed by a space.